The Reluctant Vegetarian Cookbook

THE RELUCTANT VEGETARIAN COOKBOOK

A Restaurateur's Recipes

Simon Hope

Illustrations by Jenny Dartford

HEINEMANN : LONDON

William Heinemann Ltd
10 Upper Grosvenor Street, London W1X 9PA

LONDON MELBOURNE TORONTO
JOHANNESBURG AUCKLAND

© Simon Hope 1985

First published 1985

Reprinted 1985 (three times)

All illustrations by Jenny Dartford

0 434 34667 5

Typeset by Inforum Ltd, Portsmouth
Printed in England by
Redwood Burn Ltd, Trowbridge

Contents

Normal Oven Temperature Guide (approximations)

Description	°C — Celsius	°F — Fahrenheit	Regulo 1—9
Very hot	230–260°	450–500°	8–9
Hot	205–230°	400–450°	6–7
Moderately hot	175–205°	350–400°	5
Moderate	150–175°	300–350°	3–4
Cool	120–150°	250–300°	1–2
Very cool	120° and below	250° and below	½ and below

Preface

Vegetarian cookery is perhaps the only truly international cuisine in the world, encompassing dishes from many countries and even different regions from within those countries. It is important to remember this because, as a result, it caters for many religious, political and sectarian needs. At the same time it opens up a new cuisine for all those reluctant vegetarians who simply want a pleasant and varied addition to their diet which is both inexpensive and nutritious.

Most of the vegetarian dishes included in the recipe part of the book have origins firmly rooted in simple concepts that have evolved from peasant economies throughout the world. In any society where meat is scarce or expensive the mass of the people adopt and develop dishes in which the emphasis falls on what surrounds the more expensive ingredient – in other words they make what they can't afford go further. The pasta dishes of Italy, the puddings and pies of England, the rice dishes of the East, and even the hamburger of America, are all examples of making an expensive commodity, whether it be meat or fish, go further by padding it out with cheaper fillers. In the examples quoted, with the exception of the hamburger, the idea is simple – surround your expensive ingredient with a thick tasty sauce, then mop it up with pasta, pastry or rice. In the case of the hamburger, it is more often than not the cheapest bits of meat ground up so that really only the flavour still remains, padded out with a cheap bulk filler, seasoned so that the bad quality meat is disguised, shaped and served between what must be one of the cheapest staples of the Western world – bread.

What reluctant vegetarians all over the world must ask themselves is, 'Is it worth so much trouble, time and expense?' Surely most of our food has travelled so far from its original ingredients – ingredients which we can no longer really afford. Wouldn't it be better to start afresh? Why not create a new cuisine which uses less expensive and unadulterated components, but which we still enjoy? In fact we are better off because we have not only replaced bad quality, expensive meat or fish products with an unending variety of vegetables, grains, beans, pulses and pastas, but we have also re-introduced into our lives something which has been long forgotten – inspiration.

Reluctant vegetarians know that somehow their diets are meant to be more varied and more fun, but are perhaps daunted by the prospect of cooking without meat. *What do we do instead, isn't it complicated, doesn't it take much more time?'* Read on and all will be revealed.

Put simply, vegetarian food is influenced primarily by two very different international cuisines. We look to the Far East and especially China for a fast and therefore nutritious approach to preparing and cooking vegetables and some light but very tasty sauces. This aspect of vegetarian cooking is developed in the chapter on stir-fried vegetables and is extremely important to the successful reluctant vegetarian cook. Then we look to Europe and particularly France, because France combines Mediterranean cookery with that of Northern Europe producing robust sauces and using familiar food presentation. We take the best ideas from both cuisines and amalgamate them while at the same time we draw inspiration from every country and region in the world, not only in terms of cooking techniques but also for our ingredients.

With a vast array of ideas, ingredients and knowledge we start to create dishes that are, in essence, international creations in themselves, not poor substitutes for the real thing.

The internationality of vegetarian food is felt throughout our entire repertoire, from starters to sweets and cakes. The reluctant vegetarian may well feel that at the moment meals at home are more like rituals. They can become wonderful, interesting and even exciting experiences because in creating vegetarian dishes the imagination can actually start to work again. Rather than making what you cannot afford go further, make what you can afford an exciting part of everyday life.

Chapter 1

Influences on Vegetarian Cookery

Seasonal and climatic influences

The climate is of enormous importance to the cook who wishes to cook without meat, for the climate affects the choice, quality, availability and therefore price, of fresh fruit and vegetables and occasionally grains, beans, pulses, nuts and dried fruits. Of course, the limitations placed on your purchases depend largely on where you live in the world and the time of year. Any good cook will work alongside the climate, sometimes cursing it but more often than not praising it. Even in mid-winter in England summer has begun elsewhere in the world. More important, the vegetables at home do have special qualities, not only in taste and quality but appropriateness when eaten in season.

To use frozen or tinned foods as a hedge against seasonal influences on availability is a false economy. Tinned fruit or vegetables are generally awful with the exception perhaps of some Italian tomatoes. Frozen fruit and vegetables after defrosting never cook to a satisfactory standard. To make matters worse, both are extremely expensive. Frozen fruit may be acceptable but only for flavouring a dish; it can never replace the fresh items in season. It is far better to buy with the seasons, if not always with those of your own country, with those of countries that are near enough to supply a decent-quality product that will still be reasonably fresh when it reaches you. Locally grown produce can simply never be beaten for flavour, nutrition and usually price. So, give up the supermarket and start a relationship with your local greengrocer.

Today, many different vegetables are available at a price throughout the year. It is advisable, nevertheless, to cut down on those vegetables or fruits that are out of season, locally or nationally. There are two reasons for this. Firstly the vegetables will have travelled a long way to reach you; artificially prepared in all sorts of nasty ways, and often sprayed with dangerous chemicals. They will usually lack flavour, vitality and therefore goodness. Secondly, they will be comparatively expensive. I am not saying never buy these goods; in mid-winter it is necessary to do so for the sake of variety, but be careful how you buy them. If you can get them cheaply, all the better. Imported fruit and vegetables will often deteriorate quickly once they have been removed from their controlled environment. To buy produce cheaply that has only just started to deteriorate will add variety and flavour to your diet, but be under no illusions about it – just use it for what it is worth and balance it with fresher produce that is still available locally or the whole range of other ingredients which are dry and safe to store for longer periods of time. This point is discussed more fully in the vegetable chopping section, and exact details given on a range of fruit and vegetables.

It is always best to use seasonal vegetables, as they are inexpensive, fresh and nutritious, with little wastage. In season, vegetables and fruit deserve special attention, so create your dishes around the best and most reasonable produce. That way not only will your diet be better but your cost of living will also come down. If you simply follow the natural cycle of growth for both fruits and vegetables, the quality of food you eat should always be of the highest standard, provided it is treated correctly.

Influence of the seasons

Spring

Spring is the time of growth. Vegetables that are picked are young, sweet and tender. Popular varieties of vegetables gradually break the surface of the soil. The weather is still changeable and winter casseroles and stews may not yet be completely redundant, but it is generally warmer and drier and so some lighter summer dishes could be called for. Let the vegetables create dishes themselves, light and fresh but still with a wholesome earth flavour. They will need less cooking time than most winter vegetables, but still require longer than the vegetable crops of summer. The variety of vegetables available is still not great, so use grains, beans, pulses and pastas for bulk, nutrition and your pocket.

Summer

Summer should be a time of total indulgence for the thrifty vegetarian cook. There is a vast array of vegetables, vegetable fruits and soft fruit. Forget grains, beans and pulses, if you wish, and concentrate on the art of cooking with vegetables or fruits alone. The result will be light, colourful, refreshing food that is ideal for a hot summer's day. Remember summer fruits and vegetables have a high water content and so must be prepared carefully and quickly and cooked sparingly. Otherwise, forget cooking completely and create colourful and attractive salads, chilled soups, starters and sweets. Concentrate flavours in unusual dressings that are as light as they are piquant. Make sweets that are full of mouth-watering soft fruits and naturally sweetened by their own juices.

Autumn

Autumn is the time of 'mists and mellow fruitfulness'. The orchards dominate the sweet department. In savouries and salads we still find a good variety of summer vegetables that have grown to their full extent. As vegetables grow, their skins become tougher and more blighted, their flesh harder and more often bruised. Autumn vegetables, while abundant, require more preparation and slightly longer cooking. Consequently, we see a return to thicker, more sustaining dishes for cool autumn evenings with perhaps still some lighter dishes for the warmer days.

Winter

Suddenly autumn is over and most vegetables have returned to the ground, roots predominate in the market, supported by tasteless produce grown under glass. Summer continues elsewhere in the world. In the kitchen we must return to grains, beans, pulses and pastas that naturally create hot, thick and sustaining food, every bit as

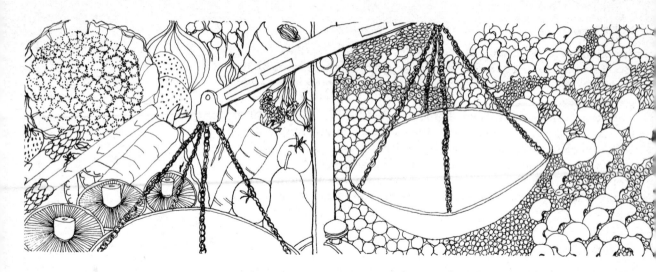

exciting as its summer counterpart, but in every way suited to cold and often wet days. Attention must be paid to creating a wide selection of flavours through stocks, sauces, seasonings and the many ingredients that are easily available in winter and summer.

Influence of balance

The influence of balance in a meal that is well thought out and prepared should be noticed only in its subtlety. In other words, after an excellent lunch you should feel that the whole experience was lovely, not that the cook had carefully balanced this dish against that. Balance is something you can learn to feel but not set out to create. A perfectly balanced meal may seem contrived while a perfectly wonderful meal twists and turns balance to its own ends.

It follows that you should never re-create a recipe blindly – alter it, adjust it, even re-structure it to suit your own purposes. After all, a recipe is only someone else's interpretation of how a dish should be and it is you who must eat the finished result. Think of the recipe as a blank canvas and then start to paint a picture. Of course, if you don't know how to 'paint', then the end result will not be satisfactory. So here are a few points that may help a reluctant vegetarian formulate an approach to what he wants a dish to be like.

Before preparing your meal, look out of the window and see what the weather is like, then devise your menu, bearing in mind what raw materials you have available.

The number of courses involved in the meal will determine the sort of quantity each dish will contain.

Next, and this is the most difficult part, decide what effect each course may have on the one it follows and its role in the meal as a whole. Having thought carefully at this stage, you may wish to change one or two courses. For instance, split-pea and leek soup followed by barley roast with cheese and mushroom sauce followed by chocolate banana sponge with cashew sauce may seriously prevent any further activity for the rest of the day.

Then look at the individual dishes to balance texture, colour and nutrition with the desired finished effect. This will help you decide on the ratio of certain ingredients within the dish. To complicate matters further, you must also consider the nature of the sauces involved, especially with regard to the thickening agent and the influence of seasoning and sweetening in any part of the dish.

It sounds difficult, but really it boils down to having a feeling for food. Once you are happy with what you make, and have learnt the basic disciplines, then the theories of cooking fade into the background and leave you the most important aspect – creativity.

One thing I must emphasize. Do not get bogged down with nutritional factors. Counting calories, vitamins, proteins, essential minerals, etc. can all go by the wayside if you eat freshly prepared fresh food every day. Simply putting into practice what the book suggests will ensure your future health. Most diet plans are a temporary part of your life – often boring and arduous, expensive and at best impractical. Learning how to create exciting food without meat and using plenty of unrefined foods, whether it be alongside or instead of your present way of eating, will ensure your fitness and help avoid the terrific cost of manufacturers' food products.

Chapter 2
Vegetable and Fruit Preparation

Introduction

The preparation of fruit and vegetables for use in both cooked and uncooked dishes is extremely important for many reasons. In Chapter 1 we discussed balance and how a dish depends not only on its ingredients, but also on the shape, size, and colour of those ingredients which give the dish a fundamental structure and perhaps more importantly, an attractive character of its own. The methods by which fruit and vegetables are prepared and cut therefore, will ultimately determine how the dish looks, how easy it is to serve and eat, its nutritional content and bias. A sound knowledge of vegetable preparation will also ensure economic use of fruit and vegetables, with minimal wastage and maximum speed, dexterity and nutrition.

To enjoy the best of the vegetable or fruit content of a dish, first of all look carefully at their condition. Seasonal influences have already been discussed and ideally only the finest vegetables and fruit should be used. However in practice this is not always possible. For taste and nutrition nothing can beat the vegetable or fruit that is picked and eaten within a few hours, but that doesn't mean to say that produce which comes from the other side of the world, has been stored, and may well be past its best when eaten, should be written off completely. When I buy fruit and vegetables at the market, although keeping a firm eye on freshness and variety, I will often purchase produce in bulk which may have only one or two days of its edible life left. Produce like this is often 10–50 per cent of the original cost price and leaves me with more money to spend on the exotic and rare vegetables and fruit which can lift a more ordinary dish into the realms of the gourmet. Attention to preparation of second-grade fruit and vegetables, combined with careful cooking, will help the weekly food bills and increase the range of your diet.

If buying or picking young fresh vegetables, try to interfere with them as little as possible during preparation. Their vitality, goodness, and taste will all be there, so the less you do to them the better. An obvious all-year-round example is button mushrooms. These tiny mouth-watering fungi need no preparation, except a good washing. Remember, most vitamins are water-soluble and as soon as you cut a vegetable the vitamins begin to leak out with the juice from the cut edges. Therefore, speed in vegetable and fruit preparation is essential. The quicker they are prepared and cooked or eaten, the better they will taste and the better they will be for you. Of course, rules are made to be broken and some interesting ways of breaking them will be shown later in the book. Never, ever peel young vegetables (there are a few odd exceptions) for 90 per cent of the vitamins and protein are stored in that very bit most people strip off. In fact, even older vegetables, with the exception of woody roots, need nothing doing to their skins apart from a good scrubbing. Skin blights, bruises and eyes should be cut out but even an old parsnip will, if prepared, chopped, and cooked correctly, enhance and even dominate a dish should you wish it.

The shape and size you choose for your vegetable will determine how long that vegetable takes to cook. Bearing this in mind you can mentally construct an approach to cooking any particular dish. Root vegetables generally take longest to cook and old root vegetables take longer than young, but by slicing them thinly their cooking time will be reduced automatically and their individual flavours retained. An example of this technique is given in recipe 244 – Leek and Parsnip Crumble – a dish almost entirely created from root vegetables which is very cheap in winter and yet absolutely delicious. Green vegetables take far less time to cook and are often the main character vegetable in a dish. Preparation of these then must give priority to shape; the size can be just as you like. At the restaurant we have to think of interesting mouthfuls, big enough to get your teeth into but not so big as to be unwieldy.

Using a variety of chopping techniques when creating a dish can give it a vivid and interesting texture, but care should be taken not to make a dish too complicated and confusing to look at. We always pay special attention to the feature vegetable or fruit allowing the other ingredients to form a background to it. On the other hand a Chinese-influenced casserole should look oriental and should be cooked quickly in the Chinese way. Vegetables are generally cut to a similar size, diagonally sliced, stripped or cubed – rather spikey looking. We tend to use Chinese styles of chopping and Chinese choppers for chopping. This 'diagonal' approach to cutting vegetables and fruit ensures a larger area being exposed to heat in the pan, decreasing cooking time, so increasing nutritional value.

Of course when cooking is not involved in the preparation of a dish you have a much freer range, so long as what you prepare is eaten reasonably quickly or prevented from oxidizing (*see* p. 60). All sorts of shapes and sizes can go into making salads, starters, titbits and some cold sweets, attractive to the eye and interesting to eat. I am continually astounded by the wealth of 'health food' restaurants that destroy salad vegetables by passing them through a mincing machine – the resulting product being more akin to damp tissue paper than a crisp salad, and its nutritional value about the same. Some of the more dainty vegetable shapes like matchsticks, small cubes, and thin squares, may also be dropped into a clear vegetable soup simply to add colour and texture or sprinkled on side dishes to give eye appeal.

In an ideal world storing vegetables prior to preparation would be avoided. It is certainly not absolutely necessary to have a fridge, just somewhere dark and cool (about 8°C). If you have time buy from a market every one or two days; in this way you can keep in touch with seasons and pick up bargains. The fresher they are the less you have to think about, in terms of preparation. On the whole, vegetables and fruit will keep better if they have been topped and tailed, as these are generally the first parts to go soft – keep all the trimmings for your stockpot.

Equipment needed for fruit and vegetable preparation

Whatever you do, don't go out and buy lots of new equipment – you're probably happiest with what you have already. However, here are some useful items with tips for maintaining them:

Knives   You need only two knives, the first being a small Chinese chopper. These cost about £1.50 from most Chinese supermarkets and have a blunt end, so there is little risk of stabbing anyone! They are made from one piece of steel or iron and hold a very keen edge. Look after your knife and it will repay you a hundredfold – in speed and accuracy. After every use sharpen it on a whetstone (from most hardware stores) and oil it with vegetable cooking oil as otherwise it will go rusty.

The second knife you will need is a small 3-inch paring knife which is useful for more dainty work and cutting out blemishes. Care for it as for the first knife.

Grater   The easiest to use are flat rectangular ones.

Flippy peeler   Much faster and less wasteful than the conventional potato peeler.

Chopping board   Preferably made from one piece of wood (the harder the better – teak if possible). Avoid immersing in water.

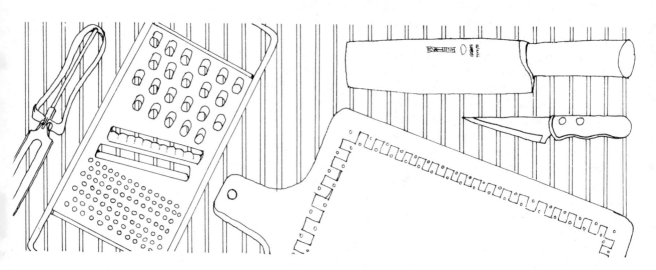

Chopping techniques

In the following pages you will find different ways of preparing vegetables, illustrated by one vegetable. Each chopping technique will be lettered and cross-referred to throughout the book. For example, chopping technique A in which a leek is sliced simply into rounds may be applied equally to all root vegetables – courgettes, aubergines, etc. The chapter finishes with a section in which common fruits and vegetables, not illustrated, will be described with some useful information and suggested chopping techniques. Eventually of course, the decision as to how you prepare your vegetables and fruit will lie with you. My intention is to lay some simple foundations upon which you can experiment.

The individual information about each vegetable or fruit is simply to help you decide when to buy and what to watch for when preparing. Certain vegetables and fruits do need special care and attention which I feel is relevant to include at this point. Hopefully by the end of the chapter you will know a bit more about vegetables and fruit in general. There is a vast array of shapes and sizes to give a dish colour and texture whilst retaining maximum nutritional content. Some vegetables and fruit do not fit into any particular classification and these will be dealt with individually in the illustrated examples.

In the course of preparation you will be handling extremely sharp knives (I hope). Common sense, of course, rules their use but if you follow these guidelines there is a good chance of you leaving the kitchen with fingers and fingernails intact:

1   Establish a safe home for knives out of reach of children. Each blade should be completely isolated from another, with sharp edges and points covered. A wooden knife rack that sheathes each blade is ideal and if used carefully the wood will not dull a finely honed edge, as will any metal contact.

2   When chopping any vegetable or fruit, hold it firmly with thumb and first two fingers. Try to keep the tips of your fingers tucked in at right angles to the surface you are cutting. This will seem awkward at first but comes easily with practice. Next time you chop a cucumber try this; being long and thin it is the ideal shape for practice. The advantages of this technique are twofold. Firstly, with fingers turned in it is almost impossible to chop your fingers off. Secondly, using the tips of the fingers at right angles to the vegetable or fruit means you can bring the blade of the knife into contact with them forming a firm and accurate block against which to chop. After a while this will increase speed and accuracy in chopping.

3   Try to get into the habit of carrying pointed knives by the handle with the point aimed at the ground. I have seen many accidents when people have been hurt through someone carrying a knife as though they were going into battle!

4   Use the tip of the knife only for fine work. Commence your slicing action with the tip of the knife on the board and bring the heel of the knife down with a rolling movement. For particularly tough vegetables, use the heel of the knife mostly as there is greater power there.

Chopping technique A – full moons

Vegetable example – the leek

The leek is a member of the onion family and is widely available through autumn, winter and spring. They are rich in vitamin A, and vitamin C, sulphur, potassium, and calcium – most of which are in the green leaves which are often trimmed off and thrown away. Leeks have a wonderful individual flavour and every part of the leek can be used in cooking. What you do with the different parts of the leek depends on its age and size. A very young leek can be used entirely, apart from perhaps the tip from which it shoots tiny hair-like roots. If the green leaves are long, woody and discoloured trim these off. The nearer you approach the dense white succulent stem the more tender and sweet the leaves become and as much as possible should be used in cooking your dish. Whatever you do don't throw the trimmings away, as they are a vital part of any vegetable stockpot (see recipes 1–4). Leeks have for so long been associated with stews and lengthy cooking procedures (of which they can form a valid part), that it seems forgotten that while young they are delicious when eaten slightly crunchy, they may be cooked in no longer than five minutes with a little very hot oil and tamari, together with some honey and lemon juice. The resulting dish is fresh, nutritious and succulent.

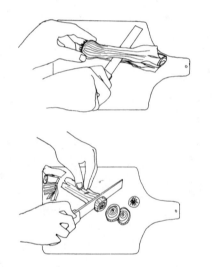

Wash the entire leek then discard any discoloured outer leaves – but retain for your stockpot, although if they're really bad don't be ashamed to throw them away. Leeks tend to have dirt and grit inside the actual green leaves down to the more dense white stem. To clean this part take a sharp pointed knife and make a lateral incision through the leek's centre (as illustrated).

Trim both ends of the leek economically and save for the stockpot.

For the full moon shapes keep the knife at right angles to the leek and slice through the vegetable. The width of your full moon will be related to the size of the leek and its status in the dish you are cooking. If it's going to be a feature vegetable in the dish it will keep its shape better if cut into larger slices – bear this in mind when cooking the dish.

Chopping technique A.1

An extension of chopping technique A would be the half moon which obviously involves simple bisection of the vegetable prior to chopping, this will be referred to in the book as chopping technique A.1.

Other chopping techniques readily applicable to the leek include B, 3.1, D and G.

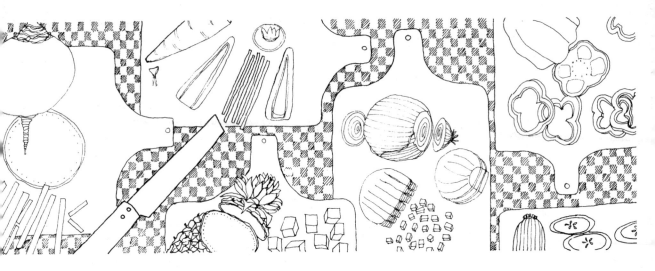

Chopping technique B – the ellipse

Vegetable example – the courgette

The courgette is really a baby marrow and may be best thought of as a vegetable fruit. As with most vegetable fruits it mainly contains water (94 per cent) together with a little protein and very few calories. It does, however, add wonderful texture and colour to any dish if treated gently, prepared attractively and cooked minimally. Courgettes are one of the vegetables we tend to add literally five minutes before serving or finishing a hot dish. They are available almost throughout the year, though sometimes there is a gap between our own season finishing and the African one starting. Out of the English and French summer season, courgettes do tend to be rather expensive, but surprisingly they are of good quality. Courgettes are extremely easy and quick to prepare and should be cooked as soon as possible, otherwise the small amount of goodness they do contain will flow out in their large water content. Sometimes the outer skin is blemished and although not dangerous these should be sparingly trimmed. Occasionally, the skin does have a bitter taste which can be removed by sprinkling salt over the prepared vegetable and later washing it off. If possible avoid this as the less water contact the courgette has the more chance it has of retaining some of its goodness. Courgettes do have a very delicate flavour which can only be retained through fast preparation and cooking. Like aubergines they do have the ability to absorb flavour and so can take on any characteristics of a dish that you wish.

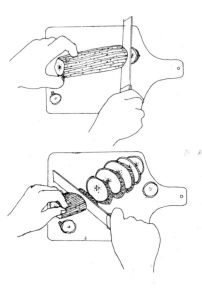

Wash the courgettes quickly and trim the worst blemishes then, top and tail.

To form an ellipse shape: using the Chinese chopper slice through the courgette on a slant. The thickness of the slices will again depend on the size of the courgette and the cooking process to follow.

Sliced courgettes can make an interesting salad if blanched quickly in boiling water and marinated for a few hours before serving.

Chopping technique B.1

This again, is identical to chopping technique B with the bisection of the vegetable lengthwise prior to cutting.

Other chopping techniques applicable to the courgette include A, A.1, D, F, H, and H.1

Chopping technique C – chunks

Fruit example – the pineapple

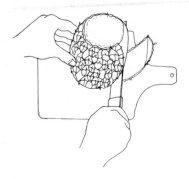

The pineapple is, of course, regarded in England as an exotic fruit, and rightly so, it is rather expensive but available all year round. It is rich in flavour when ripe and an excellent source of vitamin C (two-thirds of which is lost in tinned pineapple). When buying a pineapple it is vital to test for ripeness. To do this simply remove one of the inner spiky leaves from the top. If the leaf comes out too quickly the pineapple is over ripe and may have even started fermenting – this can probably be purchased cheaply. If it won't come out at all the pineapple is not ripe and, therefore, not worth buying. The ideal is in-between, slight resistance but eventual slow withdrawal. Like most fruits, once prepared it will quickly start to deteriorate, first losing its vitamin content and later by fermenting in its own high sugar reserves. To combat this leave preparation until the last minute, just prior to eating, and ensure it is tossed in lemon juice once prepared, the acid in the lemon juice will help prevent the oxidation which leads to fermentation. If you do have to store the pineapple after preparation keep it somewhere cool – ideally a fridge. I have included the pineapple in this section because in its preparation we see a peeling technique which is applicable to all citrus fruits and results in minimal wastage while removing the bitter, inedible skin or pith. In addition, the end shape 'the chunk' is commonly used, especially with root vegetables in substantial winter stews.

First wash the pineapple quickly in case it has been sprayed with anything nasty that might rub off on your board. Next take your Chinese chopper and remove the green top of the pineapple. Now stand the pineapple on its end and, using the centre of the knife, carefully make an incision just beneath the skin removing it from one end to the other in strips.

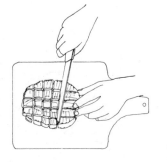

Now the pineapple is skinless but should resemble its original shape. Still standing on its end slice the pineapple clean down the centre – in half.

Supporting one half still end-on with your hand – but fingers well out of the way – make a slice the thickness of the chunk required parallel to the dissecting stroke. Repeat this process with the rest of that half. Then again with the other half. It may be necessary to lay the pineapple down at some point.

Cut into strips lengthways and then crossways to form cubes of reasonably equal size.

Chopping technique D – long thin strips (julienne)

Vegetable example – the carrot

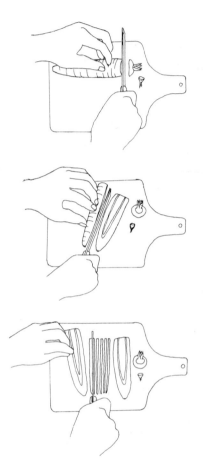

The carrot is probably the most popular of all root vegetables. Providing colour, bite, and taste, it also makes a dish nutritious with its high carotene content that is turned into Vitamin A in the body. Carrots are best eaten young as are all root vegetables, and ideally should have the minimum of preparation. At 'Food For Friends' we are always loathe to peel any vegetable for most of the taste and goodness is stored in or just under the skin. However, when using old carrots it is sometimes necessary to trim discoloured or woody parts although very seldom necessary to peel it completely. We prefer to adjust the role of the vegetable in a dish to its age and state of decay.

Because of its shape, size and colour the carrot is probably the most flexible of all vegetables. Perhaps, its versatility is the reason for its common use in savoury dishes, from salads to stews.

Cooking should be minimal, a carrot should always have plenty of bite when eaten. If water is the cooking medium use it sparingly, a saucepan with a tight fitting lid will enable you almost to steam the carrots in their own juices, so conserving the flavour, nutrition, and colour. If butter or vegetable margarine are used the same principles apply.

As the season progresses the carrots will become larger, tougher and more marked – making them suitable for more rigorous and elaborate preparation and longer cooking. These are the carrots which form the base of so many casseroles, bakes, and dressed salads – it is such a carrot that I have chosen to demonstrate a classical French vegetable shape, the julienne, or long thin strip. If you must cook them some time after preparation, toss the prepared carrots in lemon juice to prevent discoloration and to help preserve nutritional content.

Wash the carrots thoroughly and pare any discoloration or woody parts reasonably ruthlessly. Next, top and tail the carrots, remembering to retain all trimmings for your stockpot.

Slice the carrots lengthways, with a Chinese chopper or long knife. The more you do this the finer you'll be able to cut the strips.

Now you have a series of longitudinal sections of carrot. Lay these flat on your board and slice thinly again lengthways.

This style of chopping is useful for crudités, salads, and to add an unusual oriental feel to sauces and casseroles.

Other chopping techniques applicable to the carrot include A, A.1, B, B.1, D, F, G, H and H.1.

Chopping technique E – rings

Vegetable example – the green pepper

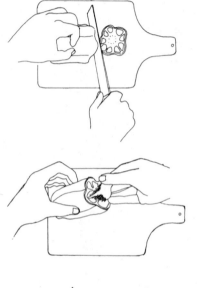

Like the courgette, the green pepper is a vegetable fruit (really an under-ripe red pepper). It comes from a large family of peppers, or capsicums to give them the correct name, of many different shapes, sizes and strengths. Because it has not yet ripened, the green pepper is much more pungent and slightly bitter compared with the sweet red pepper. Nevertheless, it is succulent eaten raw and retains this feature as long as it is not overcooked. Like most vegetable fruits, it has an extremely high water content so preparation and cooking times again should be kept to a minimum. Some green peppers are occasionally tougher and more bitter than others, probably through being picked far too young. These can withstand longer cooking (in fact they taste better) and should be added early in the cooking process.

Green peppers are not indigenous to Europe and their part in a wholefood diet might be in dispute were it not for the individuality of their colour, shape, and flavour in so many dishes. The majority are forced under glass, so are available all year round, if you can afford them. Probably the best time to buy is at the height of the Canaries season during April or during the June–August period when you will find Italian, Spanish and English outdoor varieties reasonably inexpensive.

Once purchased store in a cool place, preferably a refrigerator. Before preparing them make sure your knife is extra sharp, as a dull blade can bruise the delicate flesh causing discoloration. Large green peppers provide excellent receptacles for a tasty stuffing (see recipe 165) with almost no preparation.

The vegetable chopping style I have chosen for green peppers is used simply because it is only this vegetable and its cousins, plus perhaps onions, that have the prerequisites for the style. (Onions, of course, can be divided after slicing to produce the same effect.)

Wash the green pepper thoroughly and, using your Chinese chopper, economically slice off the stalk end of the vegetable, keeping it for your stockpot.

Using either your fingers or a small sharp knife, remove the seeds and white pith from the centre of the green pepper and discard.

Holding the closed end of the green pepper firmly in one hand – remember to keep your fingers out of the way – slice carefully across and through the green pepper and lo and behold you have a ring.

Rings are best used as an interesting shape in salads, or to decorate the tops of quiches, pizzas and bakes, in casseroles or stews they tend to break or lose their shape quickly.

Other vegetable chopping techniques suitable for the green pepper include D and G.

Chopping technique F – the wedge

Vegetable example – the tomato

The tomato is probably the best known and most widely used of all vegetable fruits. Its distinctive flavour and colour lead it to be used both raw and as a cooked vegetable fruit. The quality of tomatoes varies enormously and, unfortunately, the varieties generally on sale are often below standard, both in type and quality. This is largely the result of mass production and forced growth with emphasis being placed on heavy yield and transportability rather than flavour. Ideally, a tomato should be picked fresh and ripe from the vine and eaten immediately. Tomatoes are available all year round and are generally moderately expensive, except during the English season – June to September. Eaten fresh and ripe the tomato is a good source of carotene and Vitamin C, uncooked it is also very low in calories.

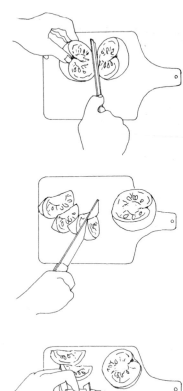

For cooking I would suggest, at the risk of ire from the wholefood community, that tinned tomatoes are the best and most economical to use. We find Italian tinned varieties, in particular, having good flavour with less of the 'tinned' taste than other types. In any case, 'tinniness' can be removed by the addition of a little sugar or honey and vinegar. It does after all, seem a shame to subject such a wonderful vegetable fruit full of so much goodness to any cooking procedures, unless damaged.

If tinned tomatoes are totally unacceptable to your philosophy of life then use tomato purée or home-made tomato concassée, both of which are, in effect, condensed forms of tomato colour and taste, though considerably more expensive.

Tomatoes, of course, consist largely of water, so it is best to keep preparation and preparation time to a bare minimum to retain flavour and nutrition. If unripe they should be stored in a cool, dry, and dark place; here, they will ripen successfully and will not wrinkle as they do in sunlight. When ripe they should be eaten very quickly, and if stored kept in the salad compartment of a fridge.

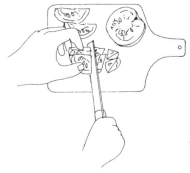

If you are on a macro-biotic regime then tomatoes are not for you. Their yin nature and relationship to the deadly nightshade and other poisonous plants (all Solanaceae) render them unacceptable. Without debating the rationale behind eating or not eating certain foods, I would suggest that any animal is healthier eating produce grown on the surrounding land rather than foods imported from thousands of miles away in the name of a balanced diet.

I have chosen the tomato to demonstrate the wedge style of chopping vegetables – simply because it is spherical. This style and shape of preparation is applicable to any vegetable or fruit which has at least one circular cross-section. Each wedge can then be cut into divisions according to need. The tomato should be cut as little as possible as the smaller the pieces the more it will disintegrate.

Wash the tomato thoroughly and remove the stalk. Using a sharp knife bisect the tomato.

Taking each hemisphere in turn cut the tomato into wedges – the size depending on the initial size of the tomato and the desired effect.

Each wedge may then be further sub-divided although, in the case of the tomato, I would not suggest this, except for decorative purposes.

Other vegetable chopping techniques suitable for the tomato are A and A.1.

Chopping technique G – fine chopping

Vegetable example – the onion

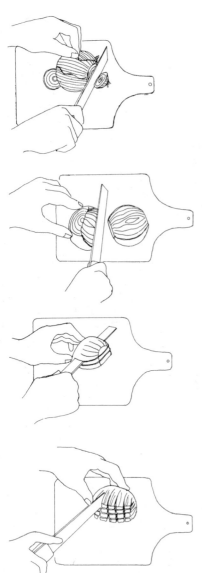

The onion is probably the most popular and commonly used vegetable throughout the world. Perhaps its very popularity explains why so many myths and uses for it have emerged. In fact, the onion on its own has very little nutritional content. It is extremely low in calories and only has a small vitamin C content. It does however, have a very strong flavour and smell which are extremely useful in cooking or if using it as a raw salad vegetable.

Onions are available cheaply throughout the year, though varying in size, taste, and colour according to the season and country of origin. English onions are generally small and will keep well. The larger varieties, such as Spanish onions, because of their greater water content, will tend to go soft quickly and spoil easily. In general, the darker the flesh of the onion the stronger the flavour will be, red onions being the most flavoursome of all. If possible then, as with most of the vegetables I have described, do not keep them any longer than you have to. Although onions usually keep better than most vegetables and salad vegetables, they are always available so keep your purchases to a bare minimum and avoid spongy or sprouted onions. When storing keep in a cool dry area which is well ventilated and, if you can, keep them separated.

The vegetable chopping technique for the onion is common only to the onion and white cabbage. However, it does provide useful practice for increasing your dexterity with a sharp knife.

Top and tail the onion, keeping wastage to a minimum and retaining as much of the root intact as possible. Do not peel as this is easier when the onion has been halved. Washing is not necessary as all the outer skin will be removed and discarded.

Divide the onion in half and remove the dry outer skin, leaving the first layer that is completely unblemished exposed.

Place the onion half flat on your chopping board and, using a sharp knife slice inwards towards the root. It is important not to slice completely through the onion as the root will then hold the vegetable together, allowing you to perform the next two stages with greater ease. Make several parallel incisions to the first one.

Still holding the onion firmly by its root end, slice down through the onion at right angles to your first incision, careful not to cut the root

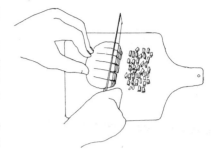

and repeat leaving the onion at the end of the process, still held together by the root.

Still holding the root end of the onion with your non-cutting hand, slice downwards perpendicularly to the preceding incisions moving with each slice towards the root end of the vegetable. Usually, you are left with a small amount of root that has not been touched. This can be chopped to a suitable size or used for your stockpot.

Bear in mind what role the onion is playing in the dish you are preparing. Usually, onion is best remaining in the background of a dish, adding lots of flavour, but rarely a feature vegetable in itself.

Other vegetable chopping techniques suitable for the onion include A, A.1, D, and E.

Chopping technique H – batons and matchsticks

Vegetable example – the turnip

Root vegetables, like the turnip, were among the first vegetables eaten by prehistoric man. The reason being that they store comparatively well and are generally available through much of the year. Their nutritional content varies from root to root and decreases considerably with age. Eaten best when young, the turnip contains almost no carotene but some vitamin C, it has very little calorific content but is fairly high in minerals. Again, the useful part of the turnip is the skin so this should be left intact whenever possible. However, the older they become the more woody the skin, it is at this stage that some amount of peeling becomes necessary. Without their skin most root vegetables tend to discolour very quickly, so should be cooked immediately or sprinkled with salt or lemon juice. As a last resort they could be submerged in salted water.

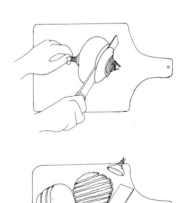

The turnip does have an interesting flavour all of its own, and provides a good deal of bulk to any dish, but, personally, I don't think any main savoury dish should over-emphasize turnips. It will make a lovely soup, if well flavoured with other ingredients (see recipe 185). My favourite turnips are the baby ones which are available in April and May. They are so sweet and delicious that they can be eaten raw as a salad vegetable, or as a feature vegetable in fresh spring casseroles, bakes or soups.

Anyway, being relatively un-nutritious and inexpensive they make wonderful practice material. The technique described is one very commonly used for potato chips. If the same technique is used, but the vegetable chopped much more finely, the resulting matchsticks make an unusual garnish for salads or give clear soups an interesting texture. The same technique can be used for any vegetable, fruit or tuber that has a firm and substantial flesh. Any trimmings you do get from your turnip should be retained and added to the stockpot.

Wash and scrub the turnip thoroughly. Top and tail it then deal with

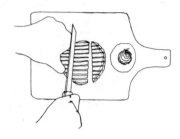

blemishes and assess the woodiness of the skin before considering peeling. Sometimes, long cooking will tenderize a slightly woody skin. If it is too far gone then do your worst and trim it off, without any misgivings.

Using a Chinese chopper divide the turnip in half crossways. Make another slice crossways through the turnip at the thickness required for either baton or matchstick.

Place your cross-section flat on the board and make a series of parallel incisions through it, creating batons. If matchsticks are wanted make the incisions closer and cut the whole cross-section into two or three pieces depending on the size of the turnip.

Throughout the rest of the book, chopping technique H refers to the method used for cutting baton shapes, and chopping technique H.1 to that used for matchstick shapes.

Other vegetable chopping techniques suitable for the turnip include A, A.1, B, B.1, D, F, and G.

Chopping technique I – florets

Vegetable example – the cauliflower

The cauliflower is a beautiful, delicate vegetable, so often treated roughly, overprepared and overcooked. It is a member of a large group of leafy vegetables known as the brassicas, which include broccoli, kale, Chinese cabbage and spinach, as well as more common varieties of cabbage and 'greens'. All of this family are rich in nutrients, especially vitamin C and carotene – cauliflowers being an exceptionally good source of vitamin C. However, as with all foods rich in vitamin C the care with which you prepare and cook them will determine how much benefit you receive. The cauliflower, especially, needs very little preparation and can be cooked whole or in florets, as will be demonstrated, using very little water. At 'Food for Friends' we like to cook the cauliflower as little as possible, for no more than 5 minutes, so as not to destroy its distinctive shape, flavour and firm texture. Cauliflowers quickly change from being just cooked to overcooked so, bearing in mind their nutritional content, always undercook and eat immediately.

Cauliflowers also make an unusual and useful salad vegetable and they are perfectly delicious eaten raw. If you doubt this, try scalding them with boiling water, then drain, cool immediately and eat. Alternatively, using the same technique, having poured off the water used to scald the vegetable, replace it with a chosen marinade. Scalding will help its ability to absorb some of the marinade and will slightly change the cauliflower's taste and texture for its new role.

Cauliflower is available throughout the year, though tends to vary in price and quality according to the seasons. Around Christmas it is usually at its peak price, about double the normal price for other times of the year. Quality varies enormously, the ideal cauliflower is medium-sized, with a clear pale cream colour and tightly bunched florets. As the cauliflower grows old the florets will appear more jaundiced and may develop small fungal spots. They may also start to grow apart, making the whole vegetable look slightly bedraggled. There is nothing wrong with these cauliflowers, and often they still have a lot of flavour. However, the deterioration in shape makes them better suited for use in soups or sauces.

Make a transverse slice through the bottom part of the cauliflower. This will remove all of the unnecessary green leaves. Wash the head thoroughly.

If cooking the cauliflower whole, remove the core using a sharp pointed vegetable knife in a circular cutting motion. This will ensure the cauliflower cooks evenly.

To produce florets, simply cut each floret off from base to centre working inwards. Leave as much of the small stalk attached to each floret as you think appropriate. In a few instances you may wish to bisect particularly large florets, but this will increase the tendency to deteriorate during cooking. It is only recommended when preparing cauliflower for soup.

The central core that is left is delicious eaten raw, with a crisp mustard-like flavour; otherwise – into the stockpot with it.

This vegetable chopping technique is particularly applicable to calabrese (Italian broccoli) and purple sprouting broccoli.

Chapter 3
Sauces

Introduction

Sauces are the fundamental building blocks upon which many savoury vegetarian dishes are based. People who cook with meat tend to rely upon the flavour of the particular type of meat they are using to dominate the whole dish. Sauces then become regarded as accompaniments or extensions of the meat being used. They may add balance, colour and texture to a meat dish, but generally take on a supportive role in the end product. At least, this is the theory, in actual fact sauces tend to disguise most meat dishes in which they are used, and most basic sauces are vegetarian.

The role of the sauce in vegetarian cookery is to act as a catalyst; unchanging itself, it gives the rest of the ingredients a common identity while enabling them to retain their individual characteristics. To do this effectively there are several factors to take into account. For instance, vegetables will overcook quickly if stewed in a thin sauce. This hypothesis may suggest that it is better to reheat vegetables, for an oven-baked dish say, in a thick sauce. This is true, but only to some extent, for the problem can be avoided completely if enough thought is put into your cooking. From the nutritional point of view, it is bad policy to reheat vegetables. If you really want a thin sauce in your bake, cook the sauce separately, cut the vegetables into large chunks and add to the prepared sauce when it is boiling, for a few minutes. Then remove from the heat and finish the dish off quickly in its bake tin with a suitable topping in a hot oven. Using this method you are really only finishing cooking the vegetables and, at the same time, cooking the topping.

Another important factor to bear in mind is presentation. Too thin a sauce will not lift the vegetables so they may be totally submerged. Too thick a sauce may mask the vegetables in a different way, hiding attractive ingredients; it may even dry up if reheated.

Once again, balance is the ultimate aim, with the scales tipped to your own personal tastes. First of all consider the vegetable/fruit, beans/peas/grains or pasta you will be using. Having decided where the emphasis is going to lie, decide on the nature of the sauce, will it be simple or rich, thick, thin or medium, little or abundant. Then consider what effect bringing all the ingredients together will have and how they will be cooked. Look out of the window and see if it is hot or cold, dry or rainy. Not until all of these factors have been mentally assessed should you decide on the exact nature of your sauce. On paper it sounds like decisions, decisions, but it soon becomes instinctive.

The sauces we use originally came from all over the world. So, in using a particular sauce, I find it helpful to imagine which fruits and vegetables the people of that particular country might use and either use the same or adapt other vegetables for the same purpose. For example, Italy brings visions of tomatoes, garlic, herbs, pepper and pasta, while India reeks of coriander, cumin, turmeric, garam masala and lentils; Africa makes one think of chilli and peanuts; the Middle East chick-peas and tahini, and so on. To simplify the chapter I have highlighted only two fundamental influences in our cooking, these being Chinese and European. Sauces from these two areas demonstrate various different types of sauces, from the simplest Chinese shoyu-based sauce through to the most rich and intricate French sauces. Using this method, I have been able to distinguish six basic different approaches to vegetarian sauces and have provided examples later in the chapter.

The chapter will also give you a simple guide to different herbs, spices, natural flavourings and oils which are all easily available and, if used correctly, can turn an ordinary sauce into something really special. I won't attempt to give you their Latin names, just a little background knowledge, when to add them to your cooking and how they might taste. There are few firm rules regarding the addition of different herbs, spices and flavourings to your dish, but, for example, you get a much nicer flavour if you add oregano to a dish just before serving than if you stew it for hours. More subtle ways of flavouring dishes are to use different oils at the stir-fry stage of preparation. For instance a West Indian dish can really come alive with the use of coconut oil.

We will also explore the various ways in which sauces are thickened, their advantages and disadvantages, and their suitability to the end purpose, relating specifically to the Chinese/European approach to sauce cooking.

Finally we will move on to the basic stockpot, a viable feature in everybody's kitchen and an alternative to revolting little cubes or packets of monosodium glutamate.

The aim of this chapter on sauces is to encourage experimentation in cooking, based on sound knowledge and flair.

Unusual additions to sauces

Tamari, shoyu and soya sauce

These are all basically the same product yet totally different in quality. They are all fermented soya bean products. Tamari is the best, but also the most expensive and least widely available. It is thick, dark brown and should be used more sparingly than shoyu or soya sauce, as it has a stronger flavour. We use shoyu, which is reasonably pure and less expensive than tamari. I have found some brands labelled soya sauce not worth buying as they contain mostly chemicals and caramel and this cheap flavour comes through in cooking.

Use any of these products sparingly as their flavour is usually best used in a supportive role, rather than as the dominating feature. For best results, shoyu should be added to vegetables when they are very hot (see stir-fry recipe 177). However, Shoyu may be used like any other condiment in the final stages of seasoning your dish.

Miso

Miso comes from the same stable as tamari and shoyu. It is a paste of fermented soya bean and wheat, and may be black or white. It has an even stronger flavour and smell than tamari so should be used sparingly. The rich flavour of miso is useful for stocks, soups and pâtés. If adding miso to a hot liquid make sure it is never boiled for this will kill enzymes in the product which are beneficial to digestion and will also mar the flavour. Not everyone will like miso at first, because it is so strong; try using it sparingly at first and don't tell anyone, soon people will come to love it.

Tahini

Tahini is a paste of sesame seeds and sesame oil, it is usually white or brown. It originates from the Middle East and has a slightly bitter edge to it, though this is usually lost in cooking. Its creamy consistency makes it not only an unusual flavouring but also a thickening agent. It is quite easily available and is worth buying if only to make hummous.

Peanut butter

Peanut butter is worth buying only from wholefood shops, the supermarket brands are very disappointing. I never liked it as a child but, as an addition to a sauce, it is quite unique. It adds a peanut flavour while at the same time thickening the sauce considerably. When making a peanut sauce it is best to add it with the tamari at the stir-fry stage, then gently stir the rest of the liquid into it trying to avoid lumps. The end sauce should taste nothing like peanut butter; often spicy, it will combine excellently with wine, cider or fruit juice to give an African or Indonesian touch to a meal.

Seaweed

There are lots of varieties of seaweed. We find nori easiest as it comes in sheets and is quick to cook while retaining a distinctive fishy flavour. Japanese seaweed is nothing like that which we find on Brighton beach, it is grown in special underwater farms, is clean and easy to use. It may be dropped into a soup just before serving (especially nice in miso soup), or grilled and sprinkled over hot rice or vegetables.

Herbs and spices

The addition of herbs and spices to a sauce can 'make or break it'. For a long time, people have used old standards, like 'mixed herbs', 'curry powder', bay leaves, ginger and cinnamon, while ignoring the vast array of other easily available herbs and spices which are both special in their own right and may be combined to your personal requirements or to emphasize a certain aspect of a dish. Once again it is a question of balance or imbalance. Only experience will tell you exactly how you like your dish seasoned and this short section on herbs and spices is just to give advance warning of what you can expect from them.

There are no hard and fast rules, just tips to get the best flavours out of your herbs and spices. When creating a dish it is especially important to keep in mind an overall direction to work to, whether geographical, seasonal or personal. The herbs and spices, and how you use them, will either add to or take away from your desired end result.

Herbs are best used fresh and, if dried, the leaves or flowers are generally used rather than the stems. However, herbs are not all green deciduous plants – some are shrubs, some trees. It is important to bear in mind from what part of which plant the condiment comes as this will affect its role in the dish. For instance, marjoram, a soft, green-leaved plant, may be eaten along with the rest of the dish, whereas the bay leaf must be left well alone as it is bitter and inedible.

Spices should always be freshly ground. If this is impracticable then purchase in small quantities from wholefood or Indian shops. Spices purchased in packets are very inferior as regards flavour. Try to store for as little time as possible.

Herbs and spices should never be kept in glass jars, as they are very sensitive to light. Keep in stone jars or in a dark cupboard. Fresh herbs and spices are also highly nutritious, containing many common and rare vitamins as well as minerals. However, some are also dangerous if eaten in too great a quantity or too regularly.

Herbs

Tarragon

Tarragon is often of poor quality, containing a lot of wood, which is not worth buying. You should purchase only the leaves; either dried, freeze-dried or fresh, the latter being best but most expensive. Tarragon has a strong flavour, so be careful not to use too much. Fresh or dry, it can be added at any stage to your sauce, but the longer it is cooked the more flavour it exudes. Again, it is best added at the stir-fry/sautée stage. It is especially nice used in conjunction with wine and vinegar, for both tomato and white sauces. It is one of the four 'Fines Herbes'.

Chervil

Chervil is again a leaf and may be treated and used in a similar way to tarragon. It too is a 'Fine Herbe' and is not bitter like tarragon, but rather sweet. Because of this, it is often used with tarragon on the old sweet and sour principle. Again it has considerable versatility and may be used in a wide range of mostly European sauces.

Fennel

Fennel may be mistaken for dill. We generally use the leaves as a herb and the seeds for spice. Leaves are usually dry while the seeds are ground. Both leaf and seed are very sweet and the aniseed flavour is an acquired taste, so experiment continuously. Fennel leaves should be added to sauces quite late in cooking, the seeds make an interesting addition to pastry, whether sweet or savoury.

Marjoram

Marjoram is a leaf herb, grey-green in colour, and delicate enough to be added at any stage in cooking. Used moderately, it will add a light piquancy to many sauces, especially those involving the use of tomatoes. Used to excess, marjoram will make a sauce bitter as it contains a high level of tannin. Marjoram is one of the only herbs that can be used successfully in European, African, Asian and American-influenced dishes. Funnily enough, it is also usually one of the dreaded 'mixed herb' bunch.

Thyme

Thyme, again a leaf, is finer than marjoram but of similar colour. It is probably one of the most commonly used herbs in the history of cooking. We use dried thyme almost exclusively in this country, though fresh it is a wonderful addition to salads. Like marjoram it has a high tannin content, so be careful not to add too much to a sauce and make it bitter. Thyme is especially nice used in North African or European-influenced cookery.

Rosemary

Rosemary is the leaf of a shrub and very few gardens in England are without a rosemary bush. Usually used either whole or crushed, fresh or dry, rosemary is a particularly pungent herb and can easily dominate a sauce, but used sparingly it will enhance and even stimulate the appetite. It's tough composition means it has to be well cooked and should be added at the very beginning of any dish, another reason to cut down on the quantity used. Rosemary is used primarily in central European and Mediterranean-based recipes.

Dill

Dill comes in several forms. Dill weed is the fine hair-like leaves of the dill plant, it is usually available either dried or freeze-dried. Dill seeds are more bitter and suitable only for pickling. If fresh dill is available the whole leaf may be used and the stalks retained for pickling. Dill has a very strong flavour whether weed or seed, so should be used with caution. Many people find it too pungent in hot dishes. Used sparingly and with the right ingredients it can make a dish distinctive and tasty. It is also always a useful addition to mayonnaise. Dill originated from the Middle and Far East and so it is particularly suitable for Arabic and central European dishes.

Basil

Basil is a sweet leaf herb and may be used fresh or dry in salads and sauces. It has a pungent aroma rather like nutmeg which will be retained as long as the herb is not overcooked. Originally from India, it reached the whole of Europe and is equally delicious in spicy Middle Eastern food or in more traditional French tomato sauces.

Sage

Sage is the crinkled leaf of a shrub, grey-green or silver in colour with a distinctive flavour and smell. It is another herb that should be used cautiously or else its pungency will totally dominate the surrounding dish. It is spicy and has a high tannin content. Over-use will make a dish too bitter and aromatic. Sage is native to the Mediterranean and has long been used as an ingredient for stuffings, it is also delicious in basic sauces so long as it is not overdone.

Mint

Mint is probably one of the most commonly used herbs in England, whether peppermint or spearmint. We usually only use the leaves, except if brewing tea when the stalk is also useful. Mint may be one of the most common herbs but it is also one of the most underestimated. For a long time its sole purpose has been to accompany lamb or flavour new potatoes. In small quantities, however, it is an exciting addition to sauces and can form the base of some interesting Middle Eastern and Greek dips.

Oregano

Oregano is also known as wild marjoram. It is very spicy and an absolute must with almost any tomato dish, be it cooked or raw. We use the stalks and leaves of this delicate grey-green herb. If thrown into your sauce just before serving you will retain all of its flavour and aroma. For a tomato salad simply sprinkle it on according to taste, though a great deal may be a little too pungent.

Parsley

Parsley is another extremely common English herb although it is native to the Mediterranean. Apart from mint, it is perhaps the only bulky herb that is widely available. As it has a delicate flavour you can use a lot of it, both to flavour a sauce, and also to colour and garnish it. We use mostly the leaves but the finer stalks are also useful as long as they are chopped. The longer stalks are valuable for the stockpot. It is never necessary to chop parsley except for presentation purposes; flavour and nutrition will be retained if it is stripped by hand, colour and bulk will be kept if it is not added until the last possible moment to your sauce. Parsley is one of the infamous 'Mixed Herbs' which I do not like; never use dried and cut parsley unless you absolutely have no choice.

Bay leaf

The bay leaf is a tough, coarse leaf of the bay tree which is a shrub. Bay leaves are one of the few cases where it does not matter whether you use them fresh or dry. They are obtainable whole or in pieces, and fresh or dry. They take a long time to release their flavour and when they do it is very strong, as they cannot be eaten it does not matter which you use. Used correctly, bay leaves can add a lot of depth to a stock or sauce. Over-used they will totally destroy all other flavours in the dish.

Spices

Black and white pepper

Black and white pepper come from the same plant. Black pepper is harvested before the berries are ripe while white pepper is harvested after the berries have ripened. The difference between the two is in the flavour. Black pepper is much stronger in taste and aroma while white pepper is more delicate. The only reason white pepper became popular was because of the snobbish fastidiousness amongst French chefs who considered it unseemly to have little black specks in their pristine white sauces – never mind the flavour. We, of course, do not have that problem and use black pepper only. I don't think it is necessary to describe it, suffice to say it is incredibly superior when freshly ground. It is best used to your own taste. Crushed, it forms the nucleus of an exciting sauce.

Cloves

The clove we know is an unopened flower bud and may be used whole or ground. It is incredibly pungent so try not to over-do it. It is usually associated with autumn and winter sweets or punches. However, it can also be used as an interesting addition to Asian, African and West Indian-influenced dishes and is always used in a supporting role rather than dominating the dish.

Ginger

Ginger is one of the oldest spices, in terms of usage, in England, its use in cooking dates back to the Middle Ages. Consequently, it is one of the best known to English cookery. However, it seems to have been mostly associated with sweets, especially winter ones. Ginger is a root vegetable and is nicest when used fresh. Preserved, it is best used in sweet cookery. Whole, it will keep fairly well but once grated the flavour soon disappears. Because it is a root vegetable ginger should be added to the dish fairly early on in cooking. Fresh or preserved it should be grated or thinly sliced, when dried it should be in powder form. Ginger has a very strong flavour so do not use to excess. It can stand out as a flavour in its own right providing you don't overdo it.

Ginger is a grossly under-used addition to savoury dishes. Originating in the tropics it will blend well with Chinese, Indian, Japanese, West African and Caribbean cookery in particular. Not only will it add a subtle glowing warmth to dishes, it will also dominate a savoury sauce in its own right.

Nutmeg

Nutmeg also originated in the tropics and has been used in England for some considerable time. Nutmegs grow on a tree rather like a plum. The fleshy part if dried and ground is called Mace while the kernel is the nutmeg. This is always grated whole for use in cooking. Nutmeg is usually associated with sweet cookery, but it has a very strong flavour which can be used to spice white sauces delicately, notably cheese sauces. Over-used nutmeg can ruin a dish, so be cautious. Never buy ground nutmeg when you can grate a whole one. Nutmeg can be added at any time to your dish.

Cinnamon

Cinnamon is another tree-spice. This time however, it is the bark that is used. After drying, the bark rolls itself into tightly packed scrolls. These may be broken down to flavour dishes or ground into a powder. Cinnamon has an extremely strong and distinctive taste which is delicious when used subtly. Again, it is associated with winter puddings especially where these consist of apples, cakes or pastries. It may be used as a savoury additive however, especially in Chinese and Indian cooking. Cinnamon is best added at the beginning of cooking in order to benefit from its full flavour.

Allspice

Allspice is better known as the pimento (in fact the berry). It is pungent to taste and is prepared in a similar way to black pepper. Indigenous to Central America, Mexico and Jamaica allspice has become associated with hot savoury dishes, especially those involving chilli. It is also commonly known as a member of the boring 'Mixed Spice' combination.

Chillies

Chillies are a hot variety of pimento. They are used whole, fresh, dried or powdered. Grown in nearly every country that has a Mediterranean climate, they have become especially associated with South America and Mexico, although originally from Spain and Portugal. Chillies may be red or green, the red being notoriously hot. A simple way to reduce the viciousness of chillies is to remove their seeds prior to cooking. For best results fresh or dry chillies should be added in the initial phase of cooking the dish. Chillies are probably the most widely used spice in the world. Do not forget to appreciate a mild chilli as much as a hot one.

Cayenne

The cayenne pepper is basically exactly the same as the chilli. Cayenne is in fact, ground chilli.

Coriander

The plant looks more like a herb than most spices but it is the dry, round seed pods that are whole coriander. Whole coriander is often used for pickling, while freshly ground it adds a distinctive flavour to sweets or, more commonly, savouries. Coriander leaves can also be used as a seasoning though these are harder to come by. It originates from the Middle East and India, but today is much more widely available. Not only will it provide an interesting accent in curries, but it will also enhance South American and the more spicy Russian dishes.

Coriander should be added in the initial phases of cooking, but be careful not to over-use it.

Turmeric

Turmeric, like ginger, is a root spice. Rarely seen as a root in England, turmeric is usually powdered and so the fresher the better, try not to store it. Turmeric has been used in Europe for centuries, not only as a flavouring, but also as a colouring and it is often seen as a cheap version of saffron. It is fat-soluble and so should always be added to a dish at the stir-frying stage. It has a distinct spicy flavour and is extremely aromatic – apart from giving all it touches a yellow/orange tinge. Turmeric is an intrinsic part of the awful 'curry powder', however a curry mix with turmeric as a dominant ingredient can be extremely tasty, unusual and potentially mild.

Cardamom

The cardamom we use are seeds, either whole or ground. It may be used in sweets or in the South East Asian sauces we prepare, as well as cakes and pastries. Pungent and strong, it is easy to over-use.

Aniseed

Aniseed must be remembered as distinct from star anise. However, both are similar to taste and have similar uses. Both are excellent additions to sweets and pastries, while also adding depth to curries, chilli and Chinese dishes. Add sparingly in the early stages of cooking and use to taste. Strangely, aniseed belongs to the carrot family.

Cumin

Cumin is another member of the carrot family akin to aniseed, and, though milder, is used in the same context. We use the seed pods either whole or ground. Add early in the cooking process.

Saffron

Saffron is the stamen of the crocus. It is incredibly expensive and, of

course, totally over-rated. If you are going to use it treat it like gold-dust – it costs about the same. It has a very delicate flavour but does impart a beautiful colour. Saffron should be added at the end of the cooking process, except when colouring rice.

Paprika

Paprika is simply the dried pods of the largest and mildest varieties of capsicum. Cayenne and chilli are the smaller more pungent versions. After drying, the pods are ground and it is in this form that it is most commonly purchased. Because paprika is mild, it may be used not just for its distinctive flavour but also to add a rich orange-red colour to a dish. Paprika may be added in the early stages of preparing a dish, usually during any stir-fry procedure. It may also be used to adjust a sauce before serving. Generally, more flavour comes through with longer cooking, so last-minute additions must be noticeably greater to achieve the same effect. Paprika is synonymous with goulash and is best used in conjunction with tomatoes.

Mustard

We use mostly black mustard, either whole, ground or in its yellow form. In very common use it also has thickening properties when powdered. Mustard is far too strong to take full advantage of it as a thickening agent, and this property is primarily used in the preparation of table mustard or prior to its addition to a sauce. Mustard, as you all know, has a distinctive hot, spicy flavour. When using it in a sauce, the aim is to retain the clarity of the mustard flavour, while tempering it to the average palate. Most people prefer chilli to the fierce heat of mustard, and it is best to add mustard in the form of a paste to your dish at the stir-fry stage, coating the vegetable in a thin layer of mustard, a little of which is absorbed. The rest will combine with the whole dish to support, rather than dominate the final sauce.

Mustard may also be used as a substitute for ginger in some areas of sweet cookery.

Oils

Oils are all too rarely used to add extra flavour to dishes, with the possible exception of olive oil. The most common barrier is expense. The cheapest vegetable oils are chemically treated and frankly will do nothing extra for a dish except make it taste chemical; most of us put up with this out of necessity. More expensive ones are the chemically treated corn oil, olive oil, peanut oil, sunflower oil, safflower oil, coconut oil and sesame oil. These do retain some original flavour and aroma but most is submerged beneath that chemical taste. As oil is so expensive anyway it is best to stick to your regular variety for day-to-day cooking, but for special occasions splash out on a cold-processed oil, suitable for the dish you are serving. Cold-processed oils are extremely expensive but worth every penny in flavour, aroma and nutritional content; they cook well too. It is very important to choose an oil appropriate to the other ingredients in the dish. For instance, it is not advisable to use strong-flavoured olive oil in a delicate white mushroom sauce, for all you will taste is olive oil.

Oil should be stored in a cool, dark place, preferably the fridge. We never really have the problem of re-using oil as most of our dishes use only a little. Personally, I do not like the idea of deep-frying when usually shallow-frying can be just as effective. If you do want to re-use oil make sure it is strained immediately of all impurities then cooled and restored in the fridge as soon as possible.

When heating oil keep a careful eye on the temperature it has reached. Too hot, oil will damage anything put into it and may even burst into flames, depending on the ignition point. Too cold, and the ingredients will start to absorb oil making them unpleasant to eat. Oils should be heated quickly over a medium-high flame, and tested regularly with a trimming from your vegetable preparation. As soon as the oil begins to bubble in the presence of your vegetable trimming it is hot enough and the flame should be turned down to medium-low, to prevent over-heating. Changing the temperature of the oil will ultimately change the nature of the whole dish – just be careful and sensible.

Oil, of course, has emulsifying properties when mixed vigorously in the presence of a little acid, such as lemon juice or vinegar. This property is generally utilized in the preparation of salad dressings. The emulsified state is temporary and so dressings should not be mixed until a short while before serving. Oil, with a little acid, may also be added gently to egg yolk to form mayonnaise (see recipe 59). The process of thickening a sauce with an egg yolk will be discussed shortly; it is a much more permanent liaison if kept in the right conditions.

There follow a few notes on the oils more commonly available. I feel it is worth saving up and buying the cold-processed varieties instead of the chemically extracted varieties for special occasions. Always try to use a good oil for salad dressings where the flavour is even more noticeable. Strangely, Greek olive oil is the most widely available cold-processed oil, as the Greeks have not yet stopped using the process in favour of chemical extraction.

Corn oil

Corn oil is probably the most generally used oil, for the simple reason that it neither adds to or takes away from the flavour of a sauce or dressing; it is rather bland. So use it if you want to be safe.

Olive oil

Olive oil is probably one of the strongest flavoured oils. Only buy it if it is a deep green colour, preferably opaque. This means it has not been refined and will retain a wonderful flavour. Olive oil is especially good in hot Mediterranean dishes and those involving herbs, garlic and tomatoes. It is also the best to use in a salad dressing.

Coconut oil

Coconut oil is rather pricey, but has an extraordinary strong coconut smell and flavour. Used in spicy Indian or West Indian dishes you will probably not need to add any coconut cream to the recipe.

Peanut oil

Peanut oil is fairly bland, but very re-usable. It may be worth using in Indonesian or African dishes that involve peanuts or even your nut roast, depending on how rich you feel.

Safflower oil

Safflower oil is highly nutritious but it has no outstanding flavour, so use it if you want to feel better.

Sesame oil

Sesame oil is good because it does not need refrigerating. It also retains a noticeable sesame flavour. It is especially pleasant in African, Chinese, Malaysian or Middle Eastern dishes. It will add depth to any dish that involves tahini, and is nice in its own right with stir-fried vegetables.

Sunflower oil

Sunflower oil is good for you but not quite as good as safflower oil, it is rather bland and rather expensive, but suitable for those on a health kick.

Soya oil

Soya oil has a terrible smell and I would advise not using it.

Thickening sauces

This section discusses the major thickening agents used in both hot and cold, sweet and savoury vegetarian food. It covers the use of each agent, the food for which it is most suitable, at what stage the thickening is best performed, and what the end product should look like. Sauces are thickened for a variety of reasons and purposes, so it is important to bear these in mind when choosing a thickening medium. Your choice of medium will ultimately affect the flavour and presentation of the whole dish.

Roux

To make one litre of sauce:

Stage	Ingredient	Quantity	Method
1	Butter/vegetable margarine	90 g	*Melt fat in a heavy saucepan.*
2	100% wholewheat flour	90 g	*Add flour and mix in well, heat gently for 5–10 minutes (stirring regularly) or until the flour starts to change colour.*

When the roux is ready set it aside to cool for a few minutes, before gradually adding a litre of the chosen boiling liquid to avoid lumps.

Roux are particularly useful for thickening milk-based sauces. The resulting sauce is thick but may be further diluted to suit its purpose. After a sauce has been thickened with a roux, particularly milk sauces, the cooking process should effectively be brought to a halt. Thick sauces like these may be reheated to some extent but cannot be thoroughly worked without the risk of burning, scalding or curdling.

Roux-based sauces are usually flavoured after thickening, although some alteration of the milk/stock may be favoured prior to thickening, it will not drastically influence the end result.

The béchamel is the classic roux sauce (see recipe 34), although some heavy-duty tomato sauces may be thickened in the same way. Béchamel is usually a fairly bland, delicate white sauce, to which a myriad of ingredients may be added to form endless varieties of sauce (see recipes 34–53).

Roux are primarily used to thicken before seasoning, and may be diluted or left thick depending on what is needed. They are capable of supporting a bulky casserole or bake and take up any flavour you wish in a sauce. Although the final sauce should not be overcooked, it may be kept at an ambient temperature for some time.

The main drawbacks of roux sauces are that they tend to go on thickening and often burn if you're not careful. Conversely, if they are diluted to too great an extent the only way of re-thickening is to add the whole sauce to another roux. Roux are one of the most widely used thickening agents and are usable in sweet as well as savoury cooking, although the roux is perhaps a little clumsy for delicate sweet flavours.

Cornflour

To make one litre of sauce reasonably thick, blend a generous, but not heaped, dessertspoon of cornflour with a little water and stir into boiling liquid. It will thicken almost immediately and may be kept hot indefinitely in a closed container with a gentle heat. Left open on too high heat, cornflour-thickened sauces will generally become jelly-like before burning.

Cornflour is unfortunately very refined and very white – in fact it is pure starch. It is widely available and fairly cheap and easy to use, its main disadvantage being its glutinous consistency and flavour. Sauces which have been thickened with cornflour do have an unfortunately floury feel to them and this can ruin a carefully prepared sauce.

Cornflour should ideally be added only just before serving. Unlike the roux, cornflour-based sauces are constructed prior to thickening and are only adjusted after the cornflour has been added. As the effect of thickening is instant (providing the basic sauce is boiling) and easy to control, cornflour has become a popular thickening agent though I would say it is rather over-used. As I have said the floury after-taste of cornflour can ruin the end result of your sauce, so we tend to use cornflour to thicken only the spiciest and sharpest of sauces. For instance, a sweet and sour or chilli sauce is so distinctive that the cornflour after-taste will fade into the background. Cornflour is generally unsuccessful used with dairy products. With these, use a more natural starch flour, like potato or arrowroot. They can be used in exactly the same way as cornflour, but will not add any unpleasant glutinous aftertaste, and though a little more expensive and less easy to obtain than cornflour are well worth the time and expense. Cornflower and arrowroot are particularly useful for preparing glazes and sauces in sweet cookery.

Seaweed

Seaweed in the form of agar agar is an excellent thickener and, if chilled, will set. It is therefore a marvellous vegetarian alternative to gelatine, though in the presence of even the slightest warmth it will start to melt. Its applications to both sweet and savoury cookery are numerous, but usually only for cold dishes. Agar agar is rather expensive so its use should be confined to very special things like pâtés, mousses, sweet flans and jellies.

The most easily available and usable agar agar is powdered or flaked. The exact quantities used will usually vary from brand to brand but, basically, it is a question of adding a small amount to boiling water, then continuing to simmer for 10 minutes. It may then be added to the dish requiring it and will thicken up as it cools.

Agar agar does have a slight after-taste, but then so does gelatine – most people don't notice it. Agar agar is also extremely useful in glazes and other decorative work, especially for cold buffets.

Eggs

If you have a strong wrist and plenty of time you may make a thick sauce with egg yolks. It's a similar principle to making mayonnaise, the main difference being that the resulting sauce is hot and very temperamental. I think it is easiest demonstrated with a basic hollandaise sauce (recipe for one litre):

Stage	Ingredients	Quantity	Method
1	Butter/margarine	1 kg	*Melt the butter/margarine in a bowl or pan sitting in another pan of boiling water (a bain-marie). Be sure not to allow the butter to boil as this will separate out the hot milk solids.*
2	Ground black peppercorns	15	*Reduce the vinegar with peppercorns in a separate pan.*
	Cider/wine vinegar	66 ml	*Allow to cool and then add 50 ml of water.*
3	Egg yolks	10	*Place the pan containing the vinegar and peppercorns in your bain-marie and add the egg yolks whisking the mixture continuously, until the mixture has doubled in volume and has a smooth but fluffy texture. Then remove from the bain-marie and allow to cool to lukewarm whisking continuously.*
4			*Finally add the cool, melted butter gradually and then season.*
5	Lemon juice	2 lemons	*Finish by adding the lemon juice and be careful to keep at an even temperature from 85–98°F (30–37°C, blood heat).*

Sauces thickened with eggs are jolly difficult aren't they? They are also very tiring, very expensive, very rich and difficult to keep. Do them only on very special occasions and always use nice fresh free-range eggs.

Natural ways of thickening

I prefer this approach to thickening sauces, although these methods are not always practical or possible. Here are a few suggested alternative thickening techniques.

Reduction

Any liquid may be reduced by simmering it fairly vigorously for a considerable length of time. Even milk can be reduced this way but it takes so long that it is really impracticable. Tomato sauces lend themselves best to this method of thickening – not only do they become thicker, but also more tasty as the flavour becomes concentrated with the evaporation of the water. Likewise, sauces that revolve around alcohol are best when reduced as much as possible to bring out the true essence of the particular drink. The advantages of reducing as opposed to thickening are thus manifold, but limited to sauces that don't involve dairy produce and preferably have some kind of vegetable content, especially if it consists of tomatoes. Because they are cooked for a long time and have no artificial thickener at all, the basic taste is infinitely superior to most other sauces.

Purées of roots and tubers

Purées of root vegetables and tubers, especially potatoes, may be used as thickeners, simply stirred into the sauce. However, they are rather clumsy for use in fine sauces and are best used in soups and casseroles.

Root vegetables and tubers have a high carbohydrate content which is released through cooking and when mashed, these will effectively thicken any surrounding liquid, though only to a limited degree.

Lentils and smaller grains

These may be used in the same way as roots and tubers, and serve the same purpose. Puréed beans will also have a similar effect. They should all be well cooked, even overcooked, to make certain that they release starch into the surrounding liquid, thus thickening it. This, too, is a clumsy thickening procedure, but is perfect for soups and winter casseroles.

Peanut butter, tahini and tomato paste

These three and many other weird and wonderful pastes will also thicken sauces, while adding their own particular character to the sauce. For maximum effect, they should be added at the stir-fry stage in cooking the sauce, and when hot, the liquid to be thickened should be added gradually. Peanut butter especially will go on and on thickening if the liquid is added very gradually, and care should be taken not to make it too thick. Pastes have the advantage of not being discriminatory and will thicken any liquid, even milk. The only disadvantage is a mixed blessing, their flavour will affect the dish and so is usually used as an integral part of the sauce to be thickened.

Basic stocks

Stocks are very satisfying to use in a kitchen – there are few rules regarding what you should put into them. It seems so tidy and economical to have somewhere to throw almost all your trimmings, knowing they will be well used. For stocks are useful and will add a lot of flavour to either soups, sauces or casseroles. Why use plain water when with a little forethought and no extra work you could be using a tasty, healthy stock?

At home you may say it is impracticable but, once prepared, a basic vegetable stock will keep for a week in the fridge and at the end of that period can be re-boiled with new additions almost indefinitely.

The thing is not to think too seriously about stocks, just throw your vegetable trimmings into some simmering water while preparing your meal. Add whatever herbs come easily to hand, don't try to create a stock, it will create itself. Never boil it violently, just let it simmer in the background for as long as you like.

A very few bits of vegetables do nothing for a stockpot and should be excluded: onion and garlic skins, and the centre of green peppers, for they are rather bitter. But, as I said, do not worry too much.

There are several stocks that can be made very quickly, if you have forgotten to store one in your fridge. These tend to rely on powerful flavourings, like miso, tamari and Yeastex and so are not always desirable. However, speed is sometimes essential and they are certainly better than plain water.

Here follows a basic vegetable stock recipe and some quick stocks. Try not to follow them too closely as they are only broad outlines, specifically useful for cross-reference throughout the book.

1 Vegetable stock

Stage	Ingredients	Quantity	Method
1	Cold water	Enough to cover vegetables	Add salt and bring to the boil in a large saucepan.
2	Vegetable trimmings, old vegetables, yesterday's stew, handy herbs, salt and pepper		Place in the large saucepan, checking boiling water covers vegetables. Simmer gently for no less than 30 minutes. When ready, or needed for use adjust seasoning and strain. Discard the vegetables or use for compost in garden.

2 Quick tamari stock

1 litre

Stage	Ingredients	Quantity	Method
1	Cold water	1 l	Bring to boil in suitable pan and simmer.
	Salt	1 tsp	
2	Onions	1 large	Add to the boiling salted water.
	Carrots	2 medium	
	Celery	3 stalks	
3	Tamari/shoyu	2 tbsp	Add to vegetables and simmer for at least 15 minutes.
	Ginger	5 g – grated	
	Parsley	3 sprigs	

3 Quick miso stock

Miso has a dominating, unusual flavour making it unsuitable for general use as a stock, but very important in light Japanese-style soups in particular.

Use 1 litre of tamari stock (2) having substituted 2 tablespoons of miso for tamari. 10 g of nori seaweed may also be added. Miso stock should never be boiled.

4 Quick Yeastex stock

Yeastex is basically a yeast extract, like Marmite. It may be used in the same context as miso to form a distinctive, yet quick stock. Substitute 1 tablespoon of Yeastex for tamari in the tamari stock (2). The resulting stock is very meaty and not to be recommended for regular use.

Basic sauces

Sauce preparation gives you, the cook, an ideal opportunity to experiment and add your own personal touch to dishes. Do not blindly follow recipes; add things that you are particularly fond of and take away those you dislike. The recipe need only be used for background information regarding the general direction or purpose of a sauce.

For clarification I have divided sauces into the following basic sections:

1 Tomato sauces – sauces entirely based around tomato flavour.
2 Tomato and alcohol sauces – alcohol can radically change the whole direction of a sauce and so, while really a sub-section of tomato sauces, they deserve a separate mention.
3 Tomato-related sauces – those which use tomatoes (usually tomato paste) only for background taste allowing other flavours to dominate the dish.
4 Stock-based sauces – sometimes it is nice to get away from rich, tomato or white sauces and simply use a good stock. Many of our standard casseroles are flavoured in this way.
5 Stock-based sauces with alcohol – in these sauces alcohol, usually red or white wine, is introduced to a basic stock in such a way that it becomes a fundamental part of it.
6 White sauces – these are all basically variations of a standard béchamel sauce, giving the cook an immense spectrum of tastes with very little extra work.
7 White sauces with alcohol – several notable white sauces, stroganoff for example, use alcohol. This sub-section will give you some experience of the kinds of alcohol suitable for white sauces, and how they are best introduced to a béchamel.

Tomato sauces

When using tinned tomatoes always cancel out the tinny taste with a little vinegar and sugar. Fresh tomatoes may be used in place of tinned tomatoes when available, although it is best to skin them first, and it is not necessary to add the vinegar. You will find tomato sauce recipes 5 and 6 are referred to quite often. To facilitate using the recipes, first look to see if Recipes 5 or 6 are included and start them cooking first. Even better, make a large batch and store it in the fridge or freezer.

5 Basic tomato sauce A

1 litre

Stage	Ingredients	Quantity	Method
1	Vegetable oil Onion, finely chopped Garlic, finely chopped	50 ml 2 large 3 cloves	Heat the oil in a pan, add the onion and garlic and cook gently.
2	Wine vinegar Sugar/honey	200 ml 2 tsp/1 dsp	Add the wine vinegar and sugar or honey, bring to the boil and reduce by ²/₃.
3	Tinned tomatoes	1 large tin (approx ½ kg)	Crush by hand and add to the rest of the ingredients. Season with salt, pepper and tamari then simmer until thickened naturally. Skinned fresh tomatoes may be submitted for tinned and the vinegar omitted.

6 Basic tomato sauce B

1 litre

Stage	Ingredients	Quantity	Method
1	Vegetable oil Onions ⎫ Celery ⎬ finely chopped Carrots ⎭ Marjoram Basil Bay leaf Garlic, crushed	50 ml 1 large 1 stalk 1 medium 2 tsp 2 tsp 1 2 cloves	Heat the oil in a pan. Add the onions, celery and carrots with the herbs and garlic and stir-fry until the onions are soft.
2	Cider vinegar Sugar/honey Tomato purée	200 ml 2 tsp/1 dsp 2 tbsp	Add the cider vinegar and sugar or honey, bring to the boil and reduce to ¹/₃, then stir in the tomato purée.
3	Tinned tomatoes Vegetable stock	1 medium tin 300 ml	Crush the tomatoes by hand and add slowly to the rest of the ingredients, stirring continuously. Pour in the vegetable stock and simmer until reduced to a suitable thickness. Adjust seasoning with salt and pepper and tamari.

7 Créole sauce

½ litre

Stage	Ingredients	Quantity	Method
1	Vegetable oil (coconut or sesame) Green pepper ⎫ Red pepper ⎬ finely chopped Aubergine ⎭ Chilli, fresh, dry or ground	50 ml 1 small 1 small 1 small To taste	Heat the oil in a deep pan, and add the green peppers, red peppers, chilli and aubergines. Stir-fry until all the ingredients are going soft.
2	Tamari Tomato sauce A (5)	Dash ½ l	Add a dash of tamari followed by the tomato sauce. Bring to the boil and re-adjust seasoning.
3	Yoghurt/sour cream	100 ml	Before serving, add yoghurt or sour cream (optional).

8 Ragout sauce   ½ litre

Stage	Ingredients	Quantity	Method
1	Vegetable oil	50 ml	Heat the oil in a pan. Add the onion, carrots, herbs, garlic and pepper and sautée until very hot, stirring regularly.
	Onions ⎱ roughly	1 large	
	Carrots ⎰ chopped	2 medium	
	Marjoram	1 tsp	
	Basil	1 tsp	
	Thyme	1 tsp	
	Parsley	3 sprigs	
	Bay leaf	1	
	Garlic, crushed	3 cloves	
	Peppercorns, crushed	3	
2	Tamari	1 tbsp	Add the tamari to the vegetables and allow to be absorbed. Then stir in the tomato paste.
	Tomato paste	2 large tbsp	
3	Vegetable stock	½ l	Add the vegetable stock and bring to the boil, adjust seasoning adding salt, pepper and tamari. Simmer gently for as long as you like. Thicken if necessary, preferably with potato flour, arrowroot or cornflour.

9 Provençale sauce   ½ litre

Stage	Ingredients	Quantity	Method
1	Olive oil	50 ml	Gently heat the oil in a pan (be careful as olive oil becomes very hot very quickly). Stir in the garlic and cook very gently.
	Garlic	5 cloves, or to taste	
2	White wine vinegar	100 ml	Add to the garlic mixture and reduce by $2/3$.
	Sugar	1 tsp	
3	Tomato sauce A (5)	½ l	Stir into mixture, bring to the boil and adjust seasoning with salt, pepper and tamari, serve immediately. For a very garlicky taste, add the garlic at the end.

10 Neapolitan sauce   ½ litre

Stage	Ingredients	Quantity	Method
1	Olive oil	50 ml	Heat the olive oil in a pan. Add the onion, green pepper, garlic and basil. Sautée until onion begins to soften.
	Onion, roughly chopped	1 large	
	Green pepper, roughly chopped	1 large	
	Garlic, crushed	3–4 cloves	
	Basil	1 dsp	
2	Red wine vinegar	200 ml	Add vinegar and sugar or honey and bring to the boil, then reduce by $2/3$.
	Sugar/honey	2 tsp/1 dsp	
3	Tomato paste	2 dsp	Stir in tomato paste and, when hot, add the crushed tinned tomatoes and bring to the boil. Simmer and adjust seasoning with salt, pepper and tamari.
	Tinned tomatoes	1 large tin	
4	Mushrooms	100 g	Before serving throw in a few mushrooms, parsley and oregano. A little parmesan may also be added if desired.
	Parsley	A few sprigs	
	Oregano	1 dsp	

11 Goulash sauce

½ litre

Stage	Ingredients	Quantity	Method
1	Vegetable oil (sesame or sunflower)	50 ml	Heat oil in a pan. Add the onion, green pepper and paprika, then sautée until onion is soft.
	Onion	1 large	
	Green pepper } chopped	1 medium	
	Red pepper	1 medium	
	Paprika	1 dsp	
2	Tomato sauce B (6)	½ l	Stir into pepper and onion and adjust seasoning with salt, pepper and tamuri.

12 Ghuvetch sauce

½ litre

Stage	Ingredients	Quantity	Method
1	Vegetable oil (sesame or sunflower)	50 ml	Heat oil in pan. Then add onion, carrot, green pepper and dill. Cook gently until the onion is softening.
	Onion	1 medium	
	Carrot } chopped	1 medium	
	Green pepper	1 medium	
	Dill weed	3 tsp	
2	Tomato sauce A (5) (or tomato purée)	¼ l	Stir into mixture and bring to the boil.
3	Vegetable stock	¼ l	Bring to the boil and add to the rest of the sauce. If sauce is still too thin, thicken with arrowroot or reduce by heating for a considerable time. Adjust seasoning with salt, pepper and tamari.

13 Niçoise sauce

½ litre

Stage	Ingredients	Quantity	Method
1	Olive oil	50 ml	Heat the oil in a pan. Add the onions and herbs. Cook gently until the onions are soft.
	Onions, red, coarsely chopped	2 large	
	Thyme	1 tsp	
	Basil	2 tsp	
2	Tomato sauce A (5)	½ l	Add to mixture and bring to the boil, then reduce slightly or thicken with arrowroot or cornflour. Adjust seasoning with salt, pepper and tamari.
	Vegetable stock	200 ml	

14 Ratatouille sauce

Stage	Ingredient	Quantity	Method
1	Olive oil	50 ml	Heat the oil in a pan and sautée the onion, green pepper and tomatoes with the herbs and sugar or honey, until all are starting to soften.
	Onion	1 large	
	Green pepper } chopped	1 large	
	Fresh tomatoes, skinned	2 large	
	Basil	2 tsp	
	Marjoram	2 tsp	
	Sugar/honey	2 tsp/1 dsp	
2	Cider vinegar	200 ml	Add cider vinegar and reduce by 2/3, then stir in tomato paste and reheat until bubbling. Add crushed tinned tomatoes.
	Tomato paste	2 dsp	
	Tinned tomatoes	1 medium tin	
3	Garlic, crushed	4 cloves	Before serving, stir in garlic, herbs and tamari. Adjust seasoning, with salt, pepper and tamari.
	Oregano	1 tbsp	
	Parsley	3 sprigs	
	Tamari	2 tbsp	

15 Celery and tomato sauce

Stage	Ingredients	Quantity	Method
1	Vegetable oil	50 ml	Heat the oil and add the onion, carrots, celery and celery seed, and thyme. Sautée until onion begins to soften.
	Onion	1 medium	
	Carrot } chopped	1 large	
	Celery	3 sticks	
	Celery seeds, ground	1 tsp	
	Thyme	2 tsp	
2	Tomato sauce A (5)	½ l	Stir in tomato sauce and stock. Bring to the boil and simmer until sauce is thick. This sauce needs a lot of cooking to bring out the flavour of celery.
	Vegetable stock (1)	¼ l	

Tomato sauces with the addition of alcohol

In most of the tomato sauces already described vinegar has been used.
Wine may be added in place of vinegar at the same stage in cooking.
Generally with alcohol, the stronger it is the less it needs cooking.
Wine being a comparatively dilute form of alcohol needs to be reduced
by at least a half for its flavour really to come through. Stronger alcohol
needs little or no reduction and should be added just before serving.

16 Red wine ratatouille sauce

½ litre

As for Ratatouille sauce (14), but with the substitution of
300 ml of red wine for the cider vinegar.

17 Chasseur sauce

½ litre

Stage	Ingredients	Quantity	Method
1	Butter/good vegetable margarine	25 g	*Melt the butter in a saucepan and add the mushrooms, shallots and tarragon; then cook gently, without colouring for 5 minutes.*
	Mushrooms, finely sliced	100 g	
	Shallots/spring onions, chopped	25 g	
	Tarragon	1 tsp	
2	Dry white wine	100 ml	*Add the white wine and increase the heat to reduce by ½.*
3	Tomato sauce A (5)	½ l	*Stir in and bring to the boil. Adjust seasoning with salt and pepper, then serve or use.*

18 Bourguignonne sauce

½ litre

Stage	Ingredients	Quantity	Method
1	Butter/vegetable oil	25 g/50 ml	*Heat the butter in a saucepan. Add the onion, carrot and herbs, the sautée until onion is soft.*
	Onion	1 large	
	Carrot	1 large	
	Parsley	2 sprigs	
	Thyme	1 tsp	
	Marjoram	1 tsp	
	Basil	1 tsp	
2	Red wine	300 ml	*Add and reduce by ½.*
	Basic tomato sauce A or tomato sauce	2 tbsp	*Add tomato sauce/purée*
3	Quick tamari sauce	700 ml	*Add and bring to the boil.*
4	Mushrooms	100 g	*Stir in mushrooms and parsley and, if necessary, thicken with arrowroot or cornflower. Adjust seasoning with salt, pepper and tamari.*
	Fresh parsley	3 sprigs	

19 Scallopini

½ litre

Stage	Ingredients	Quantity	Method
1	Olive oil	50 ml	Heat the olive oil in a saucepan. Add onion, green pepper and herbs, then cook until the onion is soft.
	Onion } sliced	1 large	
	Green pepper } sliced	1 large	
	Basil	2 tsp	
	Bay leaf	1	
2	Tomato purée	2 tbsp	Stir tomato purée into rest of ingredients. Add marsala and reduce by ½. In separate pan, bring lemon juice and vegetable stock to the boil and add to rest of ingredients. Add parsley before serving. Thicken with arrowroot or cornflour.
	Marsala	200 ml	
	Juice of lemon	1	
	Vegetable stock (1)	½ l	
	Parsley	2 sprigs	

Distant cousins of the tomato sauce

20 Sweet and sour sauce

½ litre

Stage	Ingredients	Quantity	Method
1	Sesame oil	50 ml	Heat the oil in a saucepan. Add onion, carrots, green pepper, pineapple, chilli, garlic and ginger. Sautée until onion softens.
	Onion } cut into juliennes	1 large	
	Carrots } cut into juliennes	2 medium	
	Green pepper } cut into juliennes	1 large	
	Pineapple, small chunks	50 g	
	Chilli	½ tsp	
	Garlic	3 cloves	
	Ginger	½ tsp	
2	Tamari	2 tbsp	Add tamari and Worcestershire sauce and stir-fry.
	Worcestershire sauce	1 dsp	
3	Wine vinegar	200 ml	Add and reduce vinegar by ½. Add honey or brown sugar.
	Honey/brown sugar	2 dsp	
4	Tomato paste	1 tbsp	Stir in tomato paste and add either boiling water, juice or stock. Adjust seasoning with salt, pepper and tamari, and thicken if necessary with arrowroot or cornflower.
	Pineapple juice/orange juice/water/vegetable stock (2)	½ l	

21a Chilli sauce

½ litre

Stage	Ingredients	Quantity	Method
1	Olive oil	50 ml	Heat oil in a saucepan. Add onions, carrots, green and red pepper, garlic, chilli. Cook gently for 8 minutes.
	Onion } roughly chopped	1 medium	
	Carrot } roughly chopped	1 large	
	Red pepper } roughly chopped	1 large	
	Garlic, crushed	3 cloves	
	Fresh chilli or chilli powder	¼ or ½ tsp	
2	Tomato paste	2 tbsp	Stir in tomato paste and orange juice and bring to the boil.
	Fresh orange juice	200 ml	
3	Vegetable stock	400 ml	Bring vegetable stock to the boil and add to rest of sauce. Adjust seasoning with salt and pepper and thicken with arrowroot or cornflour.

21b Mexican chilli sauce   ½ litre

Stage	Ingredients	Quantity	Method
1	Olive oil	50 ml	*Heat oil in a saucepan. Add onion, green or red peppers,*
	Onion	1 large	*garlic, herbs and spices and cook gently, stirring frequently.*
	Green/red } chopped		
	peppers	2 medium	
	Garlic, crushed	4 cloves	
	Cumin	1 tsp	
	Coriander	¼ tsp	
	Cayenne	¼ tsp	
	Black pepper	¼ tsp	
	Chilli, fresh or dry	½ tsp	
2	Red wine	200 ml	*Add to sauce and reduce by ½.*
3	Tomato purée	2 tbsp	*Stir in tomato purée and sugar and bring to the boil.*
4	Tinned tomatoes	1 large tin	*Add tomatoes and lemon juice*
	Juice of lemon	1	*and bring sauce to the boil, adjust seasoning, and thicken if necessary with arrowroot or cornflour.*

21c West Indian chilli sauce   ½ litre

Stage	Ingredients	Quantity	Method
1	Coconut oil	50 ml	*Heat oil in saucepan. Add onion, green pepper, pineapple,*
	Onion	1 medium	*garlic, thyme and chilli, then cook gently until onion is soft.*
	Green pepper } chopped	1 large	
	Pineapple, small cubes	50 g	
	Garlic, crushed	4 cloves	
	Thyme	1 tsp	
	Chilli	½ tsp	
2	Juice of lemon	1	*Add juices and coconut cream then bring to the boil.*
	Coconut cream	50 g	
3	Tomato paste	2 tbsp	*Stir in tomato paste, tamari and sugar and cook for 2 minutes.*
	Tamari	1 tbsp	
	Sugar	2 tsp	
4	Tinned tomatoes	1 large tin	*Add tomatoes and banana, then bring to the boil. Thicken with potato flour, cornflour or arrowroot, and adjust seasoning with salt, pepper and tamari.*
	Banana (sliced)	1	

21d Indonesian chilli sauce   ½ litre

Stage	Ingredients	Quantity	Method
1	Peanut oil	50 ml	*Heat oil in a saucepan. Add onion, pineapple, apple, chilli*
	Onion, chopped	1 large	*and garlic. Saútée until onions are soft.*
	Pineapple, diced	200 g	
	Apple, chunks	100 g	
	Chilli	½ tsp	
	Garlic, crushed	4 cloves	
2	Tamari	2 tbsp	*Add tamari and sugar and bring to the boil.*
	Sugar (brown)	2 tsp	
3	Peanut butter	2 dsp	*Add and stir in well.*

4	Tomato sauce B (6)	½ l	*Bring to the boil and add to the mixture gradually. Allow to thicken with the peanut butter. Adjust seasoning with with salt, pepper and tamari and serve.*

22a Mild curry sauce

½ litre

Stage	Ingredients	Quantity	Method
1	Sesame oil	50 ml	*Heat oil in a saucepan. Add onions, herbs and spices and gently sautée until the onions are soft.*
	Onions, finely sliced	2 large	
	Medium curry powder	1 dsp	
	Coriander	1 tsp	
	Cumin	1 tsp	
	Garlic, crushed	3 cloves	
2	Juice of lemons	2	*Pour lemon juice and sugar/honey into mixture and bring to the boil.*
	Honey/brown sugar	1 dsp/2 tsp	
3	Tomato sauce B (6)	½ l	*Bring tomato sauce to the boil and add to the rest of the sauce. Add garam masala and adjust seasoning.*
	Garam masala	1 tsp	

22b Dahl curry sauce

½ litre

Stage	Ingredients	Quantity	Method
1	Sesame oil	50 ml	*Heat oil in a saucepan. Add onion, green pepper, spices and garlic, then sautée gently until onions are soft.*
	Onion } chopped	1 large	
	Green pepper	1 large	
	Cumin	½ tsp	
	Coriander	½ tsp	
	Chilli	½ tsp	
	Garam masala	1 tsp	
	Garlic, crushed	4 cloves	
2	Juice of lemons	2	*Add lemon juice and bring to the boil.*
3	Tomato paste	2 dsp	*Stir into mixture.*
4	Vegetable stock (2) or lentil water	½ l	*Bring vegetable stock to the boil and add to sauce gradually. Adjust seasoning with salt, pepper and tamari, then thicken if necessary, but as this sauce may often be used with lentils I would not advise it.*

22c West Indian fruit curry sauce

½ litre

Stage	Ingredients	Quantity	Method
1	Coconut oil	50 ml	*Heat the oil in a saucepan. Add onion, green pepper, fruit, spices and garlic, then cook until onions are soft.*
	Onion } chopped	1 medium	
	Green pepper	1 medium	
	Pineapple/apple, cubed	100 g	
	Garlic, crushed	3 cloves	
	Chilli	½ tsp	
	Cumin	½ tsp	
	Coriander	1 tsp	
	Garam masala		
2	Tamari	1 tbsp	*Add Tamari and bring to the boil, stir in coconut cream.*
	Coconut cream	50 g	

3	Tomato purée	2 dsp	Stir in tomato purée.
4	Orange/apple juice	½ l	Bring to boil and add gradually. Throw banana in prior to serving.
	Banana, sliced	1	

22d African curry sauce

½ **litre**

As for Indonesian chilli sauce (21d) with the addition of 1 dsp of curry powder in Stage 1, and 50 g of sultanas and the juice of 1 lemon added in Stage 3.

23 Devilled sauce

½ **litre**

Stage	Ingredients	Quantity	Method
1	Vegetable oil	50 ml	Heat oil in saucepan. Add shallots, spices and herbs, then cook gently until onions are soft.
	Shallots/spring onions, chopped	200 g	
	Peppercorns, crushed	5	
	Bay leaf	1	
	French mustard	1 tbsp	
	Thyme/chervil	2 tsp	
2	Red wine	200 ml	Add wine and reduce by ½.
3	Tomato purée	2 tbsp	Stir into mixture.
4	Vegetable stock (2)	½ l	Bring to the boil and add to sauce gradually. Thicken with potato flour, cornflour or arrowroot and adjust seasoning.

24 Boston sauce

½ **litre**

Stage	Ingredients	Quantity	Method
1	Vegetable oil	50 ml	Heat the oil in a saucepan. Add the onion, carrot, green pepper and bay leaf then sautée until onions are soft.
	Onions	1 medium	
	Carrot	1 medium	
	Green pepper	1 medium	
	Bay leaf	1	
2	Malt vinegar/red wine	200 ml	Add and reduce by ½.
3	Molasses	2 dsp	Stir molasses, tomato purée and tamari into mixture and bring to the boil.
	Tomato purée	2 dsp	
	Tamari	1 tbsp	
4	Tomato sauce A (5)	¼ l	Combine tomato sauce with vegetable stock and bring to the boil. Add to sauce and thicken with starch. Adjust seasoning, and stir in garlic just before serving.
	Vegetable stock (1)	¼ l	
	Garlic, crushed	3 cloves	

Stock-based sauces

Stock-based sauces may be thick and warming or thin and delicate, though full of flavour. They make a subtle change from rich tomato or white sauces.

25 Irish sauce

½ **litre**

Stage	Ingredients	Quantity	Method
1	Vegetable oil	50 ml	Heat oil in a saucepan. Add and stir-fry, onion, celery, leek,

	Onion ⎫	1 medium	*potatoes, and herbs. Cook until onions are soft.*
	Celery ⎬ chopped	1 stalk	
	Leek ⎭	1 medium	
	Potatoes, small cubes	1 medium	
	Parsley	2 sprigs	
	Tarragon	1 tsp	
	Thyme	1 tsp	
	Mint	1 tsp	
	Bay leaf	1	
2	Tamari	2 tbsp	*Add to vegetables and bring to the boil.*
3	Vegetable stock (1)	½ l	*Bring stock to the boil and add to the mixture, thicken with potato flour or arrowroot, otherwise cornflour.*

26 Hokkien sauce ½ litre

Stage	Ingredients		Quantity	Method
1	Sesame oil		50 ml	*Heat oil in a saucepan. Add vegetables, garlic and spices and gently cook until the onions are soft.*
	Onion ⎫	chopped	1 medium	
	Carrots ⎬	into	2 medium	
	Red/green ⎭	juliennes	1 large	
	pepper			
	Garlic, crushed		3 cloves	
	Cayenne		½ tsp	
	Ginger		1 tsp	
2	Tamari		2 dsp	*Add and bring to the boil stirring continuously.*
3	Juice of lemons		2	*Add and re-boil.*
4	Vegetable stock water (2)		½ l	*Bring stock to the boil and add to the sauce. Thicken with arrowroot or cornflour and adjust seasoning with salt, pepper and tamari*

27 Hot pot sauce ½ litre

As for Irish Sauce (25), omitting mint and using Vegetable stock 4 instead of Vegetable stock 1.

28 Garlic sauce ½ litre

Stage	Ingredients	Quantity	Method
1	Vegetable stock (1)	⅔ l	*Bring stock to the boil and reduce by ⅓. Stir in garlic. Thicken with arrowroot and adjust seasoning.*
	Garlic, crushed	10 cloves	

Variation – add 100 ml sour cream.

Introducing alcohol in stock-based sauces

In these sauces the stock flavour fades into the background, allowing the alcohol to dominate completely the end product. Such a sauce is very rich and is best used sparingly. I have exemplified red wine, white wine and cider sauces but equally easy to make are sherry, brandy, marsala, madeira, port and beer sauces. So long as the alcohol you use has a definite character of its own, then try using it.

29 White wine sauce   ½ litre

Stage	Ingredients	Quantity	Method
1	White wine	300 ml	*Add wine to saucepan and reduce by ½.*
2	Vegetable stock (1)	300 ml	*Bring stock to the boil and add to the wine. Thicken with cornflour or arrowroot and adjust seasoning.*

30 Mushroom and white wine sauce   ½ litre

Sautée 1 medium onion, chopped with 150 g flat mushrooms (sliced) and add ½ litre of white wine sauce (29). Bring to the boil and adjust seasoning.

31 Creamy white wine sauce

To ½ litre of hot white wine sauce (29) add 100 ml of cream or sour cream, then add a pinch of cayenne before serving.

Variations are, of course, endless.

32 Red wine sauce   ½ litre

Stage	Ingredients	Quantity	Method
1	Vegetable oil	50 ml	*Heat oil in a saucepan. Add onions and cook gently until onions are soft.*
	Shallots/small onions, chopped	250 g	

2	Red wine	400 ml	*Add to onions and reduce by ½.*
3	Tomato sauce A (5)	100 ml	*Stir into mixture gradually.*
4	Vegetable stock (¼)	200 ml	*Boil stock and add to sauce. Adjust seasoning and thicken if*
	Cayenne	Pinch	*necessary, finish with a touch of cayenne.*

Variation: Add mushrooms in stage 1, also a little mustard. Finish with capers or chopped olives.

33 Cider sauce   ½ litre

Stage	Ingredients	Quantity	Method
1	Vegetable oil	50 ml	*Heat oil in a saucepan. Sautée vegetables and dill until onions*
	Onion	1 large	*are soft.*
	Carrot ⎱ chopped	1 large	
	Green pepper ⎰	1 large	
	Dill weed	Pinch	
2	Cider	50 ml	*Add cider and brown sugar and reduce by ½.*
	Brown sugar	1 dsp	
3	Tamari	1 tbsp	*Stir in and bring to the boil.*
4	Vegetable stock (1)	¼ l	*Bring to the boil and add to sauce. Thicken with potato flour or*
	Parsley	2 sprigs	*arrowroot or cornflour. Adjust seasoning.*

White sauces

Most of the white sauces in this section are based on milk or milk products. Using milk alone makes any sauce rather rich and heavy so I would suggest you mix the milk with vegetable stock to make up the required volume. For variety you may also wish to add yoghurt, cream or sour cream and these must always be added just before serving as too much extra heat will curdle them and spoil the effect of the sauce. Likewise with grated cheese, cream cheese or cottage cheese, try to leave their addition to any sauce until the last minute for they too will curdle with excess or prolonged heating.

Another temptation is to make excess roux, in order to make sure your sauce thickens. This may well thicken the sauce but it will also go on and on thickening and make the sauce taste almost exclusively of flour, thus being stodgy and unappealing. If, by accident, you think you have made too much roux, use what you need and put the rest in the fridge for your next sauce.

My favourite white sauces are those which are not thickened and can be prepared in literally 5 minutes. They are usually a little expensive and rich in taste but nevertheless lighter than béchamel-based sauces.

Always make sure that the milk or milk/stock mixture is almost boiling as it is added gradually to the roux, otherwise the resulting sauce will be floury and lumpy. Remember to stir the sauce continuously in this critical phase of preparation.

At 'Food For Friends' we add a dash of tamari to every white sauce as this takes the rather cloying milky flavour away.

34 Béchamel sauce   ½ litre

Stage	Ingredients	Quantity	Method
1	Butter/margarine/oil	45 g/50 ml	*Melt the butter in a pan and add the flour, allow to cook to*
	Wholewheat flour	45 g	*desired colour and then cool.*
2	Milk	½ l	*Boil milk with onion, clove and bay leaf. Gradually add to*
	Onion, finely sliced	1 large	*roux, stirring continuously with a wooden spoon.*
	Clove, powder	Hint	*Add a dash of tamari and adjust seasoning with salt and*
	Bay leaf	1	*pepper.*
	Tamari	Dash	

Béchamel may be cooked in advance and stored in the
fridge to ease preparation.

35 Tamari sauce   ½ litre

Stage	Ingredients	Quantity	Method
1	Béchamel sauce (34)	½ l	*Bring béchamel gently to the boil, stirring continuously.*
2	Tamari	1 tbsp	*Add to béchamel and adjust seasoning with salt and pepper.*

36 Tahini sauce   ½ litre

Stage	Ingredients	Quantity	Method
1	Béchamel sauce (34)	½ l	*Bring béchamel gently to the boil, stirring continuously.*
2	Tahini	100 ml	*Add tahini, mace, garlic and lemon juice to béchamel, then*
	Mace	½ tsp	*adjust seasoning with salt and pepper and serve.*
	Garlic, crushed (optional)	3 cloves	
	Juice of lemon	1	

Variation: Cheesy Tahini Sauce, substitute nutmeg for
mace and throw in a handful of grated cheese.

37 Gado Gado sauce (Peanut chilli Mark I)   ½ litre

Stage	Ingredients	Quantity	Method
1	Peanut oil	50 ml	*Heat in a saucepan. Add onions, garlic and chilli and sautée*
	Onions, sliced	2 large	*until onions are soft.*
	Garlic, crushed	4 cloves	
	Chilli	½ tsp	
2	Honey/sugar	1 dsp/2 tsp	*Stir in honey and tamari and bring to the boil.*
	Tamari	1 tbsp	
3	Peanut butter	2 tbsp	*Add peanut butter and tomato purée and mix in well.*
	Tomato purée	1 tbsp	
4	Hot milk/milk–stock	½ l	*Pour gradually into mixture stirring continuously. Adjust*
			seasoning and serve.

38 Cheese sauce

½ litre

Stage	Ingredients	Quantity	Method
1	Béchamel sauce (34)	½ l	Bring béchamel to boil stirring continuously, reduce heat
	Cheddar cheese	150 g	and add cheese, tamari and nutmeg. Adjust seasoning and
	Nutmeg	1 tsp	serve.
	Tamari	Dash	

Variations:

(a) *Cheese and mushroom sauce* (½ litre) – sautée 100 g mushrooms, sliced, in a little oil. Add béchamel and bring to the boil. Proceed as for cheese sauce, but substitute cream cheese, cottage cheese or sour cream for the cheddar then add a little cayenne or chilli.

(b) *Cheese and onion sauce* (½ litre) – as for cheese and mushroom sauce (a) but substitute 100 g onions, sliced, for mushrooms and proceed as before.

(c) *Cheese and cauliflower sauce* (½ litre) – as for cheese and mushroom sauce (a) but substitute 100 g of cauliflower, finely chopped and proceed as before.

There are endless variations of this sauce which I will leave to your imagination.

39 Mushroom sauce

½ litre

Stage	Ingredients	Quantity	Method
1	Béchamel sauce (34)	½ l	Bring to boil, stirring continuously.
2	Juice of lemons	2	Stir in lemon juice and mushrooms 5 minutes before serving.
	Mushrooms, chopped	250 g	Adjust seasoning with salt, pepper and tamari.

Variations: Try substituting different ingredients yourself.

40 Parsley sauce

½ litre

Stage	Ingredients	Quantity	Method
1	Béchamel sauce (34)	½ l	Bring to the boil, stirring frequently.
2	Parsley, roughly chopped	50 g	Add parsley and cayenne then adjust seasoning with salt,
	Cayenne	½ tsp	pepper and tamari.

Variations: will go with almost anything else.

41 Onion sauce

½ litre

Stage	Ingredients	Quantity	Method
1	Vegetable oil/butter	50 ml/25 g	Heat oil in a saucepan. Add water and onions and cook together
	Onions, sliced	300 g	until almost all water is evaporated.
	Water	200 ml	
2	Béchamel sauce (34)	½ l	Gently bring to the boil and mix in. Adjust salt, pepper and
			tamari.

Variations:

All previous variations plus:

(a) *Shallot sauce* (½ litre) – substitute 200 g shallots for onions and proceed as for onion sauce (41).

(b) *Leek sauce* (½ litre) – substitute 300 g leeks for onions and proceed as for onion sauce (41).

(c) *Garlic sauce* (½ litre) – sautée 10 cloves of crushed garlic in a little oil or butter then add béchamel sauce as in stage 2 of onion sauce (41). Season with black pepper, salt, a little cayenne and tamari.

(d) *Sage and onion sauce* (½ litre) – as for onion sauce (41) adding 1 dsp of sage to onions before cooking.

42 Lemon sauce   ½ litre

Add juice and zest of 2 lemons to tamari sauce (35). Adjust seasoning with salt and pepper and add a little ginger and chilli.

43 Curry sauce   ½ litre

Stage	Ingredients	Quantity	Method
1	Sesame oil	50 ml	Heat oil in a saucepan. Cook onion, garlic and spices until onion is soft.
	Onion	100 g	
	Garlic	3 cloves	
	Medium curry powder	1 dsp	
	Cumin	1 tsp	
2	Tomato paste	1 dsp	Stir into mixture.
3	Stock and béchamel sauce (34)	¼ l of each	Bring to the boil and add to the sauce. Add to sauce 10 minutes before serving, then adjust seasoning with salt, pepper and tamari
	Chutney/apple/dessicated coconut	100 g	

44 Celery sauce   ½ litre

As for onion sauce (41), but substituting 300 g celery for onions, and add a few dill seeds.

45 Cashew sauce   ½ litre

As for tamari sauce (35) but throw in 100 g of uncooked cashews.

Note – There are no real limits to the variations and combinations of these white sauces. In fact, any of the preceding examples could have been finished off with port, brandy, sherry, marsala, madeira or vermouth. They could even have had a dash of cream and an ounce of butter stirred into them just before serving which of course, brings us nicely on to the next section.

White sauces with alcohol

Here are just a few of the more popular white sauces we use that involve alcohol. Because more white sauces are based around dairy produce like milk, sour cream and yoghurt, in the presence of a lot of alcohol or acidity they are quite likely to curdle, which does nothing for the looks of your dish. This is why only the strongest fla-voured alcohols are used, because you don't have to add a great volume to get a great taste. Wine, however, must always be reduced before being added to a white sauce.

46 White wine sauce

½ litre

Stage	Ingredients	Quantity	Method
1	Béchamel sauce (34)	½ l	*Bring to the boil gently stirring frequently.*
2	White wine	400 ml	*Reduce wine by ½ and add to béchamel sauce. Reboil. Adjust seasoning, and a add a little cayenne.*

Variations:

(a) *Mushroom and white wine sauce (½ litre)* – substitute mushroom sauce (39) for béchamel sauce in above recipe.

(b) *Fondue sauce (½ litre)* – substitute cheese sauce (37) for béchamel and add ½ tsp cayenne and 4 cloves of crushed garlic.

(c) *Strogonoff sauce (½ litre)* – as for mushroom and white wine sauce (46a), but add 100 ml of sour cream or yoghurt just before serving. Also add an extra dash or two of tamari.

47 Red wine sauce

½ litre

Stage	Ingredients	Quantity	Method
1	Vegetable oil	50 ml	*Heat oil in a saucepan and add shallots and herbs, then cook until onions are soft.*
	Shallots/small onions, chopped	200 g	
	Bay leaf	1	
	Marjoram	3 tsp	
	Garlic, crushed	3 cloves	
2	Red wine	400 ml	*Add and reduce by ½.*
3	Tomato purée	2 dsp	*Stir into mixture.*
4	Tamari sauce (35)	½ l	*Bring to boil and add to mixture, stirring continuously. Remove from heat, adjust seasoning with salt, pepper and a little cayenne/chilli.*

Variations:

I'm sure you can think of some now, but here is a really nice one:

(a) *Hungarian red wine sauce (½ litre)* – simply add 1 dsp paprika in stage 1.

Some quick and tasty white sauces with alcohol

Heat ½ litre of tamari sauce (35) or Béchamel sauce (34),
depending on preference, then add to it:

48 Madeira sauce   ½ litre

100 ml madeira.

49 Xavier sauce   ½ litre

100 ml dry sherry.

50 Marsala sauce   ½ litre

100 ml marsala (Italian sherry).

51 Martini sauce   ½ litre

100 ml dry vermouth.

52 Warming sauce   ½ litre

100 ml brandy/whisky.

Finally, just to prove that anyone can cook a delicious
sauce in 5 minutes flat, try:

53 Mushroom boulevard sauce   ¼ litre

Stage	Ingredients	Quantity	Method
1	Butter	75 g	*Melt butter in a pan. Add mushrooms with a little lemon juice*
	Mushrooms	500 g	*and cook for 2 minutes.*
	Juice of lemon	½	
2	Dry vermouth	100 ml	*Add and reduce by ½ quickly.*
3	Sour cream/cream	¼ l	*Reduce heat and add gently to avoid curdling. Adjust*
			seasoning with salt, pepper, tamari and cayenne.

Chapter 4

Dressings and Dips

Dressings

Dressings are an integral part of some salads, while to others they are a superfluous additional flavour, almost like a dip. Most dressings not only add flavour in themselves, but contain properties that help keep salad vegetables fresher and firmer for longer after they have been prepared. Salad vegetables are generally extremely delicate having a very high water content, most are eaten raw. It is only vegetables that have been adopted by the salad department such as beetroots and potatoes that need cooking and can stand prolonged preparation. Ideally, salad vegetables should be prepared and dressed literally just before eating, but when social gatherings demand pre-preparation of salads, store these in the fridge but with their dressings separate and mix the dressing in just before serving or serve the dressing separately.

Most salad dressings are oil-based and there are a wide variety of oils you can use to add different flavours to a dressing. Generally, olive oil is the best, but its price is often prohibitive so use a good quality, preferably cold-pressed, vegetable oil or in some cases try sesame, sunflower, peanut, safflower, soya and maize oil. The reason oils are so commonly used as the base for a salad dressing is because, when emulsified in liaison with an acid such as lemon juice, cider vinegar, wine vinegar or one of the many vinegars now easily available, they form a thick protective barrier around the salad vegetables themselves. For a short time, this barrier will keep the goodness, flavour and texture of the salad vegetables where it should be, in the vegetable. Of course, eventually the juices in the vegetables will start to leak out again turning the salad dressing into a rather watery substance and leaving the vegetables soggy, dull and unattractive. The same process occurs during marination, although, in that case, the chosen vegetables are not usually of the soft salad variety and can stand a good deal of absorption without losing their texture and odour. Simple oil-based dressings benefit from being made in bulk and stored in a cool dry place, preferably the fridge. Personally speaking, I would only make one week's supply at a time. In storage the ingredients will start to 'cook' themselves (the same process as marination) imparting all of their flavour to the liquid around them.

Mayonnaise, although an oil and acid-based dressing, is made rich and creamy through the slow addition of egg yolks. It is not only a wonderful dressing in itself but can be a superb base for the development of other dressings. Mayonnaise is so simple to make it seems a shame that most people buy bottled varieties that are both bland and full of a vast array of chemical emulsifers and preservatives. Mayonnaise will store for 2–3 days in a fridge but its flavour will not improve.

Dairy-based dressings can make an ordinary salad into a gastronomic adventure. They are usually rich but, if over-used, can totally disguise the ingredients they cover and, for this reason, it is sometimes better to present a dairy-based dressing in the form of a dip. Salads

with a dairy dressing must not be left to stand as the
content of the salad can quickly dissolve the dressing a
sour. Of course, there is a wide range of dairy produce
including cream, sour cream, yoghurt and soft chees
they are really fresh if they form the bulk of the dressin
constitute a small part of the whole take the opportunity
leftovers.

Other dressings may be based on vegetables and
cooked or uncooked. Some may even be cold sauces,
relishes, the range is enormous. Always try to use fresh l
available and freshly ground spices. Remember with most
you make a mistake it is usually quite easy to cover up so don
you have to start again. Ideally, dressings should lift s
smother them so bear in mind the quality and nature of
vegetables before deciding on a suitable salad dressing. The e
my point becomes clear if you consider a real Greek salad ma
plump tomatoes, a few olives, feta cheese, unrefined oliv
squeeze of lemon juice and a sprinkling of fresh oregano – beau.y with
simplicity.

In the recipes that follow I have included those dressings which have
proven popular in the past. Even to a reluctant vegetarian the tell-tale
sign that a dressing has been good is when bread is required to mop up
the last traces.

Equipment required

Pepper and spice grinders, a sharp Chinese chopper, a paring
knife, a whisk or a blender and a grater.

Oil-based dressings

54 French dressing   ¼ litre

Stage	Ingredients	Quantity	Method
1	Vegetable oil	160 ml	*Put all the ingredients into a bowl and whisk, or blend in a*
	Cider vinegar	80 ml	*blender, until the liquid is thick. Store in a cool place and remix*
	Sugar	1 tsp	*before use.*
	French mustard (ready mixed)	2 dsp	
	Mixed herbs	1 dsp	
	Salt and pepper	1 tsp	
	Garlic	3 cloves	

55 Orange dressing

As for recipe 54 with the addition of a freshly squeezed medium orange and zest. Reduce cider vinegar to 50 ml, sugar optional.

56 Lemon and honey dressing

As for recipe 55 with 1 medium lemon instead of the orange and 1 dsp honey instead of the sugar.

57 Greek dressing

As for recipe 54, but replace vegetable oil with olive oil (or add a handful of de-stoned black olives). Replace cider vinegar with lemon juice, replace mixed herbs with oregano. Omit mustard. Garlic optional.

58 Tamari and ginger dressing   ¼ litre

Stage	Ingredients	Quantity	Method
1	Soya oil	160 ml	Blend ingredients thoroughly.
	Rice wine vinegar	60 ml	
	Tamari/shoyu		
	Fresh ginger (grated)	15 g	
	Garlic	3 cloves	

Variations

Try different oils and vinegars or lemon juice. A particularly good oil variation is sesame oil.

Note
Oil-based dressings offer many variations, experiment with different herbs and spices, the addition of miso or tahini may also provide an exciting alternative. Always use garlic according to taste, try soft or blue cheeses too.

59 Mayonnaise

¼ litre

Stage	Ingredients	Quantity	Method
1	Egg yolks	2	*Thoroughly stir dry ingredients into the egg yolks.*
	Dill	1 tsp	
	French mustard	1 tsp	
	Salt and pepper	To taste	
2	Cider vinegar/lemon juice	Dash	*Using a blender or fine whisk blend in thoroughly.*
3	Vegetable oil	¼ litre	*Add oil slowly, blending or beating continuously. As mixture thickens gradually increase the rate at which oil is being poured. When all oil is used mixture will be very thick.*
4	Egg whites	2	*Whisk until peaking then gently fold into mayonnaise mixture.*

Additions to mayonnaise
Cream, sour cream, yoghurt, cream cheese, ricotta cheese, cottage cheese, brie, roquefort, camembert cheeses, watercress, spring onions, chives, parsley, fresh tarragon, mixed herbs, chilli, tamari/shoyu/miso/tahini. Mayonnaise dressings can be made to go further with the addition of french dressing.

60 Blue cheese dressing

½ litre

Stage	Ingredients	Quantity	Method
1	Blue cheese	125 g	*Mix blue cheese thoroughly with yoghurt and french dressing.*
	Yoghurt	125 ml	
	French dressing (54)	125 ml	
2	Mayonnaise (59)	250 ml	*Fold mayonnaise into blue cheese mixture.*

61 Egg mayonnaise

To ½ litre of mayonnaise (59) add 2 chopped hard boiled eggs (cold), 50 g cottage cheese and a dash of vinaigrette, adjust seasoning, a touch of paprika is nice.

62 Egg and caper mayonnaise

Add a small handful of chopped capers to ½ litre egg mayonnaise (61).

63 Curried mayonnaise

Substitute 1 dsp of a good mild curry powder in place of dill in recipe 59.

64 Garlic mayonnaise

Add as much garlic as you prefer to mayonnaise (59), replace dill with oregano.

65 Herb mayonnaise (green mayonnaise)

Blend any selection of fresh herbs with a little french dressing and fold into mayonnaise (59). I recommend tarragon and parsley especially.

66 Red wine mayonnaise   ½ litre

Stage	Ingredients	Quantity	Method
1	Mayonnaise (59)	250 ml	*Fold mayonnaise into cold red wine sauce.*
	Red wine sauce (32)	200 ml	
2	Apricots (dry)	30 g	*Cook apricots in a little water with some sugar or honey, purée and allow to cool.*
3	Whipped cream	200 ml	*Fold apricots and whipped cream into red wine/mayonnaise mixture.*
4	Salt and pepper	To taste	*Adjust seasoning.*

A dressing like this can make many cold vegetable dishes meals in themselves. Experiment with other cold left-over sauces (they must be thick) to extend the idea.

67 Thousand island dressing   ½ litre

Stage	Ingredients	Quantity	Method
1	Red pepper	1 small	*Finely chop the ingredients, use any juices that emerge for your stockpot.*
	Green pepper	1 small	
	Green olives ⎱ optional	5	
	Capers ⎰	a few	
2	Cottage cheese	120 g	*Thoroughly mix together the cottage cheese, mayonnaise and tabasco and add the chopped vegetables.*
	Mayonnaise (59)	¼ litre	
	Tabasco	Dash	

Suggestion

Thousand Island dressing is best kept as thick as possible and used quickly because the vegetable content tends to make the dressing separate and even curdle. If it is far too thick add a little vinaigrette to dilute it.

Special points

While mayonnaise may be kept in a fridge for 2–3 days, mayonnaise-based dressing should always be used on the same day, and if stored at all always in a fridge. Mayonnaise is a great addition to many dressings but it is also very delicate so keep acid, water and vegetable content down to a bare minimum.

It is very important to remember that if your mayonnaise curdles you can use the ingredients that have curdled to form the bulk of your next attempt. However, it does mean going back to the egg yolk phase and starting the process with fresh oil, but as soon as you have formed a proper liaison (thickening) between egg yolk and oil you can commence using up the curdled mixture. It is necessary for successful mayonnaise that eggs are kept in a cool place, not the fridge, and that the air temperature is not cold, but not hot either! Likewise the oil and bowl used should neither be hot nor cold. If your bowl is cold, heat it gently with the steam.

Dairy-based dressings

68 Tsatziki

½ litre

Stage	Ingredients	Quantity	Method
1	Cucumber	½ large	*Peel the cucumber if waxed and grate, then cover with salt for 1 minute. Drain off liquid thoroughly by squeezing through a dry cloth.*
2	Yoghurt, natural	400 ml	*Crush garlic then stir into yoghurt with other ingredients.*
	Garlic	3–4 cloves	
	Salt and pepper	Dash	
	Lemon juice	½ small lemon	

Serve this chilled as a dressing or a dip (especially nice with pitta bread). Spring onion ends or chives may be added for colour if you have had to peel the cucumber. If you can, buy Greek yoghurt, as this makes it even nicer. It also makes a refreshing drink if diluted with a little water or soda water.

Variations

Tsatziki is very similar to many Middle Eastern dishes, known in India as raitas. Try the following recipes as alternatives to tsatziki.

69 Cucumber raita

As for recipe 68 but add mint and basil too. This is also good to drink.

70 Aubergine babajanou

As for recipe 68, but replace cucumber with a small aubergine. Cut the aubergine in half and baste with a little oil. Bake dry in the oven until flesh is soft, approximately 45 minutes at 350°F (180°C, Gas Mark 4). Scoop out the flesh, purée and allow to cool then proceed as for tsatziki. Again, mint is a nice addition.

71 Carrot and apple raita

As for recipe 69 but use raw carrot and apple instead of cucumber, toss the carrot and apple in a little lemon juice after grating to prevent discoloration.

72 Sour cream and spring onion dressing

½ litre

Stage	Ingredients	Quantity	Method
1	Sour cream	350 ml	*Stir ingredients together well.*
	Yoghurt	100 ml	*Season to taste.*
	Paprika/cayenne pepper	Pinch	
	Salt and pepper	Pinch	
2	Spring onions	1 bunch	*Chop spring onions and fold into mixture.*

Special points

Simple isn't it? And very nice. The variations are enormous once again. Use any soft cheese in addition to, or instead of, sour cream. Replace, or add to, the spring onions, chives, parsley, watercress, well drained but cooked spinach and, of course, garlic. For dips, cut down on or leave out the yoghurt, blend all the ingredients apart from the dairy produce and fold this into the mixture afterwards. (Both yoghurt and sour-cream will turn to liquid if put through a blender.) If the basic ingredients are rather dry and difficult to blend, add a small quantity of liquid to get them going. A little yoghurt may in this case serve the purpose.

73 Tahini and lemon dressing

½ litre

Stage	Ingredients	Quantity	Method
1	Tahini	150 g	*Stir hot water into tahini to create a thick paste — allow to cool.*
	Hot water	200 ml	
2	Lemon juice	1 lemon	*Blend with tahini paste until smooth.*
	Olive oil	100 ml	
3	Natural yoghurt	200 ml	*Fold into mixture at the end. Season to taste.*
	Garlic, crushed	3–4 cloves	
	Salt and pepper	Dash	

Special points

Although this dressing is in the dairy section it can be made without yoghurt simply by increasing the quantity of tahini and water; the ratio of tahini to water should be kept the same. If using yoghurt, make sure the tahini mixture is cool before adding it.

Optional extras

A dash of shoyu/tamari, a race of ginger, a teaspoon of honey or how about a bit of sour cream: whatever inspires you.

74 Curried mushroom dip

½ litre

Stage	Ingredients	Quantity	Method
1	Flat mushrooms, sliced thinly	105 g	*Heat the oil or butter in a pan and add the spring onion; cook for 1 minute then add the mushrooms, curry powder and sweetener if desired. Season, cook until mushrooms are soft stirring regularly, allow to cool.*
	Vegetable oil/butter	25 ml/½ oz	
	Spring onion, chopped	1	
2	Sour cream	400 ml	*Stir in sour cream and chill, sprinkling with a little paprika or chilli powder before serving.*

Optional extras

If you like things really savoury add a little shoyu/tamari with the spring onions, or the juice of half a small lemon. Substitute or supplement the sour cream with an equal quantity of cottage or cream cheese, depending on the thickness required. Mayonnaise (59) may also be added – yoghurt is good, too. It is easy to make a chilli mushroom dressing by substituting chilli powder for curry powder, it is up to you.

75 Avocado and yoghurt dressing

½ litre

Stage	Ingredients	Quantity	Method
1	Ripe avocado	1 medium	*Halve the avocado and scoop out the flesh, blend or mash immediately with lemon juice.*
	Lemon juice	½ lemon	
2	Yoghurt	400 ml	*Fold yoghurt and garlic into avocado mixture until smooth, season with chilli or cayenne pepper.*
	Garlic, crushed	3–4 cloves	
	Chilli	Pinch	
	Salt and pepper	Dash	

Special points

Avocados make excellent dressings, both thickening and providing a distinctly exotic flavour. Please don't waste good avocado in your dressing, over-ripe ones bought cheaply are more than adequate, in fact they are ideal so long as you remove the worse of the black bits.

Variations

Add half an orange, chopped, to the above recipe for 'avocado seville'. For vegans (who may be browsing through the dairy section) replace the yoghurt with 150 g of tofu, no need to use hard-pressed variety. Alternative-ly, add equal quantities of spring onions, green pepper, cucumber and tomato, finely chopped, for a miniature guacamole. See recipe 84.

Note

Although this last section has been primarily devoted to dairy-based dressings, vegans will be happy to know that tofu can form the base for just as many and varied recipes, so experiment, but adjust your seasonings accordingly. Remember any dairy-based dressings can become dips, either runny or thick, simply by altering the quantities of the prime ingredients.

Odd dressings, relishes

76 Peanut Chilli (gado gado)   ½ litre

Stage	Ingredients	Quantity	Method
1	Peanut oil	50 ml	*Heat oil gently and stir in onion, chilli, sugar/honey and shoyu, cook until onion is soft.*
	Onion, thinly sliced	1 medium	
	Chilli	½ tsp	
	Sugar/honey	2 tsp/1 dsp	
	Shoyu/tamari	1 tsp	
2	Tomato purée (optional)	1 tbsp	*Stir in and bring to the boil stirring continuously.*
	Peanut butter (smooth)	2–3 tbsp	
	Garlic	3 cloves	
3	Water, hot or cold	200 ml	*Pour on mixture and bring back to the boil stirring regularly until mixture is smooth and not too thick. Season to taste and allow to cool.*
	Milk, hot or cold	200 ml	
	Salt and pepper	Dash	

Special points

Peanut chilli originated in Indonesia and so is essentially hot (spicy). However, we Westerners tend generally to have more delicate taste buds so use the chilli to your own requirements. It is important that the consistency is smooth but fluid. If cooked too long the sauce gets thicker and thicker, and eventually lumpy, in this state the oils start separating and the whole sauce looks a bit messy. It is not necessary to use part water or part milk, either will do instead but the total volume of the liquid added should be adjusted accordingly. It is nice to add garlic near the end of preparation to obtain maximum flavour.

Variations

It is difficult to improve on this sauce, but if you roast and grate a handful of peanuts to add at the end, they will add a touch of authenticity.

77 Mushroom and tomato relish

½ litre

Stage	Ingredients	Quantity	Method
1	Olive oil	50 ml	*Heat the oil in a pan, add other ingredients and cook until the onion is soft, and cider vinegar has reduced.*
	Onion/shallots, finely chopped	1 med/4	
	Mushrooms, sliced	150 g	
	Mixed herbs	1 dsp	
	Cider vinegar	1 dsp	
	Tamari	1 tbsp	
2	Tomato purée	1 tbsp	*Stir in tomato purée.*
3	Boiling vegetable stock/ water	100 ml	*Add if sauce is too thick. Allow to cool.*

Special points

Because this is basically a tomato and mushroom sauce refer to Chapter 3 for inspiration in developing the idea. Experiment with different herbs and ingredients; celery would be a good addition, or could even replace the mushrooms for a crunch relish. The addition of a little cream, sour cream or yoghurt might also be appropriate.

78 Parsley and garlic cream

½ litre

Stage	Ingredients	Quantity	Method
1	Lima beans, dry	75 g	*Soak beans overnight then rinse and cook until soft.*
2	Vegetable stock	275 ml	*Put beans in blender and add rest of ingredients — blend until smooth, if paste is too thick dilute with more stock, allow to cool.*
	Garlic	6 cloves	
	Parsley	6 sprigs	
	Lemon juice	1 lemon	

Special points

This sort of dressing is a tasty way of using up left-over beans and obviously is almost a pâté.

Variations

Use blackeye beans instead of lima beans or even bread crumbs. Add soft cheese, sour cream, cream or yoghurt or parmesan cheese. Chives and spring onions may be used instead of parsley. Essentially, it is the garlic flavour that comes out and should be a firm favourite with lovers of the dreaded clove. It is also very similar to the next recipe.

79 Hommous

As for the above recipe (78) but replace lima beans with chickpeas (carefully washed). Replace parsley with tahini (a nice option) – 3 dsp. Vegetable stock is not necessary in hommous and the water will do to blend the chickpeas. Even a little yoghurt will not go amiss for the non-vegans – but don't forget the garlic.

Chapter 5

Beans, Pulses and Cereals –
The Tools of the Trade

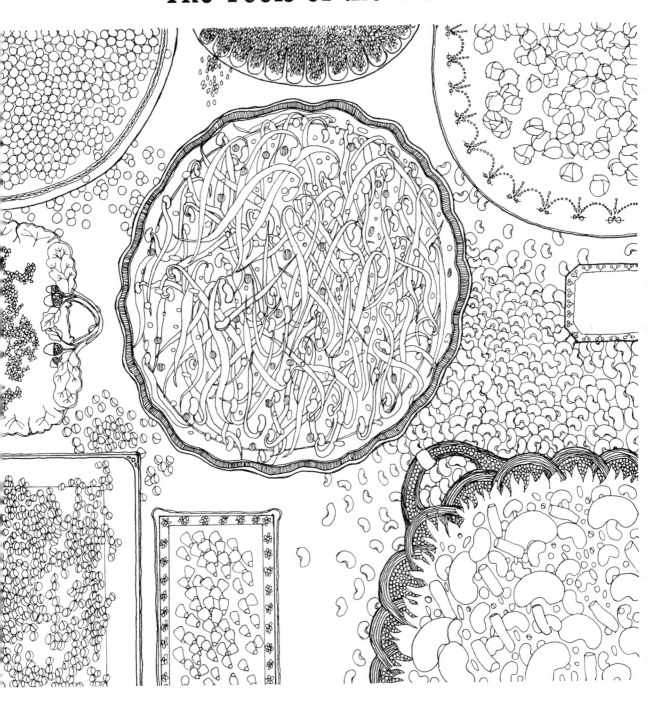

Somehow the words beans, pulses and cereals have become synonymous with vegetarianism and, to the reluctant vegetarian, there are a lot of misguided feelings about them. To be honest I'm not really a 'bean' person myself, although I love most cereals and pulses if they are properly prepared and used in the correct context. I think most of our prejudices against beans have resulted from bad experiences in their general usage. There seems to have grown up a mystique, regarding how to cook them and what they should taste like when they are cooked. This must be tempered with our experience of what has become the most common form of bean generally eaten – the baked bean in tomato sauce. In fact, the average baked bean is a poor relative of the types of bean we will be discussing later on – it has been overcooked, bleached and processed, but, and this is a big but, not only is it tasty but also cheap. It is in this context that we must see our beans; they are cheap and filling but best eaten if surrounded by a mouthwatering sauce. What is more, if they are bought, stored and prepared properly they are a valuable source of proteins, vitamins and energy. Unlike animal or dairy protein, those in beans, pulses and cereals are easily digested and don't contain nasties like cholesterol; on the contrary, some cereals are actually good for blood pressure. In addition to proteins and vitamins, these versatile commodities contain iron, potassium and calcium. A diet which includes a combination of beans, pulses, cereals and nuts of a reasonable quality will be complete.

Don't buy canned beans for, although they are easier to prepare, you lose out on much of their goodness and what little flavour they have. Try to buy fresh beans in season although they are often a bit cost-prohibitive. Dried beans, pulses and cereals are very economic purchases and can be kilo for kilo ten times cheaper than meat. Dried foods like these may already have been stored for a considerable period so keep your purchases to a bare minimum, in order to use them up regularly. Store your purchases in a dark, cool but dry place in tight sealed containers. It has become trendy to have a wide range of these goods on display in the kitchen along with the herb jars. However, as with herbs, light and heat will do nothing to help retain their nutrients or retard their aging. Just because a food is dry does not mean it is impervious to decay.

Equipment required for preparing beans, pulses and cereals

You need no special equipment to cook beans, so don't go out buying pressure cookers – they are very expensive. Of course, if you already have one then it will at least halve the cooking time of most dried beans, grains and pulses. You need a saucepan – preferably heavy as the beans take a long time to cook. For developing dishes involving dried foods it may be necessary to have a blender or a grinder – but not absolutely essential. A large colander or sieve will be handy too. Remember a little personal organization can always save the money involved when buying expensive, and often sub-standard, kitchen equipment.

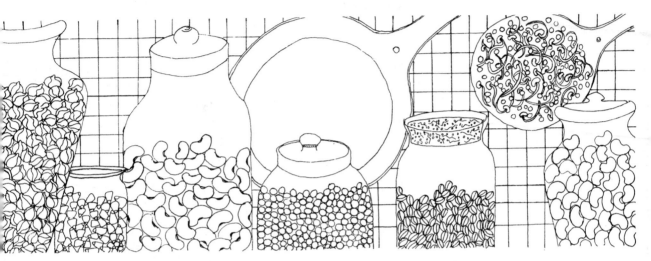

Preparation for cooking

In general, most of these products have been imported from Third World countries where, alas, cleanliness often falls by the wayside in the struggle to survive. Products from the United States and Europe are generally cleaner. Therefore, it is a good discipline to check through the goods for dirt, stones, bones and even droppings! Pick out the most obvious, then rinse the remaining beans with cold water through a sieve. Do this until you are satisfied that they are edible – remember the long cooking time will destroy anything undesirable that is not visible to the naked eye.

For most beans, and some pulses and cereals it is then best to cover them with cold water and leave them to soak for about 9 hours. This will speed up cooking time and avoid any untimely flatulence, but it is not absolutely necessary and it is best to do this over-night for lunch the following day, or first thing in the morning for evening meals. The total cooking time will be further reduced if the beans are boiled for 5 minutes prior to soaking. If the beans are soaked for too long their nutrients will begin to disperse, and this is signalled by a slight foam appearing on the surface of the water. A sign that the beans have been soaked long enough is when they split in half under the pressure of finger and thumb. Some people suggest using bicarbonate to aid soaking, but to me this seems an unnecessary destruction of the vitamins and proteins that are held within the bean. Old beans will need longer soaking than younger beans.

Dry peas, lentils and cereals do not usually need soaking unless extremely old, but like beans they do need thorough rinsing and cleaning prior to cooking.

Pressure cookers frighten a lot of people and, to those people, I would say don't use them. It is better to be happy and wait a little longer than turn yourself into a nervous wreck for the sake of an hour or two. If you do use a pressure cooker then good luck, but make sure you have read the instructions properly.

Then relax in the knowledge that not only will your dried food cook quickly and contain more goodness but it will also cause no flatulence. Personally, I feel most of this business about flatulence is more due to a radical change of diet, and would correct itself, than the poor little beans, pulses and grains that are so often blamed.

When cooking dry foods not under pressure, cook them in at least 1½–2 times their own volume in water and add a little oil as this will help them retain their goodness and stop the surface foaming. Preferably, add the dry foods to boiling rather than cold water as this will minimize uneven cooking and maximize nutritional content – never stir when cooking for this may damage their skins. If you cook too many beans don't worry, let them cool and then they will store happily in the fridge for a couple of days and may form the base of a salad, a roast, pâté or dressing.

Most beans, pulses and cereals will sprout if rinsed and stored in a muslin-covered jar. Don't forget to rinse daily and within a week you will have a delicious and unusual fresh salad vegetable.

A little about beans, pulses & cereals themselves

1 Kidney beans

Most beans that are easily available today are in the kidney bean family and are so-called because of their shape but they do vary in size, colour and texture.

(a) Red kidney beans

Really mature haricot beans (French beans). Have a lovely deep red colour and a good texture to eat. Recent scaremongering suggested they were poisonous when undercooked and this is true: however I would suggest that one would be less likely to eat undercooked kidney beans than to eat undercooked pork or chicken.

To cook these beans it is usually only necessary to soak for a couple of hours (unless they are very old), bring to the boil and simmer for 2–3 hours (again depending on age). Towards the end of your estimated cooking time check for tenderness with your fingers. If the kidney beans have started to split then alas they are overcooked.

In a pressure cooker kidney beans take 45 minutes at pressure to cook. Kidney beans have little flavour so use them in really tasty dishes or for colour and bulk in salads.

(b) Blackbeans

A cousin of red kidney beans but with a much deeper, almost black, colour. They also have a lot more flavour and their bean water is a useful addition to the stockpot. They originated in Mexico and are especially nice in Mexican or Caribbean dishes. Cook in the same manner as red beans.

(c) Flageolet beans

A light green bean with that distinctive kidney shape. Although dry they are picked younger than most other beans and are therefore more expensive but quicker to cook (they do not need soaking). They originated in Europe and are especially nice in Mediterranean-influenced dishes. They may also be eaten simply hot with butter or used as a base for a salad.

(d) Haricot beans

Usually a pale white colour, they are the elder brother of flageolets. Once soaked they will only take an hour to cook on top of the stove. Haricots vary tremendously in size, they lack flavour themselves but absorb it very well: good for casseroles, bakes and salads.

(e) Pinto beans

Yet another member of the kidney bean family. Speckled brown red on cream when dry they are a translucent pink when cooked. They cook in the same way as kidneys. They come from South America and Mexico and are good used in dishes from these areas. Pintos are also good for use in salads.

(f) Lima beans or butter beans

Practically identical except limas are usually smaller and more delicate, while butters can have a course skin. Both are usually larger than any other bean and have a pale white colour prior to cooking and a pale cream colour afterwards.

Soak butters/limas for 8–9 hours if possible then they will only take 45 minutes to cook, depending on their age. They absorb flavour well and are good nourishing bulk in a vast array of hot dishes.

2 Aduki beans

Small round beans, usually red/brown in colour over here although other colours are available. Originating in the Far East they are particularly suited to Far Eastern dishes and do add a distinctive flavour to a dish. Surrounded by a thick European sauce they make a lovely meat substitute in dishes where mincemeat is used. Adukis do not need soaking and will cook in an hour (depending on age) on top of the stove. Overcooked adukis are good for burgers, rissoles and patés.

3 Mung beans

Best sprouted, similar to an Aduki to look at but no match in flavour and green too. Use primarily in Indian dishes – cook in the same manner as Adukis.

4 Soya beans

Greyish white colour; similar shape to haricot (perhaps slightly more egg-shaped). When cooked they turn a nasty nicotine colour. Many varieties but all require soaking overnight followed by two hours cooking (one hour pressure). Add shoyu to the cooking water to counteract the awful smell they emit. Once cooked they do *not* have a pleasant flavour – I wouldn't bother using them though they are the cheapest form of protein in the world. The Chinese must have come to the same conclusion for they developed a whole list of products from soyabeans which are much more exciting to use. These include: tofu; miso; oil and flour – all of which have made an enormous contribution to vegetarian cooking today. Never use TVP; it is a waste of money.

5 Dried peas

(a) Green split-peas, yellow split-peas, marrowfat peas

Have all lost their skins, need no soaking and will dissolve upon cooking. They are excellent bases for soups, cooking water is excellent if not used for the stockpot.

(b) Blackeye peas

Sometimes called 'bean'. They retain their skin and if cooked correctly, also retain a little 'bite' when served. Uncooked they are white-grey with a black 'eye' – cooked they turn grey. Soak overnight and they only take 45 minutes – 1 hour to cook on top of the stove (no need to pressure cook). Blackeyes originate from the Caribbean, India and Africa and are excellent in Creole cooking – they are also very cheap.

(c) Chick-peas

A round hazelnut shape with a creamy brown colour. Staple food in the Middle East and great for Middle Eastern, African and Indian food. They are a reasonable price but should be checked for cleanliness and age. Very old chick-peas take ages to cook. Soak overnight then perhaps cook for 1–4 hours (take plenty of time for preparation). Extremely nutritious and best served, I feel, as hommous or in a Channah Dahl.

6 Lentils

Very cheap and very easy to cook adding flavour, bulk and plenty of protein too. Be careful to check for cleanliness.

(a) Whole lentils

Usually greeny brown or speckled, soak shortly then cook for from 45 minutes – 1½ hours. If they split they are overcooked and best used for rissoles or patés.

(b) Skinned lentils

Treat as split peas.

7 Cereals (grains)

Unrefined cereals are a great source of protein, vitamins (especially B vitamins) energy and dietary fibre. Try to find cereals that have had as little done to them as possible and similarly with products of cereals.

(a) Barley

Use pot barley (not pearl). It's cheap and easy to cook. Do not soak but simmer for 30–40 minutes (depending on age). Barley is great for soups, roasts, bakes and stuffings. It needs to be used in association with plenty of sauce and vegetables to alleviate the exercise put on your jaw.

(b) Buckwheat

Not actually a cereal but almost. It is a creeping vine native to Northern Europe and even still grows wild in Britain. In Poland and Russia it's called Kasha. It is small, brown and shaped like a beechnut; rich in protein and retin (which is good for blood pressure). It may also be ground and used as a flour: do not soak. Cover with approximately 1½ times its own volume in water (add a dash of shoyu to reduce its bitter edge), then simmer for 45 minutes or until all the water has been absorbed. This forms an extremely versatile addition to our cuisine being useful for bakes, burgers, rissoles, stuffings and roasts.

(c) Cracked Wheat (also Burghul or Bulghur)

Simply wheat that has been cracked – sometimes by boiling – sometimes by rolling. Fine cracked wheats like bulghar need only the addition of boiling water to cook them – coarser cracked wheats may need to be boiled for a few minutes. When cooked, cracked wheat should be light and fluffy and is suitable for stuffings, roasts and salads (the most famous being tabbouli).

(d) Millet

This is a very fine grain – it comes from a grass. It is a good source of protein, oils and energy. It requires slightly longer cooking than cracked wheat but may be used in the same manner.

(e) Rice

One could write a whole chapter on rice so I will stick to the basics.

There are many different varieties – again the least refined the better. We use shortgrain organic brown rice as it retains colour, nutrition and texture. If reasonably young and treated gently rice contains protein, theaming and, of course, dietary fibre. It is reasonably inexpensive, versatile and filling. To cook choose a saucepan with a lid, add your rice leaving enough room to cover it with twice its own volume of water. Add a dash of Shoyu, bring to boil with lid on and simmer until all water has gone and the rice is light and fluffy (if you dry up on water before time simply add some more – not too much!) Rice will take about 45 minutes on a low simmer.

(f) Wheat

May be hard or soft – we usually use English which is hard – but more nutritious than the soft. Whole wheat contains vitamins, energy and protein. It may be cooked in the same manner as rice and is useful for roasts, casseroles, soups and salads. Wheat may also be sprouted.

(g) Oats

Naturally do not store for long periods so are rolled on heated rollers to kill the enzyme responsible for their deterioration. This leaves us with oat flakes and they contain even so lots of vitamins, energy and fibre. Oatmeal is ground oat flakes. Store in a cool dark place and use mostly in sweets and toppings.

Conclusion

In this chapter I have only picked out a few of the most common beans, pulses and grain that we use, for the reason that they are all easily available in every town throughout the country. These three types of ingredient are fast becoming rivals to the more expensive meat products that have in the past filled the same role. The difference lies not only in their variety but in the fact that used constructively they can outstrip meat products for nutrition, availability, ease of storage and versatility. So don't be too harsh on ingredients that have been with us for many years, but have not yet come into their own. The fibre fanatics among you can relax in the knowledge that they're full of it!

One final note, the addition of salt to water used in cooking beans, pulses and cereals is not really necessary – so why bother, you will have the chance to season them later on.

Chapter 6
Starters

Introduction

The word starters encompasses a very broad spectrum of dishes appropriate to the start of a meal. It may mean anything you might have, apart from soup, before the main meal. I think the easiest way to regard a starter is to see it as being small but packed with flavour. If you wanted it to, it could even become a main meal and should be good enough and tasty enough to exist on its own, or with a small accompaniment. Given that broad generalization, almost anything can become a starter apart from heavy main course dishes. In fact most of the thicker dressings in Chapter 4 can be developed into starters, although they will need an accompaniment, such as crudités (strips of raw vegetables), fresh bread or toast, pitta bread, and so on. Likewise, some of the main course pasta dishes can become starters if the quantity is reduced.

Starters give the adventurous cook several opportunities to display his skill. First, think of starters as an individual recipe; not only will they have to taste good but they must look good. Presentation is of vital importance, from the dish the starter is in to the starter itself, how it is garnished and what it is accompanied with. Secondly, they will also set the pace of the meal so to speak, not only the general quality but, if balance is taken into account, the following course too. On a more practical note, starters can provide the ideal opportunity to use up left-overs from the day before in an exciting and useful way. Don't be ashamed to use things up, often they will provide more flavour than if they had been cooked specifically for the purpose.

Equipment required

If you have already read Chapter 4, you will probably have most of the equipment required. Get a few nice pottery dishes for preservation, but don't go mad because vegetable and fruit decoration can make up for a lot.

Starters that are dressings in disguise

There is no point in going through all the dressings again; if I highlight a few you can develop the rest. Attention will be paid to preservation and accompaniments.

80   Crudités

Crudités are the accompaniment and starter at one and the same time. Simply take a selection of fresh vegetables chosen for colour and crispness. For instance, carrots, celery, cucumber, spring onions, red and white cabbage, chinese leaves, green and red peppers, asparagus and green beans. Cut those that need cutting using chopping technique D. Arrange them attractively in a dish or jug so that they are semi-immersed in water which will keep them fresh and then choose a dip, or better several dips. Almost all of the dressings apart from French dressing would be suitable for crudités. Pour the dips into nice bowls, chill well and then garnish with fresh vegetables, olives, slices of orange or lemon, chopped nuts or perhaps simply a few fresh herbs or spices. This is a nice refreshing start to a meal that can be communal and so may break the ice.

81 The open sandwich

Perhaps 'open' to offers as the possible variations are legion. Here's one of my favourites. On to a slice of wholemeal bread – rye is nice if you can make it or get it – put a couple of lettuce leaves, then spread thickly with egg mayonnaise (51) and pile high with crisp salad vegetables, decorate with olives, sunflower seeds (roasted in tamari) (103) or just about anything you fancy. Use any dressing you like so long as it is fairly thick.

82 Marinated madness

This is based on the same principle as crudités, but marinated vegetables are used instead; for instance, the marinated florets of cauliflower (115) dipped into red wine mayonnaise (66). Concentrate on preservation. If you can, put nice crisp lettuce or alfalfa sprouts under toppings.

83 Hommous ½ litre

Here is a proper recipe for that very tasty Middle Eastern dip.

Stage	Ingredients	Quantity	Method
1	Chick peas	120 g	*Soak overnight, cook, rinse and mix in a blender with the rest of the ingredients until they form a soft creamy paste. Season with salt and pepper.*
2	Tahini	2 tbsp	
	Olive oil	4 tbsp	
	Lemon juice	1 lemon	
	Garlic	2–5 cloves	
	Salt and pepper	To taste	

Special points

If the paste is too thick dilute with chick-pea water or yoghurt. Make sure the chick-peas are well cooked.

To serve

Serve hommous in a small bowl on a base of alfalfa or crisp lettuce, garnish with a slice or wedge of lemon chopped black olives and a sprinkling of paprika.

As with tsatziki (68), cucumber raita (69) and babajanou (70), it is nice to serve hommous as a starter with some freshly baked pitta bread (136). Brush the pitta bread with a little melted butter before serving, cut the pittas into triangles and cover with a damp cloth (this stops them drying out).

Variations

(a) Replace the chick peas with the same quantity of haricot beans in recipe 84 to make haricot hommous.

(b) If you don't have time to make pitta bread, hot buttered wholewheat toast will taste just as good.

(c) Yoghurt, especially goat's or sheep's, is an excellent addition to hommous in its own right. Simply reduce the quantity of olive oil and water in the recipe and make it up with the same quantity of yoghurt.

84 Guacamole

Serves 4

Guacamole is an extension of the avocado dressing (75). It is delightful and appetising as a starter to any meal, though surprisingly filling, so don't overdo the portions.

Stage	Ingredients	Quantity	Method
1	Ripe avocado	2 large	*Scoop out the flesh of the avocados and combine with the rest of the ingredients. Try to retain the skin of the avocado if it is of good quality, as this will make an attractive receptacle in which to serve the guacamole.*
	Lemon juice	1 lemon	
	Salt and pepper	Pinch to taste	
	Garlic	3–4 cloves	
2	Spring onion/red onion	4/1 medium	*Chop fine and stir into avocado mixture.*
	Ripe green pepper/red pepper	1 medium	
	Tomatoes	2 medium	

To serve

Serve guacamole on a bed of something crisp – lettuce or alfalfa – garnish with a slice of lemon. Eat with home-made tortilla chips. If these are too much trouble go out and buy some.

Variations

(a) Fold in 100 ml of sour cream, natural yoghurt or soft cheese in stage 1.

(b) Season with chilli, for a really Mexican touch. (Although guacamole was originally used to cool your mouth down after a bowl full of highly spiced Mexican food.)

(c) Decorate with chunks of fresh orange.

85 Babajanou

½ litre

Babajanou is an extension of the aubergine dressing (70) but is extremely rich. Sometimes this starter is called mock-caviar, a name I don't like but the amount you can eat is quite similar.

Stage	Ingredients	Quantity	Method
1	Aubergine	2 med.	*Wash and then bake in a medium oven at 350°F (180°C, Gas Mark 4) for 1 hour, longer if the flesh is still not cooked. Scoop out the flesh into your blender (if you don't have a blender use a pestle and mortar.*
2	Olive oil	25 ml	*Add the rest of the ingredients and blend together to form a thick dark paste. Chill in the fridge.*
	Lemon juice	½ lemon	
	Natural yoghurt	175 ml	
	Salt and pepper	To taste	

To serve

Serve with a wedge of lemon and fingers of hot, buttered wholewheat toast or wedges of fresh pitta bread and chopped black olives.

Variations

(a) Mushroom babajanou – heat a little of the olive oil in a pan and, when hot, add 125 g flat mushrooms; cook until the mushrooms are soft. Add the mushrooms to the blender with the rest of the ingredients.

(b) Replace the natural yoghurt with goat or sheep's yoghurt.

(c) Replace the natural yoghurt with feta cheese and sheep's milk.

(d) Replace the natural yoghurt with sour cream.

(e) Replace the natural yoghurt with cottage cheese.

(f) Use any combination of the above variations that takes your fancy.

Whole mushroom starters

Whole mushrooms make an excellent vegetable for starting a meal, not only do they look and taste good but they are also light, leaving room for the courses to follow. Of course, for every recipe in which mushrooms are used other vegetables can be substituted, particularly florets of cauliflower broccoli, green beans, mange-tout, chunks of courgettes and even fresh broad beans. Do not use flat mushrooms for mushroom starters, use open cups, cups or ideally small cups (buttons), as they retain shape and texture (given minimal cooking).

86 Mushrooms in garlic
Serves 4

Stage	Ingredients	Quantity	Method
1	Vegetable oil/butter	50 ml/50 g	*Melt the butter/oil in a pan and add the mushrooms.*
	Button mushrooms	500 g	*Cook for 2 minutes on a medium heat until the mushrooms are thoroughly hot.*
2	Garlic, crushed	5 cloves	*Stir in garlic and lemon juice, allow to cook for another minute.*
	Lemon juice	½ lemon	
3	Parsley, chopped	Good handful	*Add just before serving.*

To serve

Serve in small pottery dishes with fresh wholewheat bread.

Variations

(a) Broccoli in garlic – substitute florets of broccoli for mushrooms, but cook for an extra 3 minutes in the first stage.
(b) Broccoli and mushrooms in garlic – use equal quantities of broccoli and mushrooms.
(c) Green beans in garlic – par-boil green beans for a few minutes, drain and then cook as mushrooms.
(d) Courgettes in garlic – fry the courgettes quickly, allowing them to brown on either side before adding garlic and lemon juice.
(e) Broad beans in garlic – cook broad beans prior to use then substitute for mushrooms.
(f) Mange-tout in garlic – use as for mushrooms.

87 Mushrooms in sour cream
Serves 4

Proceed as for mushrooms in garlic (86) but also add a dash of tamari with the lemon juice. Fold in 200 ml of sour cream at the end of stage 2 and reheat, but do not boil before serving. Garnish with parsley and/or fresh mixed herbs.

Variations

As for mushrooms in garlic (86) but substitute pre-cooked crunchy cauliflower florets for mushrooms.

88 Mushrooms boulevard

Proceed as for mushrooms in sour cream (87) but add 100 ml of dry vermouth and a little less lemon juice. Reduce the vermouth by 1/3 before adding the sour cream.

Variations

(a) Use double cream instead of sour cream.

(b) As for mushrooms in garlic (86), substituting pre-cooked crunchy cauliflower florets for mushrooms, either totally or in combination with other suitable vegetables.

(c) If you like parmesan cheese, then sprinkle a little on to these dishes prior to serving.

89 Curried mushrooms

As for recipe 74 but use button mushrooms instead of flat ones.

90 Stuffed mushrooms

Serves 4

Use open cup mushrooms. Remove the stalks carefully and save for your stockpot or tomorrow's bake. Rinse the mushrooms quickly and try not to damage them.

Stage	Ingredients	Quantity	Method
1	Open cut mushrooms	500 g	*Prepare for stuffing.*
2	Olive/vegetable oil/butter	50 ml/50 g	*Heat the oil/butter in a pan, add the parsley and cook for*
	Parsley, chopped	2 handfuls	*1 minute. Add the rest of the ingredients and stir to a thick but*
	Lemon juice	½ lemon	*moist consistency.*
	Garlic, minced	5 cloves	
	Bread crumbs	50 g	
	Parmesan	25 g	
	Salt and pepper	To taste	
3			*Using a teaspoon fill the mushrooms well with the mixture, then place on a lightly greased baking tray and bake in the oven for 30 minutes at 400°F (200°C, Gas Mark 6).*

Variations

(a) Serve with any dressing you like – creamy ones or cold tomato sauce (6) are especially good.

(b) After stuffing, top with a little grated cheese or mozarella.

(c) Add 90 g of cream cheese to mixture before filling the mushrooms.

(d) Add 90 g of cottage cheese to mixture before filling the mushrooms.

91 Deep-fried battered mushrooms

Deep-frying holds no mysteries and need not be dangerous if the right preparations are carried out. Always use a good quality pure vegetable oil and use only enough to submerge the ingredient, for mushrooms this is not a lot. The oil should reach 325–380°F (160–195°C) before anything is cooked in it. A simple way to test this is with a piece of bread dropped into the oil; it will sizzle if the oil is at the right temperature. As soon as the oil is hot enough turn the heat down to medium-low. When you have finished cooking always turn the heat off and just leave the oils to cool down. A frying basket is always handy but otherwise a spoon with holes in it will suffice. Put the cooked items on to kitchen paper to absorb any excess oil.

A The batter

Stage	Ingredients	Quantity	Method
1	Egg yolk	3	*Blend ingredients together.*
	Wholemeal flour (sifted)		
	Oil	25 ml	
	Water	25 ml	

Variations

(a) After coating in batter roll in breadcrumbs before frying.
(b) Add herbs, shoyu, spices, mustard to batter for extra flavour.

B The mushrooms

Trim the stalk if you like although this is not necessary, use open cups, cups or button mushrooms. Wash quickly but thoroughly and pat dry. The mushrooms must not be wet when they are fried. Dip into flour and then into the batter. Immerse the mushrooms carefully in the hot oil and cook until the batter is a golden brown colour. Serve with the dressing or dip of your choice, plain horseradish is an excellent accompaniment.

Variations

This technique is really good applied to almost any vegetable, especially aubergines, carrots, courgettes, celery, peppers, cauliflower and broccoli. Cooking times may vary but always aim to keep the vegetables fresh and succulent.

To serve

Serve piping hot with a wedge of lemon, a sprig of parsley and a little bowl of something nice to dip into.

Pâtés and mousses

Pâtés and mousses are excellent ways not only of using up left-over vegetables beans and pulses, but also of creating tasty but substantial starters. Pâtés may be made in individual cocottes or in large terrines served with hot spoons. All of the pâtés and mousses suggested are best eaten either with a salad or fingers of hot buttered toast. Like dressings and the other starters the emphasis must lie on concentrating flavour and texture; decoration is not necessary but a nice touch. Pâtés and mousses should be well chilled before serving especially if you have used agar agar to set them. Using agar agar as a setting agent for these dishes gives you the opportunity to present them attractively out of their bowls or moulds. In the end, though, it is what they taste like that counts. A short word of warning if you are using left-overs for your pâtés or mousses: don't store them for more than one day unless you have used alcohol in preparation. No additional equipment is required except perhaps some attractive earthenware dishes.

92 Carrot and sour cream mousse (an uncooked mousse)   Serves 4

Stage	Ingredients	Quantity	Method
1	Butter/vegetable margarine	50 g	*Heat the fat in a pan and add the carrots, cook very lightly for only a few minutes. Remove from heat and fold in the breadcrumbs, allow to cool before stirring in the sour cream, season with salt and pepper before adding the prepared agar agar.*
	Carrots, grated	700 g	
	Breadcrumbs	50 g	
	Sour cream	200 ml	
	Agar agar	100 ml	
	Salt and pepper	To taste	
2			*Place in greased mould and chill thoroughly for 1–2 hours.*
3	Lettuce ⎱ optional Alfalfa ⎰		*Garnish a plate with lettuce and alfalfa and turn mould out on to it. Decorate with a selection of salad vegetables.*
	Salad vegetables		

Variations

Replace some of sour cream with cottage cheese or grated cheddar cheese.

Vegetable pâtés

We have discussed varieties of aubergine starters and these can easily become pâtés if thickened with a few breadcrumbs and set with agar agar. Similarly, avocado dressing (75) will make an attractive and tasty pâté when given the same treatment. Remember when you change any dish slightly always adjust the seasoning accordingly. The main problem with most vegetable pâtés is the liquid they produce in cooking. This can be removed and used for stock or absorbed by the addition of breadcrumbs.

93 Spinach pâté   Serves 4

Stage	Ingredients	Quantity	Method
1	Butter/vegetable margarine	10 g	Melt the butter/margarine in a pan and add the spinach, cook until the spinach is soft (5 minutes), allow to cool.
	Spinach leaves	450 g	
2	Cooled melted butter/ vegetable margarine	50 g	Put cooked spinach into a blender with the melted butter and purée. Fold rest of ingredients into mixture. Season to taste.
	Sour cream	200 ml	
	Nutmeg	Pinch	
	Shoyu, optional	Dash	
	Garlic, optional	3 cloves	
	Breadcrumbs	50 g	
3	Agar agar	100 ml	Add to mixture and turn into a greased bowl for serving. Allow to chill and set in fridge before eating.

Note

Food that is set with agar agar will start to melt as soon as it is taken from the fridge so only remove just before serving.

Variations

(a) Replace spinach with mushrooms
(b) Replace spinach with cauliflower.
(c) Replace spinach with leeks.

94 Spinach mousse

As for spinach pâté (93) but add 4 egg yolks to the mixture instead of agar agar. Whip the whites until peaking and fold in carefully. Put the mixture into a buttered ovenware dish and cook at a medium-hot heat (400°F) for about an hour. Remove from oven and allow to cool before chilling. When the mousse has cooled it should be possible to turn it out on to a plate and decorate before serving.

Note

All vegetable pâtés will make cooked mousses if treated in this way. A nice addition to most cooked vegetable mousses is a handful of grated cheese added to the rest of the ingredients and perhaps a little parmesan cheese.

95 Lentil and garlic pâté   Serves 4

Lentil pâtés do not generally need thickening with extra breadcrumbs unless you do not strain off any remaining water after cooking. I usually use it for stock. Red, yellow or orange lentils are most commonly used for pâtés as they cook to a paste; split-peas are good to use for this reason too. Brown, green or speckled lentils will need to be puréed in a blender with some of their cooking water to achieve the same consistency. Lentils absorb a lot of flavour so use ingredients with strong but piquant attributes. The addition of breadcrumbs to the lentil paste is sometimes desirable to make the pâté less heavy.

Stage	Ingredients	Quantity	Method
1	Red Lentils	150 g	*Put the lentils into the boiling water and cook until most*
	Boiling water	500 ml	*of the water is absorbed (approximately 10 minutes).*
2	Olive oil	50 ml	*Combine the lentils with the rest of the ingredients either in a*
	Garlic, minced	4–5 cloves	*bowl or a blender. If the mixture is too dry add a little more olive*
	Breadcrumbs	25 g	*oil, lemon juice or lentil water. If too wet then add some more*
	Lemon juice	1 lemon	*breadcrumbs. Allow to cool.*
	Mixed herbs	1 dsp	
	Shoyu, optional	Dash	

To serve

Serve in an attractive dish garnished with salad vegetables and hot buttered toast, pitta bread or chapatis.

Variations

(a) Replace red lentils with other lentils or split-peas or buckwheat.
(b) When the mixture is cooked, beat in cream, sour cream, cream cheese, cottage cheese, blue cheese, mayonnaise (59), tofu, miso, tahini, peanut butter, grated cheese, port or red wine for example.
(c) Stir-fry a few finely chopped spring onions, chives, carrots, onion, celery, green or red peppers, mushrooms and fold into pâté – use any combination you fancy.

(d) Lentil loaves – for lentil loaves simply add 2 eggs to the mixture, beat in thoroughly and pour into a greased loaf tin. Bake at 350°C for up to an hour or until mixture is firm to touch. This can be served hot or cold in slices accompanied by a salad or a tasty sauce. If you line the loaf tin with some mushroom, or tomatoes before pouring in the mixture then this will form an attractive decoration when the loaf is turned out. For vegans, it is not always necessary to use eggs to bind a loaf, tofu can give the same effect and red lentils themselves will act as a binding agent. As with lentil pâtés, lentil loaves may be varied in the same multitudinous ways as mentioned previously (a, b and c).

96 Blackeye and mushroom pâté

This is a bean-based pâté, but the majority of applications are identical to lentil-based pâtés. Beans however, must be well cooked, even slightly over-cooked, and a blender will be necessary to create the right consistency.

Again most beans are rather bland and so form an ideal base for absorbing good flavours. Bean pâtés give the ideal opportunity of using up beans that may have been intended for another purpose, but are over-cooked.

Stage	Ingredients	Quantity	Method
1	Butter/vegetable margarine	50 g	*Heat the margarine/butter in a pan, add the mushrooms and herbs and cook until mushrooms are slightly soft.*
	Mushrooms, chopped	300 g	
	Mixed herbs	2 dsp	
2	Blackeye beans	300 g	*Place all ingredients in a blender and blend until a smooth paste, cool, add a little agar agar and set in the fridge.*
	Yoghurt	200 ml	
	Tamari	1 tbsp	
	Bread crumbs	25 g	

To serve

As for lentil pâté.

Variations

As for lentil pâté, except blackeyes can be substituted by

any other bean. Two particularly good combinations are butter bean and tofu, and aduki and apple pâté. Do try to vary your combinations to suit purpose and taste.

97 Nutty buckwheat pâté

Serves 4

Buckwheat has a nutty flavour that complements a nutty taste, it is also good as the base for a pâté, especially one where nuts are involved. Remember all the variations and permutations are the same as for lentil, bean and vegetable pâtés.

Stage	Ingredients	Quantity	Method
1	Buckwheat, cooked	500 g	*Add a dash of tamari and keep to one side.*
2	Vegetable oil	50 ml	*Heat the oil and stir-fry in the rest of the vegetables, when hot*
	Onions	1 medium	*add the shoyu, a few mixed herbs and the chilli.*
	Green pepper	1 small	
	Celery	1 stick	
	Shoyu		
	Chilli	1 tsp	
	Mixed herbs	1 dsp	
3	Tomato paste, optional	2 tbsp	*When the onions are soft add the tomato paste, peanut butter*
	Peanut butter, smooth	2 tbsb	*and chopped nuts. Add this vegetable mix to the buckwheat*
	Chopped roasted peanuts	1 tbsp	*and mix. Add the cheese to the mixture and adjust seasoning.*
	Grated cheese	125 g	*If mixture is too thick add a little hot stock or yoghurt or lemon juice.*

To serve

Serve as for other pâtés.

Variations

As for other pâtés.

Some other Starters

98 Cauliflower á la grèque

Serves 4

Stage	Ingredients	Quantity	Method
1	Cauliflower	2 large	*Cut into florets (1) and blanch in boiling water for a couple of*
	Boiling water	1 l	*minutes.*
2	Water	½ l	*Place all these ingredients into a pan and bring to the boil.*
	Oil	100 ml	
	Lemon juice	1½ lemons	
	Bay leaf	1	
	Thyme	2 tsp	
	Celery	25 g	
	Whole coriander	5	
	Black peppercorns	5	
	Salt and pepper	To taste	
3			*Place the blanched cauliflower into the boiling liquid (2) and cook until crisp but edible – a few minutes more. Leave in liquid to cool.*

To serve

Serve in a dish with a little of the cooking liquid on its own or with a sauce or dip.

Variations

(a) Substitute the cauliflower with whole globe artichokes, celery, leeks, small onions or green beans.

(b) If you're feeling very rich, substitute half the quantity of water with red or white wine.

99 Macaroni milanese

Serves 4

A cold pasta starter which can be a tasty but filling way to start a meal. Pasta is extremely quick and easy to prepare and can be made to look very attractive. It is nice if the vegetables in cold pasta dishes stay on the crisp side.

Stage	Ingredients	Quantity	Method
1	Wholewheat macaroni, cooked	300 g	*After cooking the macaroni rinse with cold water and allow to cool.*
2	Olive oil	50 ml	*Heat oil and add carrots then stir-fry. When carrots start to soften on the outside add the rest of the ingredients and continue to cook for 5 minutes stirring over a low heat.*
	Carrots (A1)	1 medium	
	Green pepper (C)	1 small	
	Red pepper (C)	1 small	
	Celery (A1)	1 stick	
	Oregano	1 tbsp	
	Salt and pepper	To taste	
3	Tomato sauce (B)	200 ml	*Heat up the tomato sauce and add to the vegetables. Combine this with the macaroni, re-season and allow to chill.*

To serve

Simply serve in a dish with the option of parmesan, perhaps garnished with a few salad vegetables.

Variations

(a) Substitute macaroni with any other form of pasta you think appropriate; for example, tagliatelle, spaghetti, canneloni, pasta shells and spinach pasta are good to use.

(b) Substitute tomato sauce B with any sauce you think appropriate. If using a roux-based sauce such as Cheese Sauce (38) add some cream, sour cream or yoghurt after cooking to stop the sauce becoming too thick. Garlic is always nice in any pasta dish.

100 Wellington rolls

Serves 4

Wellington rolls are really roly-polys and delicious served hot or cold. On their own or with a sauce or dressing, they just about constitute a starter; with a salad they are definitely a 'finisher'. Welly Rolls, as they have become known, can contain a wide variety of fillings but the most popular is given in the recipe below. Welly rolls have an added advantage in being able to be picked up, so they are excellent substitutes for boring old vol-au-vents at buffets.

Stage	Ingredients	Quantity	Method
1	Potatoes, cooked (C)	150 g	*While the potatoes are still hot add the spring onions, grated cheese, chilli and seasoning, mix together thoroughly (slightly over-cooked old potatoes are best in this recipe).*
	Spring onions (G)	3–4	
	Grated cheese	150 g	
	Chilli	Pinch	
	Salt and pepper	To taste	
2	Puff pastry/quiche pastry (142)	150 g	*Roll pastry into a rectangle and spread potato mixture over it, leaving about an inch on all sides. Take a narrow side of the rectangle and roll the pastry up. If you wish slice the top with a knife diagonally.*
3	Pastry glaze (133)		*Brush the surface with your pastry glaze and transfer the roly poly to a greased baking sheet. Bake in the oven for 45 minutes at 350–400°F (180–200°C, Gas mark 4–6) until pastry is cooked.*

To serve

Present the welly roll on a bed of lettuce surrounded by salad vegetables. Cut the roll diagonally into 4–6 pieces.

Variations

(a) Add the following ingredients to the potato mixture: mushrooms, green/red peppers, celery and/or other dairy cheeses.

(b) Replace the potato mixture with ratatouille (14) and cheese or any other sauce that is thick enough.

(c) Instead of roly polys use this concept to make savoury tarts. Grease a tart tin and use the pastry for lining the tart moulds. Fill the tarts with welly roll mixture and either leave open or cover with a small circle of pastry.

Conclusion

The whole subject of starters is enormous – the combinations and permutations are endless, so do experiment, adapt and you'll be surprised how easy it is, so long as the ingredients are right and you always follow the basic disciplines. I haven't even mentioned rissoles and burgers as starters because they are simply extensions of the pâtés which have been shaped, covered in breadcrumbs and fried or baked. The addition of sauces and dips should only be necessary when the starters are perhaps rather dry.

Chapter 7

Salads

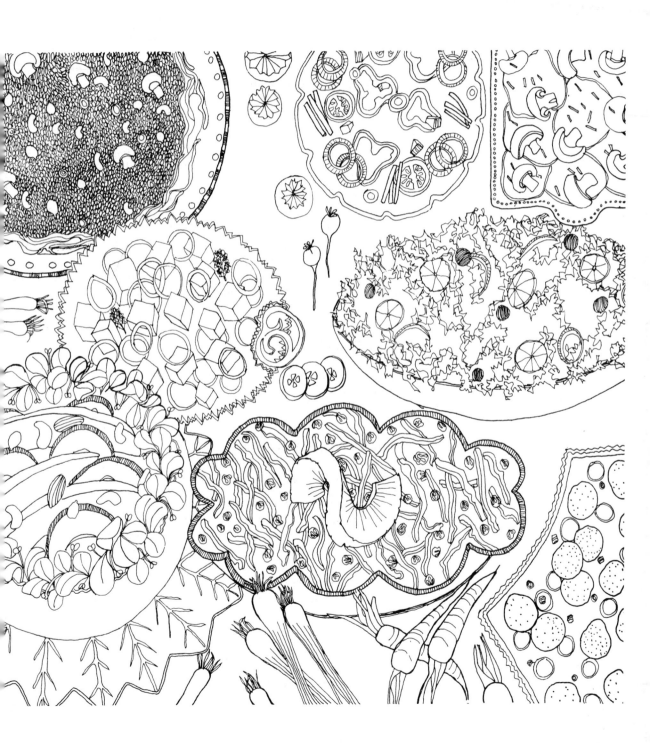

Introduction

The reluctant vegetarian may well be thinking to himself 'Hah! this is what it's really all about, vegetarians eat mostly salads; I'm not really a salad person, therefore how can I enjoy vegetarian food?' Don't worry, when we talk about salads we're not talking about limp lettuce, cress, 2 slices of cucumber, a wedge of tomato and some grated carrot. No, our salads are like the rest of our food – exciting experiments in colour, flavour, texture, shape and appropriateness. Our salads can become starters in their own right, an addition to a main course, a main course or a between course, even something to finish a meal. Salads may be simple or elaborate, whatever is needed to suit the occasion and season. Having already read the introduction to the chapter on vegetable preparation and the chapter on salad dressings you're ready to attempt your first salad anyway, so why write a chapter on salads? Really, the recipes are just a guide to a few ideas that have worked in the past. I hate the idea of quantifying the ingredients in a salad – it is better to be flexible in what you do and not to worry if you haven't got one of the ingredients to hand. In other words, follow the basic disciplines of preparation, remember the nature of the ingredients (Chapter 2), use a suitable dressing and start creating. I think first of all, however, it may be handy to outline a few of the ingredients that a salad can contain, a few additions which you might otherwise forget and then a few accompaniments to sprinkle on top of salads.

Equipment required

No additional equipment is required, except perhaps attractive salad bowls or plates for serving.

Raw vegetable ingredients

Refer to chopping section for preparation.

Lettuce (lots of different varieties), spring cabbage, savoy cabbage, white cabbage, red cabbage, chinese leaves, spinach, kale, silverbeet, celery, fennel, endive, chicory, cucumber, tomatoes, peppers (green, red and yellow, etc.), mustard and cress, watercress, alfalfa sprouts (any other bean sprouts), radish (different varieties), celeriac, baby turnips, carrots, spring onions, onions (various), parsnips (young), mushrooms, garlic. All fruits.

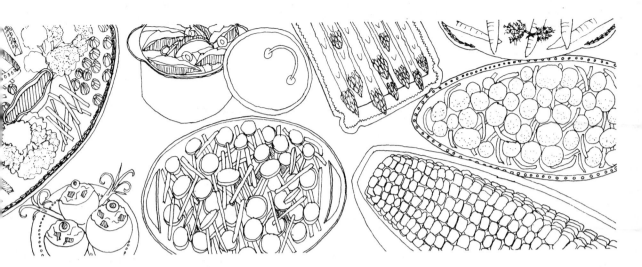

Cooked or marinated vegetable ingredients

Cauliflower, courgettes, broccoli, leeks, French beans, runner beans, broad beans, old and new potatoes, Jerusalem artichokes, beetroot, brussel sprouts, asparagus, globe artichoke hearts, sweetcorn.

Cooked dry ingredients

All dried beans and chick-peas, green/brown/speckled lentils, pastas, wholewheat, cracked wheat, cous-cous, barley, any roasted nuts and seeds.

Uncooked dry ingredients

Sultanas, raisins, apricots, peaches, currants, (you may wish to soak apricots or peaches before use), nuts and seeds.

Things to mix in or sprinkle over your salads

These ingredients are completely inessential to a salad but can lift a good salad into the realms of the gourmet.

101 Olives

Try to buy Greek olives as these are usually best. If they are kept in brine wash them before use. Olives may be black, green or stuffed and can be used whole or chopped to add colour to a salad.

102 Capers

Use and prepare in the same way as olives.

103 Tamari-roasted sunflower seeds

Stage	Ingredients	Quantity	Method
1	Shoyu/tamari Sunflower seeds	1 tbsp Good handful	*Heat the tamari in a pan. When it is starting to boil add the sunflower seeds and stir so that all the seeds are coated. Place the seeds in a tray and roast them in a hot oven for 5 minutes. Serve hot or cold with your salads or as snacks at parties.*

Variations

Substitute sunflower seeds with peanuts, cashew nuts, almonds or sesame seeds.

Note – all of these ingredients may also be used uncooked in salads, whole or grated, or just plain roasted. But tamari roasting is a very simple way of making something very addictive.

104 Poppy seeds

Simply roast and sprinkle.

105 Cheesy garlic croutons

These are a great way to use up yesterday's bread and make something really tasty too. Mash as many cloves of garlic as you think you will like into some butter or vegetable margarine. Toast one side of a piece of old bread and spread the other with the garlic butter, then sprinkle with grated cheese. Oil a baking sheet well and place the toast on to it. Roast in the oven until the cheese is golden brown. Allow to cool before cutting into small cubes. Use these in, on top or beside salads or for party snacks.

Variations

(a) Omit the cheese for garlic croutons.
(b) Add a few sweet herbs like oregano for herby garlic croutons.
(c) Mix a little french mustard into the garlic butter for mustard croutons.

Note – Croutons are best if crisp externally but softer inside so don't over-roast them.

106 Sprouted beans/pulses/cereals

These should be very young sprouts to which the bean, lentil or grain is still attached. Sprinkle over or mix in with the salad.

107 Other additions to salads

(a) Crumbled Danish blue or stilton into the salad.
(b) Cubed or grated cheddar or any other hard cheese.
(c) Marinated tofu – fried golden brown and added to the salad.

(d) Fresh and dried herbs and spices – Fresh herbs and whole spices are always the best to use in salads, but they are extremely pungent so should be used with care. Dried herbs and ground spices have less flavour, but may still be used successfully. Here are some herbs and spices you may wish to use in your salads – if you can get them fresh or whole all well and good, but don't worry if you can't.

Herbs – Mint, parsley, oregano, thyme, chives, basil, dill, fennel, tarragon, chervil, marjoram, coriander leaves, sage.

Spices – coriander seeds, mustard, chilli, cayenne, paprika, cumin, garam masala, fenugreek, allspice.

Conclusion

Salads, whether presented in bowls or on plates, should always be attractive. Use the whole range of chopping techniques to achieve a varied but harmonious texture in the salad. Leave dressing the salad till the last possible moment, it is as important not to over-dress a salad as it is not to underdress one. So add your dressing cautiously until you achieve the combination you prefer. Some people like lots of dressing – be flexible, be adventurous but always follow the basic principles already discussed.

Now we move on to recipes, although I have left the quantification to you the major ingredient will be at the top and a suggested chopping technique will be along side. Remember, the whole idea now is to get away from thinking in terms of recipes and more in terms of creativity. I have chosen a selection of salads that cover most of the ingredients already mentioned. I have suggested a dressing but again, it is up to you – you are the cook make it how you like it.

Salad recipes

108 Lettuce salads

Ingredients

Lettuce
Tips
1. Try to buy fresh, crisp lettuce in season.
2. Wash thoroughly and pat dry (see Chapter 2).
3. Never cut lettuce, tear it.

Suggested Dressing

French dressings (54) are best for lettuce, creamier dressings make it go limp. Try adding mixed herbs (1 tsp) to the French dressing as this is particularly nice with lettuce.

Variations

(a) Substitute any of the leaf vegetables already mentioned for lettuce.
(b) Mix lettuce with different leaf vegetables.
(c) Add any selection of other salad vegetables to the lettuce.

When adding vegetables to lettuce do so just before serving with the dressing so that the lettuce does not go soggy. Try tomatoes (A thin), cucumbers (A thin, A1 thin, B thin, B1 thin, H), peppers (D,C,H), radish (whole or halved), watercress (roughly chopped). I'm sure you are getting the idea by now – the variations and combinations are endless.

109 Tomato salads

(i)   Greek salad

Ingredients

Tomatoes
Olives
Small red onion
Oregano
Salt and pepper

Suggested Dressing

Greek (57)

Slice the tomatoes thickly or chop roughly. Finely mince the onion, scatter with a few olives – season and sprinkle with oregano. Add the dressing just before serving.

Variations

(a) Crumble feta cheese over salad.
(b) Add a few cucumber chunks or chopped green peppers to the salad.

(ii)   Tomato and cabbage salad

Ingredients	Suggested Dressing
Tomatoes (F)	French dressing (54) or any variation you fancy, Lemon and Honey (56) would be nice.
White cabbage (D)	
Celery (B thin)	
Black olives	
Cucumber (B thin) – only a small amount for colour.	
Add tomatoes to other ingredients, add dressing before serving.	

110 Cabbage salads

White and red cabbage salads seem to be generally very popular – they are easy to make and yield a lot of bulk quickly. Here are two combinations that go well with cabbage (white, red or mixed) as the bulk of the salad.

(i)   Waldorf salad

Ingredients	Suggested Dressing
White cabbage (D)	(a) Mayonnaise (59) with a dash of fresh cream as well (optional) (b) Sour cream and spring onion (72)
Celery	
Eating apples	
Sultanas	
White grapes	
Blanched walnuts	

(ii)   Coleslaw

Ingredients	Suggested Dressing
White cabbage (D)	Mix equal quantities of French dressing (54) and mayonnaise (59).
Onion (G)	
Carrots (D)	

111   Carrot salads

Carrots have the advantage over white cabbage of having their own distinctive colour. The vegetable preparation section tells you how to use carrots to their best. They provide good cheap bulk that is reasonably nutritious as well but, of course, a lot is lost in their shredding. Very young carrots tend to be a little watery – older ones tend to be wooden, so if possible use medium-aged carrots. Carrots do have their own special flavour, but this can become a bit boring so use a fruity dressing with them. The recipe that follows is one for carrot salad that I have most commonly used.

Ingredients	Suggested Dressing
Carrots (D) or grated	Lemon and Honey Dressing (56) or Orange (55)
Sultanas	
Roasted peanuts	

Unlike most delicate salad vegetables carrots must be dressed or at least tossed in lemon juice immediately they are prepared, to prevent discoloration.

Variations

Add any of the following: watercress, parsley, cress, toasted sunflower seeds, any bean, seed, lentil or grain sprouts.

112 Cucumber salads

Always prepare cucumbers as suggested in the chopping section; remember it is always best to remove a waxed skin. Tsatziki (68) is essentially a cucumber salad, rather than grating the cucumber chunk it or slice it. Somehow, cucumbers always seem to go well with yoghurt and cream dressings – here is an alternative.

Ingredients

Cucumbers (A thin)
Green peppers (D)
Spring onions (G)

Suggested Dressing

(a) French dressing (54) made with white wine vinegar instead of cider vinegar. Add a dash of lemon juice.
(b) Mix equal quantities of mayonnaise (59) with yoghurt and a little extra dill and perhaps a touch of fresh mint.

Variations

Keep cucumber as dominant ingredient and add a combination of all salad vegetables particularly green ones.

Add toasted sunflower seeds and croutons, too.

113 Mung beansprout salad

Mung bean sprouts are probably the largest of the sprout family. Their flavour is easily tainted so always rinse them before use. This salad is both crunchy, refreshing and tasty.

Ingredients

Mung bean sprouts
Green pepper (D)
Carrot (D)
Hard boiled eggs (chopped)
Tamari-roasted peanuts (grated)

Suggested Dressing

(a) Peanut chilli (76)
(b) Blue cheese (60)
(c) Orange (55)

Variations

Add other sprouted grains, lentils, beans and seeds (whole), radish, cucumber, tomatoes, etc . . , toasted sesame seeds, croutons, etc.

114 Leek salad

The leeks can be prepared as for Cauliflower à la Gréque (98), or otherwise simply stir-fried in butter with lemon juice, tamari and seasoning. Alternatively, they can simply be plunged into boiling water for a couple of minutes. Leeks used in salad should remain fairly crisp, but definitely cooked, unless extremely young.

Ingredients

Leeks
Tomatoes (a few)
Toasted cashews

Suggested Dressing

(a) French dressing (54) and variations.
(b) Red wine mayonnaise (66).
(c) Sour cream (72) and variations.
(d) Mayonnaise (59) and variations.

115 Cauliflower salads

Prepare as for leek salad (114); try similar variations and combinations. Dressings should probably be creamier than for leeks.

116 Brussel sprout salads

Prepare as for leek salad (114). Brussel sprouts are nice marinated in a herby French dressing or served with a light peanut sauce/dressing.

117 Green bean salads

Use French beans, runner beans, bobby or stringless beans. Top and tail if necessary – I like to leave these beans whole if possible, then prepare as for leek salad (114). The marinade procedure is not absolutely necessary. Green beans are nice with a wide variety of dressings, most have already been mentioned. Green beans are nice on their own or with a selection of other salad vegetables – tomatoes are particularly appropriate, probably best cut in the F style. Likewise, mushroom and tomato dressing (77) is a tasty dressing to use, or simply make a very thick garlic French dressing (54) and sprinkle a little parmesan cheese over the beans before serving. When using ingredients that are rather special like green beans I always feel you owe it to the vegetable to keep the salad as simple as possible.

118 Courgette salads

Cut the courgettes moderately thin (A, A1, B, B1) then prepare everything as for leek salad (114), but reduce all contact with heat by half so that the courgettes are still à la dente in the salad. Courgettes are really versatile when it comes to dressings. I would normally say 'keep it simple' like orange dressing (55), if I didn't know that courgettes were delicious with the whole spectrum of dairy-based dressings and mayonnaise, but please do not over-dress. Combine the courgettes with few other ingredients perhaps beansprouts, tomato or radish.

119 Mushroom salads

Open or closed cup mushrooms are especially good for salads, button mushrooms have very little flavour but may be used whole, flat mushrooms go limp and unattractive when dressed. Mushrooms need no marinading and should be used raw or quickly tossed in a little melted vegetable margarine/butter, shoyu and lemon juice – do this only if you are using whole mushrooms in the salad. Mushrooms should be thickly sliced or just halved, if not used whole, otherwise they will soon disintegrate – some people do like mushrooms to be thinly sliced and, while I wouldn't dream of changing lifelong habits, I would suggest a thick dressing like sour cream (72) and variations to help support them. Used whole, they need a really tasty French dressing (54) or a dressing based on it such as tamari and ginger (58) or perhaps a yoghurt-based dressing – tsataki (68). Try turning mushroom and tomato dressing (77) into a salad in its own right. Keep the other ingredients in a mushroom salad simple, chosen from beansprouts, radishes, red and green peppers, roasted sunflower seeds, cashews or peanuts, fresh tarragon and parsley. Remember it is always best to include lemon juice to stop the mushrooms discolouring.

120 Broccoli salads

Proceed as for cauliflower salad (115) but be careful not to overcook; use less water or just gently stir-fry. Broccoli salads are nicest on their own with the simplest of dressings, or perhaps with mushroom in a sour cream and shoyu dressing sprinkled with a few tamari-roasted sunflower seeds. As with all these recipes, do try a selection from the raw vegetable ingredients section at the beginning of this chapter to suit your own purpose.

121 Beetroot salads

Beetroots should be prepared in accordance with the vegetable preparation section and sliced using method A or chopped using C or H method. Beetroots have a distinctive colour, but at certain times of year can be a bit bland and woody, so here are some suggested other ingredients that can help liven up beetroot.

Ingredients – choose a selection

Spring onion, radish, watercress, celery, alfalfa, mustard and cress, green peppers, green beans, sweetcorn, roasted peanuts, sultanas

Suggested Dressings

Orange dressing (55)
Red wine mayonnaise (66)
Tsatziki (68) and variations
Sour cream (72) and variations
Peanut chilli (76) – thinner than usual.

122 Potato salad

This recipe for potato salad is actually quite famous. First refer to the Chapter 2 section on preparing potatoes and cut into large chunks (C); small new potatoes should not be cut at all. This salad is so good that I am not going to give you any variations.

Ingredients

Potatoes
Celery   } either/or
Spring onions
Seasoning

Dressing

Garlic mayonnaise (64)
plus a little French dressing (54) for lubrication.

123 Jerusalem artichoke salad

As for potato salad (122) but using Jerusalem artichokes instead of potatoes.

124 Rice salads

Rice salads should be noticeable for their colour and texture. Vegetables should be finely chopped (G,D,H and small C) to complement the size of the grain. The crunchier they are the better. The rice should never be stodgy.

Ingredients

Rice with any combination of white cabbage, red cabbage, celery, carrots, radish, spring onion, tomato, cucumber, green and red peppers, beetroot, mushrooms, beansprouts, celeriac, cauliflower, sweetcorn, sultanas, raisins, roasted nuts, seeds, etc., apple, pineapple, oranges, small chunks of cheese or tofu.

Suggested Dressings

French dressing (54)
Orange dressing (55)
Curried French dressing (54)
Lemon and honey dressing (56)
Tamari and ginger dressing (58)
Mayonnaise and creamy dressings can make rice salads look a bit stodgy but tahini and lemon (73) is a good alternative.

125 Bean salads

Use the whole range of beans in your bean salads. You can use up beans left over from savoury dishes, but not if they have been overcooked, as it is important that beans used to make salads are cooked to perfection. As we know from Chapter 5, there are many different varieties, sizes, colours, and textures to choose from, so vary the content of the salad and use chopping styles to complement any particular bean you are using. Similarly, it is possible to create a salad with several varieties of bean in equal proportions, a salad like this can look very attractive. Like rice, bean salads are best dressed with light but very tasty dressings, thick dressings make beans rather stodgy. Always provide a good vegetable content in a bean salad or else you may find your guests getting too full too quickly. Often the best bean salads have a sort of poetic justice about them – combinations like red kidney beans with fresh green beans, or mung beans with mung bean sprouts seem almost made for each other. Whichever ingredients you choose, always try to combine beans with some crunchy vegetable or with nuts or seeds for these will give a pleasant variation in texture.

Ingredients

Beans – choose any bean or combination of beans for colour and size.
Vegetables – use a wide range of chopping techniques particularly D, C (small), F, G and H.
White and red cabbage, spinach, celery, chicory, cucumber, tomatoes, red and green peppers, mustard and cress, watercress, beansprouts, alfalfa, radish, celeriac, baby turnip, carrots, spring onions, onions, mushrooms, garlic, grapes, oranges, melon, apple, pineapple, dried fruits, sweetcorn, roasted nuts, seeds, croutons, olives, parsley, fresh herbs, small chunks of cheese or tofu.

Suggested Dressings

French dressing (54) or curry, chilli, and garlic.
Orange dressing (55)
Lemon and Honey dressing (156)
Tamari and ginger dressing (58)
Peanut chilli (76)
Tomato and mushroom (77)

126 Lentil salads

It is only possible to use green, brown or speckled lentils for salads. They must be carefully cooked so that the skins remain intact. After cooking, rinse immediately in cold water to prevent any over-softening. Lentils don't have a lot of variation in colour so combine them with more colourful vegetables (lentil sprouts are a nice addition to lentil salads). Apart from the above, follow the same rules as for rice salads (124) and bean salads (125).

127 Wheat and barley salads

Follow the same rules as for rice salads (124). You will find wheat and barley a lot more chewy than rice, beans or lentils; too much sometimes so be careful to cook them properly. Wheat salads, especially, can have a thick dairy or creamy dressing and this may be desirable to off-set their jaw-aching potential.

128 Tabbouli

Tabbouli should only be made with bulgher wheat, but if you cannot get it most other cracked wheats will do. Prepare the bulgher as stated in Chapter 5.

Ingredients	Suggested Dressings
Spring onion (G) Green pepper (D) Cucumber (H) Celery (H) Tomato (F or G) Red cabbage (H)	Lemon and honey dressing (56), but omit the honey and add fresh mint and garlic. Use olive oil if possible.

129 Pasta salads

We have already mentioned macaroni milanese (99) as a starter and most pasta salads may be used in this way. They are very filling so go easy on the pasta and concentrate on flavour. Use primarily shortcut macaroni and pasta shells and always cook à la dente. Pasta needs a crunch with it like rice, beans and lentils so choose your ingredients accordingly (see recipes 124 and 125). Parmesan cheese is a nice addition to pasta salads as are many of the creamy and cheesy dressings. I recommend the following dressings:

Red wine mayonnaise (66)
Blue cheese dressing (60)
Sour cream and spring onion (72)
Mushroom and tomato dressing (77)
Peanut chilli dressing (76)
Plus any of the variations of French dressing (54, 55, 56 and 57) and mayonnaise (59).

Conclusion

Salads are very much a question of personal taste and I only hope to have spurred your imagination by showing you the enormous variety of salads that are literally at your fingertips. Do experiment to find your own favourites.

Chapter 8

Bread and pastry

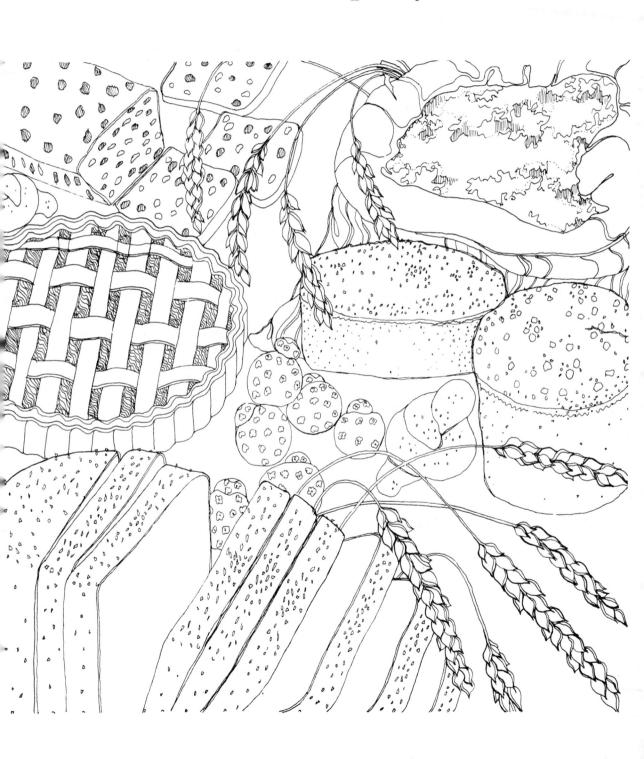

Introduction

We use only wholewheat flour because it has not been stripped of i flavour, colour and nutrients. White flours are so refined that it stipulated by law that the nutrients that have been taken out have to l added back. Wholewheat flour contains iron, calcium, protein, sever B vitamins and, of course, bran. The bran is vital to many of o digestive processes. White flours have no bran and are therefore le easy to digest with the result that our digestive systems tend to get la: and sometimes diseased.

Bran, alas, tends to make flour heavy and in the past this has led some disastrous culinary examples of wholewheat baking – mc people and especially reluctant vegetarians, may consider wholewhe bread and pastry as being solid, unsubtle and often indigestibl Usually this is not the fault of the flour (although milling process have greatly improved for wholewheat flour in the past decade), but the cook. Many people try to use wholewheat flour as a direct subs tute for white flour, and this is where they go wrong. The two flou are completely different and so your approach to cooking with the must differ too. It is impossible to bake successful wholewheat Fren bread, puff pastry, and croissants because the flour, even finely mille is too coarse and the end result is always a poor substitute for the re thing. Wholewheat flour is probably more akin to the flour o ancestors used and so is excellent used in recipes for basic breads ai pastries. Ironically, wholewheat flour is still more expensive than mc white flours – a reflection on the way society can create demand fo product that is totally stripped of all its goodness.

Bread

Unleavened bread is simply a paste of flour and water that was and baked on or in hot stones and has been made for centuries. Most bread we eat today also contains a raising agent and is therefore much lighter and easier to eat. Cooking fresh bread at home is such a joy one wonders why it has gone out of fashion. Baking bread is probably one of the only culinary experiences that involves all the senses in our bodies, touch, sight, smell – even the sound of it as you knead it is comforting. It is also essential to bake bread in a warm, but not hot atmosphere, so it is a very satisfying way to start the day. If you have a dough hook and a mixing machine the work is even less, though these are not essential. In fact, a wooden board, one side kept exclusively for bread, and a pair of hands are the only basic tools you require. If you want to be precise, then use scales and measuring cups, otherwise all you need is a large mixing bowl and of course bread tins; a pastry brush is handy too. The most important aspect of bread is the ingredients – let's look at them first.

Flour

We shall be using wholewheat flour that has been stoneground not steel-rolled, a blend of Canadian hard wheat and British soft wheat is best. Hard flour has a high gluten content which helps the bread to rise while all British flour may be used successfully, but will generally make a denser bread. Whichever flour you use the essential thing is that at least you will have home-baked bread. Flour which has been freshly milled is always best, so don't store it for too long at home. Stoneground flour retains much more goodness than the more efficient steel-rolled flours but it is usually coarser. You can also use varying degrees of wholewheat flour from which a certain percentage of bran has been removed. I have always used so-called 100% flour which still contains all the bran and been quite satisfied with the results. Ideally, bread flour should not be fine or coarse but somewhere in the middle, fine flour makes the dough too elastic, coarse flour makes it too crumbly. If you cannot get a medium flour like Jordan's 100% then mix a fine flour like soya flour with a coarse flour.

Water

Use slightly warm tap water for bread if you trust it as this will help the dough mix more evenly.

Yeast

The way in which you use yeast is as important as the flour you choose. I have always found fresh yeast far superior to dried yeast and it can be bought from most bakeries or delicatessens. If you do use dried yeast then use half the quantity given for fresh yeast in any standard recipe for wholemeal flour. Most wholewheat bread recipes will use twice the amount of yeast for the same recipe using white flour. This allows for the extra power needed to lift the heavier wholewheat flour without incurring a yeasty flavour in the bread. Fresh yeast may be frozen but should be used almost immediately after de-frosting; as it will keep fresh in the fridge for up to a week I wouldn't bother freezing it.

Yeast is a fungus that, in the presence of warmth, will change sucrose in solution into carbon dioxide, it is this gas that forms air bubbles in bread dough and causes it to rise. However, it is not quite as simple as that for bread making – here are the main reasons why yeast can cease to work and therefore not be successful in bread making.

1   Temperature

(a)   While finger warmth will encourage yeast to grow, if the sugar solution is too cold the yeast will simply not activate. If the sugar solution is too hot then the yeast cells will be destroyed immediately. If this happens then you must start afresh with more yeast. To avoid this happening always start your sugar solution by covering the sugar with cold water then topping up with hot water – the resultant warm sugar water should be ideal to pour over the yeast, but test first.

(b)   A yeast starter needs to be kept warm while the yeast is beginning to activate – if it is kept too warm then the yeast will again be killed. If it is not kept warm enough it will take ages to activate. Keep your starter away from any direct heat, but reasonably warm.

(c)   If the water you add to make the dough is too hot, again this will kill the yeast, use cool but not cold water at this stage to avoid it happening.

(d)   If, in rising, the dough is exposed to too much heat the yeast will again die, preventing any further rising. Bread that has not risen properly will be solid and indigestible when cooked.

(e)   If the dough has not risen properly and is put into the oven the yeast will immediately be killed with the same result as (d).

(f)   If the temperature of the oven is not hot enough when the bread is put in the yeast may continue to work rapidly for a few minutes, especially at the surface of the bread, causing the surface literally to erupt and sometimes break off completely. Alternatively, the bread may raise itself to its full extent and then collapse if the oven temperature is not correct or if it is left to rise too long.

2   Sugar/salt balance

Yeast prefers a medium pH balance and will be killed if you add too much sugar to the yeast culture or salt to the dough.

3   Air

Baking yeast works best in the absence of air, so cover your yeast culture with a damp cloth and likewise your bread when it is rising. This will give the yeast enough room to release a certain amount of carbon dioxide and start working properly. Left too long, the carbon dioxide will build up and eventually destroy the yeast, so do use your culture as soon as it starts foaming.

4   Kneading

Kneading is extremely important because it prevents carbon dioxide building up in the bread dough to a level which would destroy the yeast. I have always found one thorough kneading as efficient as two, but I will leave it up to you to decide how many you will do. Badly kneaded bread will appear compact, hard and may rise unevenly.

Treat yeast and bread dough like a baby and you can't go wrong.

Sugar

Sugar is the food of yeast but it should only be used in small amounts, demerara sugar is, of course, best – see alternatives below.

Oil

Vegetable oil is not essential to bread but will help soften the crust and improve the texture. It need not be used, especially if the bread is eaten fresh.

Salt

Salt is added to bread mostly to bring out its flavour. It must be used in small quantities and always added to the dough not the yeast culture. Salt will make the bread inedible if added in too large a quantity.

Here is a recipe for a yeast culture that is sufficient to raise two ¾ kg loaves of wholewheat bread.

130 Yeast culture

Stage	Ingredients	Quantity	Method
1	Yeast	50 g	*Crumble the yeast into a small bowl or jug.*
2	Sugar	2 tsp	*Stir the sugar into a small amount of tepid water and pour*
	Water (tepid)	200 ml	*over yeast. Place a damp cloth over the top and store in a warm place. When frothing use for bread.*

Alternative ingredients for baking breads

1   Flours – use wholewheat flour of any percentage (e.g. 85% or 100%: Jordans 100% wholewheat is excellent for bread), wholemeal flour, granary or rye flour. If flour is too coarse, add soya flour in ratio of 3 parts wholewheat flour to 1 part soya flour.
2   Water – use milk or milk/water mixed or soya milk.
3   Sugar – use honey, molasses or malt.
4   Oil – use margarine or butter for richer moister bread.
5   Yeast – use:
    (a)   Bi-carbonate of soda. This creates carbon dioxide like yeast, but should be added to dough only just before baking. Soda bread has its own distinctive flavour and it is a matter of personal taste as to whether you like it or not. Usually used for scones.
  (b) Baking powder. Only used in very simple breads, like waffles and muffins.
  (c) Sour-dough culture. This is an ordinary yeast culture that is allowed to go sour by feeding it sugar, or by mixing it with flour and storing it.

131 Sour-dough culture

Stage	Ingredients	Quantity	Method
1	Yeast culture (130) Flour	200 ml 200 ml	*Combine together and allow to ferment in a warm place for 5 days. Stir daily. Use this as a starter for sour-dough bread. Retain a piece of the dough and store to start your next loaf.*

Bread recipes

Now let's move on to some simple bread recipes. The most important is of course wholewheat bread. There are a variety of ways of decorating the surface of all breads by glazing. Glazing is in no way necessary but does add a certain something to bread in the way of presentation. Glazes can also act as a glue on which it is possible to stick a variety of seeds, grains, oats or nuts, whatever you think appropriate. After glazing some people slash the surface of the bread with a sharp knife – usually diagonally and to a depth of ¼–½ in. As the dough rises these scars grow larger and more rounded and eventually provide an attractive contrast to the glazed surface. Try some of these glazes.

132 Glaze for a crusty finish

Brush with 10 ml salt dissolved in 30 ml of water before rising in the tin.

133 Glaze for a soft finish

Brush with a beaten egg or egg and milk mixture before rising in the tin.

134 Glaze for a high gloss finish

Brush with warm honey or sugar syrup after the bread has been cooked but is still hot (this is also sticky).

Variations

(a) Use only water or only milk to glaze.
(b) Glaze the bread after shaping, but before you put it in the tin to rise. Then evenly coat the surface by rolling it from side to side in either poppy seeds, caraway seeds, celery, fennel, sesame seeds, cracked or whole wheat, or even rolled oats. Never glaze bread after it has risen you may cause permanent damage to the dough.

135 100% Wholewheat bread

Makes 2 × ¾ kg loaves

Stage	Ingredients	Quantity	Method
1	Yeast culture (130)	300 ml	*See recipe 130 – put aside to start working.*
2	Wholewheat flour Salt Oil	1.4 kg 5 tsp 100 ml	*Mix flour, salt and oil together in a large bowl.*
3	Water (tepid)	700 ml approx.	*Add the frothy yeast culture and work it into the flour. Gradually add the rest of the water and knead until the texture of the dough has reached ear lobe consistency – pinch your ear lobe gently and this is how your dough should feel.*

Then put the dough under a damp cloth in a warm place, the airing cupboard is the ideal place, until it has risen to about double its original size. Some people knock it back (knead) and put it back under a damp cloth for a second rising but, if this is done it will seldom reach the same ear lobe consistency as before. If you are only giving the dough one rising the bread is now ready for cutting and shaping. This mixture is enough for 2 large loaves, 3 small loaves or about 30 rolls. Cut the dough accordingly with a sharp knife – you must work quickly, if the dough rises a lot before you shape it it may damage the end result. I have always found it best to push all the square corners and tuck them firmly underneath, keep pushing all the edges underneath with both hands simultaneously until you have formed a round top to the dough. The loaf should now have a perfect crown and this should be uppermost when it is popped into its tin, after suitable glazings and coverings have been applied.

Shaping bread is difficult to describe verbally. If you put your hands out in front of you, close to your body, palms facing down, then allow your hands to describe a tube so that they end up together again but this time palms facing up, then you will have made the first motion of shaping bread into a loaf. Each time the palms come together facing up, your fingers should poke loose folds of dough into place on what will become the underside of the bread. Exerting a small amount of pressure on each side of the loaf at the same time will help bring the crown up.

After placing the dough in well-oiled tins the bread should be covered with a damp cloth – be careful not to let the cloth touch the surface of the bread and allow for rising, for the cloth may damage the surface of the bread. You will know it has risen when under slight finger pressure the dough springs back to shape – it will also have roughly doubled in size.

Pre-heat the oven to 450°F (230°C, Gas mark 8) and bake for approximately 40 minutes. To check the bread is cooked at the end of this time, take it out of its tin and tap the bottom. It should sound hollow and the surface crust should be lightly browned. If it isn't ready then return it to the oven for a few more minutes with the bottom uppermost until it is cooked. Allow to cool before cutting.

Bread can be shaped in many ways, some traditional and some practical. I think it is the job of a specialist bread book to describe these methods – but you can always use the same basic bread recipe. Bread rolls are really just tiny loaves and they take a lot less time to cook – 15 minutes at 450°F (230°C, Gas mark 8).

Variations

Use milk instead of water, butter/margarine instead of oil. Try different glazes and toppings – different sugars in the starter and of course, different flours. For granary bread, simply substitute granary flour for wholewheat flour. For rye bread, mix rye flour with wholewheat flour in equal quantities and substitute in the recipe.

Note

Do take care of your bread tins for they can ruin an otherwise decent loaf of bread if they haven't been looked after properly. Always brush the inside of the tin with vegetable oil, though not too much as this may fry the loaf, and take care to oil the corners of the tin. When you have finished baking your loaf should slide out easily and cleanly. Now wipe the inside of your loaf tin with some kitchen paper to remove any poppy seeds or crumbs that have collected and store in a warm dry place. It is good for the bread if the tins themselves are slightly warmed before the dough is put into them.

Conclusion

We'll finish this part of the chapter with a few other basic breads.

136 Pitta bread

Serves 4 hungry people

This bread originated in the Middle East and is an excellent accompaniment to many dips, spreads and pâtés, notably hommous.

Stage	Ingredients	Quantity	Method
1	Basic bread dough (135)	450 g	Grease a baking sheet. Knead bread dough on floured surface for 10 minutes. Cover with lightly oiled polythene and leave to rise for about 1½ hours or until it has doubled its size.
2			Knead again on a lightly floured surface for 2 minutes. Divide the dough into eight, knead each piece into a ball and then flatten to form a disc about 5 cm thick. Place on the greased baking sheet and cover with lightly oiled polythene and leave to prove in a warm place until doubled in size. Bake at 450°F (230°C, Gas Mark 8) for 10 minutes. When removed from oven, cover with a slightly damp cloth and allow to cool.

Variations

Pittas are excellent with pâtés etc., but also if you cut them in half you will find an air pocket which can be used to stuff with delicious salads and thick pâtés for a Middle Eastern sandwich.

137 Corn bread   Serves 4 hungry people

This originated in Mexico and Southern America where wheat flour is a fairly recent addition to the diet and maize flour is the traditional base for bread. It is best eaten with Mexican type food and can form the topping for Tamale pie (250). It is an unleavened bread.

Stage	Ingredients	Quantity	Method
1	Eggs	2	*Separate the eggs and whisk the whites until fluffy.*
2	Maize flour (maizemeal)	175 g	*Add the yolks to the rest of the ingredients and beat together*
	Wheat flour	55 g	*thoroughly. Fold in the whisked egg whites. Pour mixture into*
	Salt	1 tsp	*a square tin. Bake for 40 minutes at 350°F (180°C,*
	Honey	1 dsp	*Gas Mark 4).*
	Butter/oil	60 g	
	Milk	300 ml	

138 Chapattis   Serves 4 hungry people

Chapattis are good with Indian food and for dips and starters. They should be served warm. Basically, this is an unleavened bread but baking powder is used to make it more digestible.

Stage	Ingredients	Quantity	Method
1	Wholewheat flour	100 g	*Mix the dry ingredients together in a bowl.*
	Salt	Dash	
	Baking powder	1½ tsp	
2	Butter/vegetable margarine	15 g	*Rub in the fat and enough water to make a stiff dough. Knead the dough for about 10 minutes then divide into six. Shape*
	Water	6 tbsp	*each portion into a ball and flatten to about a 4 in diameter.*
	Vegetable oil	Enough for frying	*Heat the oil and fry the chapattis individually until they fluff up on both sides. Drain on kitchen paper.*

139 Pancakes and waffles   Serves 4 hungry people

Pancakes and waffles are not usually thought of as breads but they certainly are; pancakes and waffles are great eaten sweet or savoury. For savoury pancakes or waffles leave out the honey or sugar and vanilla essence in the recipe and add a dash of shoyu, herbs, garlic, cheese or anything you fancy. Also use pastry flour rather than bread flour.

Stage	Ingredients	Quantity	Method
1	Wholewheat pastry flour	350 g	*Mix together all the dry ingredients.*
	Salt	1 tsp	
	Baking powder	3 tsp	
	Sugar/honey	1 tbsp	
2	Eggs, separated	3	*Whisk the egg whites and stand to one side. Mix the egg yolks*
	Milk	350 ml	*with the milk and oil and blend with the dry ingredients. Add*
	Oil	90 ml	*a dash of vanilla. Fold the stiffened egg whites into this batter.*
	Vanilla, optional	2 drops	*Heat a little oil or butter in a frying pan and add a small quantity of the batter, see how it spreads before adding the full amount, this will save you finding your mixture is too thick or*

too thin when it is too late to put right. Cook for a few minutes on either side until golden brown. The same recipe with perhaps a little less liquid is good for waffles.

Variations

(a) No need to separate the eggs.
(b) Replace eggs with 100 ml yeast culture (130).
(c) Supplement the wholewheat flour with buckwheat flour, barley flour, cornmeal or oats.
(d) Add a fruit purée in place of milk in the recipe.

Pancakes are excellent eaten at any time of the day, whether simply with lemon juice for dessert or filled rolled and served with a sauce as a main dish. Waffles can have just as many applications.

140 Muffins

Makes 4

Muffins are usually served with sweet preserves, honey, maple syrup, cream, compôtes or yoghurts. They are also good simply with butter or vegetable margarine. They are another very simple bread.

Stage	Ingredients	Quantity	Method
1	Wholewheat flour – strong	125 g	*Combine dry ingredients.*
	– soft	125 g	
	Baking powder	2 tsp	
	Salt	Pinch	
2	Egg	1	*Combine wet ingredients. Fold wet ingredient mixture into dry ingredient mixture until consistency is just moist. Two-thirds fill a greased muffin tin. Bake at 400°F (200°C, Gas Mark 6) for 15–20 minutes.*
	Oil/maize	25 ml/50 g	
	Honey	25 ml	
	Milk	125 ml	

Variations

Substitute dry fruits, other flours, bran, buckwheat, spices. Use fruit juice instead of milk.

141 Scones

Scones are probably of Scottish origin and are perhaps the best examples of a soda bread, although they can equally well be made with yeast. Scones should be eaten immediately after they have been cooked; later, they will not compare, rather like muffins. As they can be made in only a few moments this should be no problem. Sweet scones should be served with butter, jams, honey and cream.

Stage	Ingredients	Quantity	Method
1	Wholewheat flour	200 g	*Mix the ingredients together.*
	Salt	½ tsp	
	Bi-carbonate of soda	1 tsp	
	Cream of tartar	3 tsp	
2	Butter/margarine	45 g	*Rub in the butter or margarine until mixture looks like breadcrumbs.*
3	Milk	125 ml	*Add the milk to form a soft dough. Mix with hands. Turn on to a floured surface and knead very lightly. Roll dough out to ½ in thickness and cut out rounds using a 5 cm pastry cutter (should make about 8). Place rounds on lightly floured baking sheet and sprinkle with flour or baste with egg wash (133). Bake in a hot oven for 10 minutes or until risen and golden.*

Variations

(a) Fruit scones – add 50 g of sultanas and 25 g of sugar after rubbing in the fat.

(b) Cheese scones – add a little mustard (1 tsp) at the flour stage and 75 g of grated cheese after rubbing in the fat. Sprinkle a little cheese on to the scones to distinguish them.

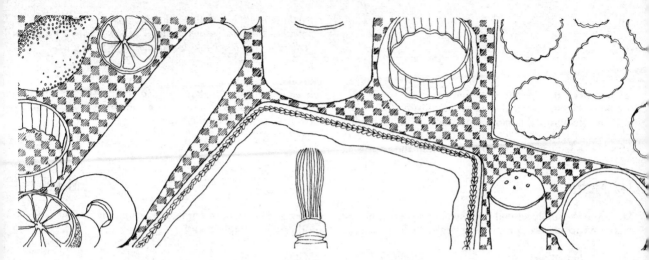

Pastry

Pastry, like bread, is based upon flour and water. The essentially different ingredient is butter, vegetable margarine or oil. While these appear in bread they are not as important as they are in pastry. Also while good bread relies on warm working conditions, good pastry needs the cold. Yeasted pastries are really basic breads that have been rolled out to act as pastry. Salt is also essential to pastry, but only for flavour.

Flour

Pastry flour should be a lot finer than bread flour. To make a flour fine means that it has to be milled several times, this breaks down the wheat and allows glutens to become active. It is these glutens in pastry flour that enable you to roll it out successfully. Pastry made with coarse flour will often cook unevenly and is extremely difficult to manage.

Butter, margarine or vegetable oil

Henceforth, these ingredients shall be known as the shortening. The more shortening you add to the pastry the more crumbly it becomes. The more crumbly it is the more difficult it is to roll out, but some would say the more delicious it is to eat. Hard vegetable margarine (there is an excellent Kosher margarine on the market) and butter produce better results than vegetable oil, which even chilled cannot really make a shortcrust pastry. However, vegetable oil pastry is good for some flans, pies, tarts and roly-polys. Cold butter or margarine make it possible to roll out what essentially would be a very short pastry given the actual proportion of fat to flour. Chilling the pastry before use also helps. If the shortening were at room temperature it would simply dissolve into the flour and be impossible to roll out. This technique is extremely important when making rough puff pastry (144).

Water

Cold water is the only other vital ingredient in pastry. Wholewheat pastry flour, because of its bran content, has the capacity to absorb perhaps more water than you would realize. Water content is very important in determining the ease with which you can roll out your pastry. For rolling out very thin pastry like that used in Apfel Strudel (307), I would advise rolling it between two sheets of aluminium foil, polythene or a damp cloth. Always roll your pastry slightly larger than is needed to allow for shrinkage in cooking and press it firmly against the side of the flan dish to prevent any trapped air expanding and stretching the cooked pastry. As with bread, it is extremely important to always have the oven at just the right temperature before inserting your pastry. When pre-cooking flan cases (without the filling) line the case with aluminium strips to prevent the sides collapsing. Blind baking, as it is called, is particularly useful when using wholewheat flour as it ensures that the pastry is properly cooked. Often with wholewheat quiches or flans the pastry at the very centre of the dish is undercooked, again it is just a question of technique. Metal flan cases should be used in preference to pottery ones as they will cook the pastry more evenly. As most quiches have a high liquid content the overall cooking time of an uncooked pastry case will be increased.

Most of the pastries we use in day-to-day cooking are of the short-crust variety, both sweet and savoury. We also use yeasted pastries, vegan pastries and we have even created a successful rough puff pastry which I think is amazing considering we do use 100% wholewheat flour. So next, we move on to a few basic recipes for pastry. Successful pastry recipes are based not only upon the type of ingredient used but also the proportions in which they are used together.

142 Shortcrust pastry

This recipe will line a 7–8 in flan dish.

Stage	Ingredients	Quantity	Method
1	Wholewheat flour	225 g	*Mix the flour and salt together.*
	Salt	Dash	
2	Vegetable margarine (preferably hard) and cold	100 g	*Rub the margarine into the flour until it resembles breadcrumbs.*
3	Water	2–3 tbsp	*Mix in the water gradually by hand or with a spoon until the dough is soft but firm enough to gather into a ball. Chill the pastry before rolling out and use it as required. Shortcrust pastry is suitable for use in all flans, quiches, pies and roly-polys mentioned later on in the book.*

Variations

(a) Substitute an egg for 1 tbsp of water – this will make a richer pastry that is more deserving of special recipes, and especially sweet recipes (do not attempt this for the first time just before guests arrive as even reducing the amount of water to compensate for egg leaves it more difficult to roll out).

(b) Substitute part of the wholemeal with soya flour in a ratio of 3 parts wholewheat flour to 1 soya flour for a lighter pastry.

143 Vegan pastry

Vegans have no problems when it comes to pastry as almost any basic pastry can be made without dairy produce by simply substituting a good quality vegetable oil/margarine. Baking powder is not essential although it is included in this recipe. Vegetable oil makes pastry very elastic, easy to roll out but slightly tougher to eat. Generally, if you are a vegan it is better to use a hard pure vegetable oil margarine (like Rakhussams). It is even more important for vegans who use vegetable oil to make sure their pastry is very cold before rolling. Again the recipe given will line a 7–8 in flan dish.

Stage	Ingredients	Quantity	Method
1	Wholemeal flour	225 g	*Combine dry ingredients.*
	Baking powder	1 tsp	
	Salt	Pinch	
2	Vegetable oil	3 tbsp	*Combine wet ingredients and add the liquid to the flour and*
	Cold water	3 tbsp	*mix thoroughly and quickly.*

Chill the pastry well and roll out for use required; it is especially good for quiches and pies.

144 Rough puff pastry

Rough puff pastry can in no way emulate the dramatic effect of its white counterpart puff pastry. Rough puff is made with wholewheat flour and, when made correctly, produces a light flaky texture that is difficult to equate with one's pre-conceived idea of wholewheat pastry. It will not rise, however. I recommend making large quantities of rough puff and freezing that which you don't use.

The work involved is more than usual but nothing too shattering. Rough puff is often used for sweet baking but may also be part of a savoury quiche, flan, roly-poly or pie. It is by far the best to use hard vegetable margarine for rough puff pastry and try to make sure all the ingredients have been well chilled before use.

Stage	Ingredients	Quantity	Method
1	Wholewheat flour	225 g	*Mix the dry ingredients together – if you like sieve the flour for*
	Baking powder (optional)	2 tsp	*a more professional result.*
	Salt	Pinch	
2	Vegetable margarine	175 g	*Divide margarine into 3 and rub $^1/_3$ into the flour. Add enough*
	Water		*water to make a soft dough. Roll the dough on a floured board into a flat oblong.*
3			*Divide the second portion of margarine into equal parts and scatter over the oblong. Fold the top edge and bottom edge of the oblong over each other to form an envelope. Repeat with the sides and roll out into another oblong.*
4			*With the third portion of margarine repeat the process. Continue rolling and folding until it is firm to handle. If it becomes sticky refridgerate it and try again later. Store in the fridge when complete. It is best to cook rough puff pastry while it is still cold so don't let it hang around after you have prepared it.*

145 Sweet pastry

Sweet pastry is exclusively used for sweets. Because it has sugar in it the pastry is often much more crumbly than other pastries. It is vital therefore, to achieve as perfect a liaison as possible between the sugar and margarine leaving no grains of sugar behind. If the sugar is not creamed well enough with the margarine it will melt in the cooking leaving the pastry with an extremely poor texture that is impossible to eat satisfactorily. The following recipe will fill a 6–7 in flan dish.

Stage	Ingredients	Quantity	Method
1	Margarine, hard	65 g	*Cream the margarine and sugar together thoroughly until a whitish colour is achieved. Fold in the wholewheat flour gently and thoroughly, add the egg yolk and enough water to make a firm dough.*
	Raw cane sugar	25 g	
	Wholewheat flour	100 g	
	Egg yolk	1 egg	
2	Water	To mix	*Roll out as required on a floured board.*

With these recipes for breads and pastries under your belt you are becoming more and more able to tackle almost anything a recipe can throw at you. Before we move on to main savoury cooking, let's just look at a few savouries that are primarily involved with pastry, bread and dough. These, of course, are pizzas, flans and quiches. Savoury roly-polys and tarts have already been mentioned in Chapter 6. Savoury and sweet pies and flans follow in Chapter 13. As we have just learned how to make pastry, let's start with quiches and flans.

Quiches and flans

Quiches were probably named after the original quiche, Quiche Lorraine. Quiches are distinguishable from flans only because they are filled essentially with a savoury egg custard and gratinated with cheese. A flan is a more general term referring to anything that is put into a flan case. Quiches and flans may be served hot or cold and, for the purpose of simplicity, we will consider them as basically the same.

Quiches and flans must have a pastry base, next there is the filling which must be sufficiently thick or set so that it does not run all over the place when the flan/quiche is cut. There may also be a topping which can add taste and attraction to the dish, but is not absolutely necessary.

I think it is simplest to discuss different recipes for each part of the quiche and then let you put them together in whatever combinations you think best. Remember quiche mixes are used to set the filling so most recipes will involve a combination of a base, quiche mix, a filling and a topping. Some recipes are vegan and for these leave out the quiche mix and any dairy based toppings and substitute with more filling and a vegan topping (if any at all).

146 The flan case

You will need a rolling pin.

Use the recipe for shortcrust pastry (142), vegan pastry (143), or rough puff pastry (144). Grease an 8 in flan tin thoroughly. Roll the pastry out so that it will cover the flan tin or dish easily. Push the pastry into the flan tin so that it will form a complete lining. With a sharp knife trim off excess pastry leaving a little to overlap. This may now be pinched between finger and thumb to make an attractive bevelled edge to the pastry. Next use a thin strip of tin foil to support the inside edge of the pastry. Make sure the base of the pastry is well pushed down in the centre and prick it a couple of times with a fork. Bake the pastry for 10 minutes in an oven pre-heated to 350°F (180°C, Gas Mark 4). The pastry case is now ready for filling.

Variations

Partially substitute flour with any of the following, cheese, cooked mashed potatoes, buckwheat flour.

Quiche and flan fillings

The majority of the filling in a quiche will always be made up of the egg and milk custard. The egg and milk custard will be affected by the rest of the filling. For instance, in a mushroom quiche, the mushrooms will impart a lot of liquid in cooking to the surrounding quiche mix, this will slow down the cooking process and may even prevent it setting at all. The answer to this problem is, of course, (especially when using the egg and milk custard) to cook any other ingredients quickly first, strain off the juice and pat them dry with a cloth. Vegetables that don't easily release their high water content, like cauliflowers, may be par-cooked before adding to the quiche mix.

147 Quiche mixes

Enough for an 8 in dish

Stage	Ingredients	Quantity	Method
1	Eggs	3	*Whist ingredients together thoroughly.*
	Milk	300 ml	
	Shoyu, optional	Dash	
	Salt and pepper	Dash	
	Nutmeg, optional	To taste	

Note

If you have any quiche mix left over save it to glaze your bread or pastry. Always give your quiche mix a thorough beating or blending just before adding to the flan case, then pop the flan quickly into the oven.

Variations

The milk may be substituted totally or partially with cream, yoghurt, tofu, sour cream, cottage cheese, cream cheese or more eggs. The eggs can also be separated, the whites whisked and folded back into the mixture to make a souffle flan. Always pour the quiche mix on top of any other filling and make sure you fill it right up to the top, otherwise the quiche will look 'mean' when it has been cooked.

Quiche fillings

These fillings are usually a vegetable or a selection of vegetables that have been stir-fried quickly and drained. They may be flavoured with herbs and spices or made crunchy with nuts and seeds. The filling always goes into the flan case before the quiche mix, but do make sure it is properly drained (remember the liquid is great for stocks, soups and casseroles).

148 Cauliflower and dill filling

Cauliflower cut into florets (I).

149 Español filling

Potatoes, tomatoes, green peppers, onions, mixed herbs and spices.

150 Leek and lemon filling

Stir-fry leeks with shoyu and lemon juice, cooked but crisp, drain off liquid.

151 Spring onion and watercress filling

Chopped but used sparingly. No need to cook.

152 Quiche chinoise

Beansprouts, red pepper, mushrooms, shoyu, a little ginger, chilli and ground aniseed. Quickly stir-fry the red peppers, mushrooms with the spices and the shoyu. Don't cook the beansprouts. Drain off any excess liquid and line flan case.

153 Spinach filling

Spinach must be cooked before adding to the flan. Use no water to cook, just a little butter. Season with nutmeg and perhaps some minced garlic. When the spinach is cooked, it must be drained very thoroughly. Chop the spinach before adding it to the flan case or, alternatively, blend the spinach, drain and whisk into the quiche mix itself.

154 Mushroom filling

Mushrooms also have a high water content and so must be cooked beforehand, it is best to use halved or whole button mushrooms, the thinner you cut them the more juice they give off. Try stir-frying the mushrooms for a minute only with a little lemon juice, some shoyu and some fresh tarragon or mixed herbs.

155 Herby onion filling

This is a good stand-by for when you have no other vegetables. Stir-fry the onions in a little vegetable oil or butter with a selection of sweet herbs, or perhaps just sage. Cook the onions until they are semi-soft, drain and add to the flan.

156 Ratatouille filling

Use the standard recipe for ratatouille (156) but use less ratatouille sauce (14) or thicken the mixture more than you would for a casserole. Make sure the aubergines are cooked but that the courgettes and green peppers are still à la dente before adding to the flan case.

157 Provençale filling

Tomatoes, green peppers and onions with the emphasis on tomatoes and plenty of garlic. Stir-fry onions and green pepper but don't cook the tomatoes. Add garlic and herbs (oregano is nice) when the peppers and onions have finished cooking.

158 Celery and celeriac filling

Grate the celeriac, cut the celery into quite fine slices (A,B). Stir-fry the celery with a little ground celery seed or mixed herbs and lemon juice. Add the celeriac and cook for a few more minutes.

159 Brussel sprouts and chestnut filling

Par-cook the brussel sprouts and chestnuts in a little water, drain well. Stir-fry with a little onion and sweet herbs before turning into the flan case.

160 Sweetcorn filling

Use fresh or frozen sweetcorn. Cook for a few minutes if fresh, if frozen just de-frost. Line flan tin and sprinkle with some basil and seasoning.

161 Courgette filling

Cut the courgettes into nice thick slices (A, A1, B, B1). Stir-fry with a few mixed herbs and garlic. Drain and add to flan case. The courgettes should still be crunchy when added to the flan case.

162 Broccoli filling

Cut into florets (I) and stir-fry with a little tamari and seasoning. Drain and add to flan case.

The variations and combinations of flan fillings are literally endless. They are determined by your flare and inventiveness, (and sometimes a lack of other ingredients, or simply using up leftovers). If you wish you can curry the ingredients or add chilli; in fact, almost any of the sauces in the sauce chapter can be used to liven up what has for so long been boring old egg flan. If you have ever wondered what to do with a leftover salad, try using it in your next quiche.

Vegans can enjoy flans too, instead of using eggs and milk they must rely on creating a thick purée to form the base, made up of beans, lentils or vegetables. Add tahini or peanut butter to help bind the mixture and grated nuts to give it bite. Retain some vegetables whole or chunky to give the flan texture and help make it just as enjoyable an eating experience as the non-vegan quiches are. Here is an example of a vegan flan.

163 Leek and tofu flan

Chop the leeks finely, retain a few larger chunks for texture. Stir-fry the finely chopped leeks with some tamari and mixed herbs. When cooked stir in some tahini or peanut butter. Blend these ingredients with tofu to form a thick purée. Add the coarsely chopped leek and decorate with sesame seeds, sunflower seeds or tomatoes.

Quiche/flan toppings

So far we have made the flan case, the quiche mix and the flan filling and filled the flan case up to the brim with the mix and the filling. Now we can top it. Once again there are a vast array of toppings at our disposal. Of course, it is not absolutely necessary to put a topping on the quiche as it will cook very well without it. But a good topping not only looks attractive but also adds another dimension to the overall taste and texture of the quiche. A topping also makes the quiche a more substantial meal, and provides a suitable, if rather unsteady, platform on which to decorate the quiche. Remember to season your toppings just as you would any other part of the dish. All of the toppings mentioned are also suitable for bakes, and will be referred to in Chapter 12.

164 Grated cheese topping

This is by far the most common topping. Use a hard cheese like cheddar, edam or mozzarella. Simply sprinkle over the quiche. The cheese will probably sink but in cooking most returns to the surface turning it a rich golden brown.

165 Cheese and breadcrumb topping

Mix equal quantities of cheese and wholemeal breadcrumbs, and sprinkle as before on top of the quiche. This forms a much more substantial crust to the quiche.

166 Cheese and blue cheese topping

Crumble some blue cheese into the grated cheese or spinkle with blue cheese only. The same can be done with parmesan.

167 Breadcrumb topping

I would advise par-cooking the quiche first before sprinkling with breadcrumbs, otherwise they will sink to the bottom.

168 Cheese, carrot and breadcrumb topping

As for cheese and breadcrumb topping (165), but add a little finely grated carrot. This topping takes slightly longer to cook but is a very attractive colour. The carrots may be substituted for by potatoes, but it is best to deep fry the potatoes quickly first and add them to the topping mix when they are crispy on the outside.

169 Cheese with seeds or nuts

Mix the cheese with any selection of roasted or tamari-roasted seeds and nuts. The larger nuts should be chopped first.

170 Cheese and herb topping

Mix grated cheese with any selection of fresh or dried herbs; some will need to be chopped.

171 Cheese and oat topping

Mix the cheese with the same quantity of oats. You may wish to stir-fry the oats quickly first. Use regular oats.

172 Inside-out toppings

Instead of lining the flan with the filling, fill the flan case with quiche mix and bake it. When it has set, pour whatever the filling would have been over the top. This is especially good with the richer more colourful fillings like ratatouille (156). Sprinkle with freshly chopped herbs, nuts or seeds.

Again the variations and permutations are endless, but as you can see Quiche Lorraine is fast disappearing into the background.

173 Pastry topping

Use thin strips of pastry to make trellis work topping.

174 Quiche or flan decorations

These may go on top of the topping, they are not essential but can make a quiche look quite beautiful. They can also help determine portion slices. Choose from the following: Tomatoes – wedged or sliced; green peppers (or red) – strips, squares or rounds; chives or spring onion ends chopped; asparagus tips – poached; green beans, whole or halved – par-cooked; cress and watercress – sprigs; parsley – chopped; sesame seed; sunflower seeds; nuts – whole, halved or chopped; radish – sliced; cauliflower or broccoli florets; wheatgerm; paprika; celery – squares or matchsticks; onion rings; any fresh herbs; leek rings; poppy seeds; caraway seeds – used sparingly. These are just a few of many and I am sure you can think of at least as many as I have.

Cooking

Now you have a complete quiche it is just a question of cooking it. Cooking times vary quite a bit, depending on what the filling is, how fresh the eggs are, and whether you pre-cook the flan case. As I recommend pre-cooking the flan case, the cooking time and oven temperature for an average egg/milk-based quiche in an 8 in flan dish (approximately ½–¾ in deep) is for 30 minutes at 375°F (190°C, Gas mark 5). Like most things there is no such thing as an average quiche, it is best to use a hot to moderately heated oven and check the quiche after half an hour. When it is ready, it will be firm all over but light. The centre of the quiche is always last to cook so let this be your guide to knowing when to take it out of the oven. If a quiche is taking a very long time to cook the surface may be in danger of burning so cover it gently with tinfoil. The key to making successful, light quiches is to do all your preparation in advance so that you can assemble it and pop it in the oven in just a few minutes. As with bread, it is vital that the oven is at the right temperature before you put in the quiche if it is to cook successfully.

Putting all these techniques and suggestions together, here is an example of a quiche recipe. Substitute your own ingredients for variety.

175 Mushroom and sour cream quiche au gratin

Stage	Ingredients	Quantity	Method
1	Rough puff pastry (144)	400 g	Grease an 8 in. flan dish. Roll out the pastry on a lightly floured board into a square approximately 9½ × 9½ in.

Lightly coat your rolling pin in flour and roll the pastry up with it. Unroll the pastry over the flan dish so that all edges of the flan dish are easily covered. Lightly push the pastry into the flan dish making sure all the metal surfaces in the flan tin are covered and the pastry fits snugly into the corners. Trim off excess pastry and use it to make a tasty little something for you, your family or friends. Make a few pricks in the pastry with a fork but only a few, and be gentle. Let the pastry rest in a cold place for 30 minutes before cooking to allow for shrinkage. Meanwhile get the rest of your ingredients prepared and heat the oven to 425°F (220°C, Gas mark 7). Line the inside edge of the pastry in the flan tin with tinfoil to prevent it collapsing, or cut a circle of greaseproof paper big enough to cover the entire flan surface and fill the centre with beans kept specifically for blind baking. When it is ready blind-bake the pastry for 10–15 minutes at 425°F (220°C, Gas mark 7). Remove from oven and carefully lift off the beans and greaseproof paper/tinfoil. If you wish you can brush the pastry with egg wash and return it to the oven for a few more minutes to give it colour.

2	Quiche mix (147) substitute milk with 100 ml sour cream and 200 ml milk	300 ml	Beat together with a whisk until slightly frothy.
3	Butter/vegetable margarine/oil	20 g/50 ml	Heat the fat in a pan and add the mushrooms and herbs. Stir-fry until hot then add the shoyu and lemon juice. Allow to cool then drain.
	mushrooms (sliced)	150 g	
	Mixed herbs	2 tsp	
	Shoyu	1 tsp	
	Lemon juice	a few drops	
4	Cheese and breadcrumbs (165)	120 g	Tip the mushrooms into the flan case, give the quiche mix one more whisk and pour over mushrooms. Sprinkle cheese and breadcrumbs on top and carefully put in middle of pre-heated oven at 375°F (190°C, Gas mark 5).

When the quiche is cooked allow it to settle for about 5 minutes in a warm place (on top of the oven) before serving, sprinkle with lots of mustard cress.

Quiches are excellent served hot or cold, on their own or in a buffet, with a salad or accompanying other hot vegetables. They are versatile, quick and can be quite exciting.

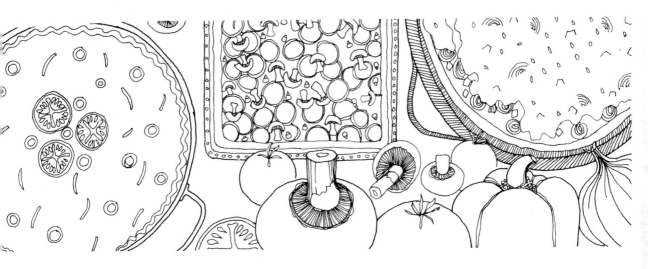

Pizzas

Until comparatively recently, pottery plates were a luxury in Western Europe that only the rich could afford. Instead people would bake round circles of bread from which to eat their food. Then if they were still hungry they could eat their plates too and enjoy a second meal with all the juices from the first course absorbed into the bread base. In Italy, this method of serving food eventually became a dish in its own right – the pizza. Pizzas are the simplest of all dishes to make, comprising a bread base on to which is spread a thick sauce, usually tomato, then any selection of vegetables that are handy and finally all this would be held together with a generous sprinkling of cheese. Some recipes put the cheese on to the sauce and then garnish the cheese with various other ingredients. The whole is then baked in the oven until the cheese has melted and lightly browned. Pizzas are best eaten hot and fresh; cold pizza is somehow irresistible too and can fill a space in a finger buffet. Why people buy frozen pizza I will never know – the bread bases are usually soggy and the toppings are at best mundane.

To cook a good pizza start thinking 'Mediterranean', of olives, peppers, chillis, plump tomatoes, mozzarella cheese, strong onions, garlic, olive oil, lemon juice, mushrooms, broccoli, spinach, courgettes, asparagus, sweetcorn, parmesan, oregano, basil, marjoram, thyme, etc. and you're almost there. You just need a large glass of Chianti to complete the picture. To the reluctant vegetarian, pizzas are a good bridging gap. They are a food form that has become generally acceptable and widely vegetarian too. Of course, they are often added to with nasties like tinned anchovies, catering-pack salami, slimy ham and even burnt bacon, but generally these things don't add anything to what would otherwise be a nice pizza.

You won't need any extra equipment, your flan tins will do. Here is a recipe for a delicious pizza, vary your fillings according to what grabs your fancy and, of course, what is in season. Remember some vegetables might need a little par-cooking before adding to the pizza.

176 Pizza neapolitan

Stage	Ingredients	Quantity	Method
1	Wholewheat bread dough (135)	¼ kg	*Follow the recipe for wholewheat bread but try to use olive oil instead of vegetable oil. Oil a flan dish (again, olive oil oil is best). On a lightly floured surface roll the dough out as thin as you can. Then line the flan dish as in quiche recipe (175). It is important to roll the dough out very thin because it will double in size when rising and could easily become too thick. Put the pizza base to one side to rise then bake for 10 minutes at 450°F (230°C, gas mark 8) until partially cooked.*
2	Tomato sauce B	250 ml	*Prepare the tomato sauce making sure all the vegetables are finely chopped. Allow the sauce to thicken naturally by reduction. It should almost be a paste when it is ready. Allow to cool. Pizza sauce is almost better if prepared a day in advance and left to chill in the fridge.*
3	Mushrooms, whole button	90 g	*Prepare the topping, you may want to stir-fry the courgettes and green peppers in olive oil with the garlic and oregano. The rest of the ingredients should not be pre-cooked.*
	Fresh tomato (A thin)	1 large	
	Green pepper (D)	1 small	
	Sweetcorn fresh/cooked/ frozen defrost	30 g	
	Courgette (B thin)	1 medium	
	cheese, grated (cheddar/ mozzarella)	90 g	
	Parmesan, grated	1 tbsp	
	Garlic, minced	3 cloves	
	Oregano	1 tsp	
	Black olives, chopped	4	
4			*Spread the par-cooked base with tomato paste. Arrange the rest of the ingredients attractively on top. Cover with the grated cheese, parmesan cheese and perhaps a little more oregano. Bake in a hot oven, 190°C for about another 10–15 minutes, or until the cheese has melted and is browning.*

Chapter 9

Stir-Fried Vegetables

The principles of stir-fried cooking are perhaps the key to successful cooking without meat. To the reluctant vegetarian, it will come as a nice surprise to discover that vegetables can play a dominating role in a dish, so long as they are not over-cooked. To understand stir-frying you have to understand the nature and character of individual vegetables and for this I refer you to Chapter 2.

In this chapter, I will describe some dishes that wholly involve stir-fried vegetables, yet the fundamental technique is at the root of all savoury cooking in this book. Broadly speaking, stir-frying is a cooking technique that ensures that a wide range of different ingredients (primarily vegetables) all end up cooked but only just cooked at the same time.

The actual process of stir-frying involves heating a small amount of oil to a reasonably high temperature, then adding to it pre-prepared vegetables in order of their individual cooking times. In other words you add the vegetables that take longest to cook first and those that need hardly any cooking last. It is best to stir the vegetables every 30 seconds or so to ensure even cooking. It is not necessary to stir all the time, otherwise nothing will be evenly cooked. If you are using a flat-bottomed pan you may wish to turn the heat down slightly; if you are using a wok you simply push the well-cooked vegetables further away from the heat centre at the base of the wok, before adding your next batch. Woks are nice to use for stir-fried dishes but not absolutely necessary. For soups, bakes, casseroles and sauces it is easier to use a conventional heavy-bottomed saucepan or casserole for any initial stir-frying. What is most important is the grading of vegetables into estimated individual cooking times so that the net result is a dish in which the vegetable ingredients retain life force and therefore shape, colour, texture, flavour and nutrition.

There are three basic criteria which you must decide before starting to stir-fry.

The vegetables

All vegetables may be stir-fried but, for a stir-fry dish in its own right, it is important to choose vegetables that are crisp and will retain their individuality in the end product, given that you cook them correctly. It is not desirable to par-cook a vegetable before stir-frying, so we also have to use vegetables that will cook, yet remain fresh, within a period of 0–10 minutes. We also choose vegetables for colour, texture, flavour and nutrition. Refer to Chapter 2 for further information.

The chopping technique

Chapter 2 tells you how important it is to prepare and cut vegetables with their end use in mind. In no other branch of our cooking is this

more important than in stir-frying, and its applications to other branches of the cuisine. It's rather like 'what comes first the chicken or the egg?' Do the chopping techniques suitable for stir-fry determine the sort of vegetables used in a stir-fry? Or, do the vegetables determine the sort of chopping technique you use? Really it is a bit of both. Some vegetables would take a long time to cook if they weren't cut to cook quickly and, if a vegetable is cooked for a long time it starts releasing its water content, at the same time losing colour, nutrition, texture and shape. It is for this reason that stir-fry is done at a high temperature and very quickly. The best chopping techniques to use are A, A1, B, B1, D, H and I. All of these expose the maximum amount of vegetable to the sealing properties of hot oil, thus ensuring their flavour remains intact and yet they will cook quickly. The vegetables should be cut thin to medium thin depending on the vegetable. Here is a selection of vegetables that are particularly nice to use in stir-fried dishes.

Very Quick Cooking	*Quick Cooking*	*Slower Cooking*
Chinese leaf	Spring onion	Onion (various)
Mushrooms	Green pepper	Celery
Beansprouts	Chard/spinach	Carrots
Mange-tout	Spring greens	Cauliflower
Bamboo shoots	Red pepper	Broccoli
Garlic	Courgettes	Green beans
Seaweed	Pineapple	Fennel
Lentil sprouts	Fresh peas	White cabbage
	Baby sweetcorn	Red cabbage
	Fresh ginger	

The flavouring

Some people would argue quite justifiably that flavouring a stir-fry should be unnecessary apart from a little salt and pepper, that you should enjoy the flavour of the individual vegetables themselves kept intact by the cooking process. While I agree that the individual flavours of the vegetables should not be disguised, it is possible subtly to bring out even more flavour without detracting from the dish. Stir-fries should only be seasoned or flavoured literally just before removing from the heat and serving. The most common addition is shoyu or tamari. A little of this added when the vegetables are at their hottest will be completely absorbed by the vegetables. If you add any liquid at all in the earlier stages of stir-frying the result will be a soggy limp mess. Seasoning and flavouring must be delicate and with a regard for the ingredients. Flavouring can be pre-determined by the type of oil used e.g. sesame.

Some nice last-minute additions to your stir-fry

Seasoning

Salt, pepper, chilli, grated ginger, five spice (use very moderately) sesame seeds (ground), fenugreek (ground), garam masala, turmeric, coriander, curry powder, paprika, nori seaweed (toasted and crumbled).

Flavouring:

Shoyu/tamari, tahini, miso, sherry, sesame oil, sunflower oil, safflower oil, vermouth, lemon juice.

Note:

If you don't have a wok, try to use a pan with a bottom that is wider than the element on which you are cooking.

Here is a recipe for a typical stir-fry as a main meal.

177　Stir-fried vegetables with rice　　　　　　　Serves 4

Stage	Ingredients	Quantity	Method
1	Sesame oil	50 ml	*Heat the oil in a pan until very hot. Add the carrots and stir-fry*
	Carrots (B1, thin)	3 medium	*for 3 minutes before adding the broccoli and celery. Stir-fry*
	Broccoli (I)	120 g	*together for another 2 minutes and push to the edges of the*
	Celery (H)	3 sticks	*pan.*
2	Red pepper (L)	2 medium	*Add pepper and courgettes to the centre of the pan and cook for*
	Courgettes (B1, thin)	90 g	*a further 2 minutes then push to the edge.*
3	Chinese leaf (B1 med)	120 g	*Add Chinese leaf to the centre of pan and stir-fry for a full minute.*
4	Mushrooms, button whole	90 g	*Add these ingredients to the pan and stir-fry for another minute.*
	Mange-tout, whole	60 g	
	Garlic (minced)		
5	Shoyu	50 ml	*When all the vegetables are hot add the shoyu, ginger and*
	Ginger (fresh grated)	1 tsp	*and seasoning. Serve immediately.*
	Salt and pepper	To taste	
6	Cooked brown rice (124)		*Stir-fries are nice served with rice or on a bed of rice.*

Variations
See vegetables suitable for stir-frying, also vary seasoning
and flavouring.

178 Tofu stir-fried vegetables

To the above recipe add 100 g of tofu. It is nice to marinate
the tofu over night in a diluted shoyu mixture, then cut
into cubes and deep fry it. It is then possible to add it to a
stir-fry at the chinese leaf stage.

By the addition of a sauce to a stir-fry we immediately
start to enter the world of casseroles and bakes. It is a
natural progression. Its important to remember, though,
what effect additional liquid will have on the individual
vegetables, and how much longer they are going to be
cooked. This is dealt with in the introductory chapter
concerning balance and will be dealt with more fully in
the chapter on bakes and casseroles themselves. It is
possible however to prepare a sauce separately and add it
hot to the stir-fried vegetables in place of shoyu at Stage 5
in recipe 177. This creates more of a stir-fry in a sauce,
than a casserole. The criteria is that the sauce should be
piquant, it should be slightly thicker than normal to allow
for the fact that the vegetables will give off some liquid,
and it should not be in great volume. I have said that the
sauce should be hot, this is not strictly true. Some very
simple sauces made purely with cream or sour cream and
perhaps a dash of alcohol should never be boiled and so
may be added cold to the stir-fry as they will only take a
few seconds to heat up. A good example of this is
mushroom and broccoli boulevard (88). Using a standard
stir-fry process involving only broccoli and mushrooms,
dry vermouth is added and reduced, brandy added for
flambé, and the whole is finished off with sour cream all
in the last minute before serving. Here are a couple of
more conventional examples.

179 Sweet and sour stir-fried vegetables

Follow the recipe for stir-fried vegetables (177) with the
addition of 50 g fresh pineapple (C small) at the chinese
leaf stage (3). Heat separately 200 ml of sweet and sour
sauce in a small pan (20). Stir this into the vegetables at
stage 5 in place of, or in addition to, shoyu and ginger.
Serve with rice.

180 Curried stir-fried vegetables

As for sweet and sour stir-fried vegetables (179) substituting 200 ml of mild curry sauce (22) for sweet and sour
sauce.

181 Chillied stir-fried vegetables

As for (179) but substitute 200 ml chilli sauce (21a).

Red wine and white wine sauces are good to use too, so
experiment, vary the vegetable content to suit your
chosen sauce. Add roasted nuts (almonds, cashews, and
peanuts are good), seeds and dry fruits.

The essential difference between stir-frying and
sautéeing is temperature. For stir-fry dishes the temperature of the cooking medium is all important, it must be
hot. Therefore oil must be used. When butter or vegetable
margarine is used the cooking temperature is a lot lower
and will not produce good stir-fries. However, the principle learnt in stir-frying with oil should be applied to
dishes that use butter or margarine, with the knowledge
that the whole process takes longer and so suitable
adjustments have to be made. If you can afford butter and
don't object to its use, or have access to a good quality
vegetable margarine, you will find the flavour they impart adds a smoothness and richness to a dish that oil
cannot. Also some vegetables will cook perfectly and
quickly in butter and margarine if prepared correctly from
a recipe that uses stir-fry techniques but butter or margarine as the cooking medium.

182 Courgettes and mushrooms in red wine

Serves 4

Stage	Ingredient	Quantity	Method
1	Butter	50 g	*Melt the butter in a pan and, when it is hot, add the courgettes and herbs and garlic. Turn the heat down slightly and continue cooking until the courgettes are starting to soften.*
	Courgettes	450 g	
	Garlic, minced	3 cloves	
	Marjoram	1 tsp	
2	Mushrooms, button whole	250 g	*Add mushrooms and continue to stir-fry for 2 minutes.*
	Lemon juice	A squeeze	
3	Red wine sauce (32)	200 ml	*Heat the sauce separately then stir into the mushroom and courgette mixture. Adjust seasoning.*
	Salt and pepper	To taste	

Serve with rice or noodles.

183 Stir-fried vegetables and noodles

Use recipe 177 for stir-fried vegetables but reduce quantity by a third. Cook 180 g of Chinese egg noodles and stir them into the stir-fry just before serving. This makes stir-fries into a really substantial meal.

Variations

As for stir-fried vegetables (177, 178, 179, 180, 181) but add noodles. Or substitute noodles with rice to make savoury rice, or substitute noodles with macaroni or tagliatelle.

You will not be able to create any good vegetarian food until you are happy with the way you approach stir-fry. It is a good way of practising and creating a tasty meal at the same time.

Chapter 10

Soups

Introduction

Soups can make appetizing ways to start a meal or can be complete meals in themselves. Soups present excellent opportunities to use up leftovers and even make a quick tasty snack. It's possible to make a soup from scratch out of raw materials just as quickly as it takes most people to open a pack of cuppa soup and drink the powdered chemicals, flavourings and preservatives therein. By now you have built up a considerable amount of knowledge about vegetables, beans, pulses, grains, pastas, stir-frying, thickening agents, sauces and stocks. Basically, you know all you need to know to create attractive and satisfying soups. In the chapter on balancing influences in cooking we mentioned the effect of the time of year and even the time of day on what you decide to cook. Thick and warming winter soups give way to thinner, fresher more attractive soups in summer and when it is very hot you may even like to try a chilled soup. So I have divided this chapter into *thick soups*, where the thickening agent not only thickens the soup but can also become the soup itself, and *thin soups*, where much more of what you learnt in the stir-fry chapter is important and the anomalous *chilled soups* which can sometimes seem more like a cross between a salad and a salad dressing than a soup.

Equipment required

No more special equipment is needed, though you may like a small ladle for tasting, and if you haven't yet got a blender you will need a sieve or a hand-mouli. A nice tureen to serve the soup from is always useful.

Thick soups

In Chapter 3 we discussed the methods of thickening sauces. The same thickening techniques apply to soups; indeed, some soups may be thought of as extended sauces. However, the emphasis in thickening soups lies not with flour-based thickeners but with natural thickeners like vegetable purées, lentil and bean purées, nut pâtés. Natural thickeners like these not only add their own flavour to a soup but they may, as we said in the introduction, become the soup itself. Many natural thickeners, however, do not have sufficient flavour to create a good soup in themselves and will need additional flavours and ingredients to make the soup as delicious as it can be. For instance, watercress and potato soup relies on the watercress for flavour and the potato for thickening, the potato does add a lardy consistency and some flavour, but primarily it forms the base upon which the soup is built. Natural thickeners can also be too thick and may need diluting with a vegetable stock (1,2,3 and 4) or milk or a mixture of both. Bean and lentil water is also a valuable addition to any soup as a substitute for stock. If the base is already very tasty you may wish to use just plain water. Cornflour is not a good thickener for thick soups because it is so glutinous. Below is a table showing the various ways in which soups can be thickened, diluted and flavoured. It also shows ingredients that can only be added just before serving to round the soup off.

Thicken With/ Soup Base	Dilute With	Flavour With	Add Before Serving
Potatoes	Veg. water	Mushrooms	Cream
Parsnips		Leeks	Sour cream
Turnips	Veg. stock (1)	Cauliflower	Cream cheese
Beetroots	Tamari stock (2)	Jerusalem artichokes	Cottage cheese
Carrots		Celery	Grated cheese
Swedes	Miso stock (3)	Garlic	Parmesan cheese
Leeks	Yeastex stock (4)	Onions (various)	Butter
Cauliflower		Watercress	Yoghurt
Jerusalem artichokes	Lentil water	Spinach	
Pumpkin	Bean water	Nuts and chestnuts	
Spinach		Herbs	
Nut pâtés	Pea water	Spices	
Lentils (various)	Milk and/or alcohol	Alcohol (various)	
Beans (various)	Apple juice	Tomato paste	
Peas		Tomatoes	
Split-peas	Orange juice	Peanut butter	
Tahini		Asparagus	
Leftovers		Lettuce	
Grains		Cabbage	
Roux		Sweetcorn	
Egg yolks		Miso	
Mushrooms		Shoyu	
Bread		Tahini	

Note

You will see that some soup bases are also classed as flavourings, in other words these ingredients are able to make a soup in their own right.

Whatever base you use for your thick soup I always think that it is just as well to start the soup with what is known as a mirepoix. This is a selection of root vegetables – any that you have around, finely diced and sautéed with herbs, bay leaf and pepper. A soup that uses a mirepoix as a starting point cannot fail to be tasty, but it is not absolutely vital, it just depends on how tasty the rest of the ingredients are.

Thick soups with a root vegetable or tuber purée base

These hearty soups are excellent winter dishes because it is the main season for root vegetables. Very few other exciting vegetables are in the shops except those that have been imported and are therefore too precious to use for soup.

184 Leek and potato soup   Serves 4

Stage	Ingredients	Quantity	Method
1	Oil/vegetable margarine/ butter	25 g	*Melt the fat in a deep pan, add the leeks and cook gently until they begin to soften. Stir occasionally with a wooden spoon.*
	White part of leek, roughly cut (use the green part for stock)	200 g	
2	Vegetable stock (1)	1¼ l	*Bring the stock to the boil and add to the leeks. Simmer for about 10 minutes.*
3	Potato, roughly chopped	200 g	*Add and continue to cook until potatoes are tender. Blend ingredients together and adjust seasoning.*
	Salt and pepper	To taste	
4	Chopped parsley		*Garnish with chopped parsley before serving.*

Special points

If the soup is too thick when it has been blended, dilute it with more vegetable stock until you achieve the desired consistency; adjust seasoning.

Variations

(a) Keep a few leeks separate from the blender and add afterwards to give the soup more texture.
(b) Substitute half the vegetable stock with milk and proceed as before.

(c) Add 100 ml of cream, sour cream, or yoghurt just before serving – do not re-boil.
(d) Watercress and potato soup – substitute for leeks with watercress, but add the watercress raw just before serving.
(e) Spinach and potato soup – Substitute for leeks with spinach and season with a little nutmeg.

185 Turnip and dill soup   Serves 4

Probably one of the nicest ways of using turnips.

Stage	Ingredients	Quantity	Method
1	Oil/vegetable margarine/ butter	25 g	*Heat the fat in a deep pan. Add the onions and sautée until softened. Add the turnips, potatoes and dill and continue to cook on a medium heat for 10 minutes.*
	Onions (G)	1 medium	
	Turnips (C)	250 g	
	Potatoes (C)	150 g	
	Dill-weed	1 dsp	
2	Shoyu	1 dsp	*Turn the heat up and add the shoyu and sherry. Reduce the sherry by half, stirring continuously.*
	Sherry	2 tbsp	
3	Vegetable stock (l)	1¼ l	*Heat the stock and add to the rest of the ingredients. Continue to cook until all ingredients are tender. Blend and adjust seasoning.*
	Salt and pepper	To taste	
4	Chopped parsley		*Sprinkle with chopped parsley before serving.*

Special points

If turnips are very old it may be necessary to remove some skin.

Variations

(a) Wholly or partially substitute vegetable stock with milk.
(b) Add cream, sour cream or yoghurt just before serving.

186 Nutty parsnip soup   **Serves 4**

Sounds unusual but somehow peanuts and parsnips might have been made for each other.

Stage	Ingredients	Quantity	Method
1	Vegetable margarine	25 g	*Melt the margarine in a deep pan. Sautée the onions and parsnips together until beginning to soften.*
	Onions (G)	1 medium	
	Parsnips (C)	300 g	
2	Smooth peanut butter	1 tbsp	*Stir in the peanut butter to coat all the vegetables. Add a little shoyu.*
	Shoyu	Dash	
3	Vegetable stock (l)	1 l	*Bring vegetable stock to boil and add gradually, allowing the peanut butter to thicken slightly. Continue cooking until all ingredients are soft. Then blend.*
4	Peanuts, roasted	25 g	*Roughly grate the peanuts and scatter on the surface just before serving.*

187 Bortsch   **Serves 4**

This is a great way to use beetroots as the base of a soup. Some beetroots are very woody; you should remove the core from these (the cores can always be put in your vegetable stock for this recipe). In fact, all the trimmings from this recipe will make excellent additions to your stockpot.

Stage	Ingredients	Quantity	Method
1	Butter	150 g	*Heat the butter in a deep pan, add the ingredients and stir-fry until all the vegetables are starting to secrete their juices. Heat the vegetable stock and add it to the rest of the ingredients with the lemon juice. Cook until the beetroot is tender. Blend and adjust seasoning. Add more vegetable stock if too thick.*
	Onion (G)	1 medium	
	Carrot (C small)	1 medium	
	Turnip (C small)	1 small	
	Celery (A small)	1 stick	
	Parsnip (C small)	1 small	
	Beetroot (C small)	450 g	
	Vegetable stock	1.75 l	
	Lemon juice	1 lemon	
	Seasoning	To taste	
2	Chopped chives		*Reheat and serve with a dollop of sour cream and sprinkle with chopped chives.*
	Sour cream		

Variations

(a) Beetroot and orange soup – replace half the volume of stock with orange juice and add the zest of 1 orange just before serving, a little tomato purée is nice too.
(b) Cream of vegetable soup – substitute beetroot with another vegetable, say leeks and omit the lemon juice. Then proceed as for Bortsch. Cream of vegetable soups may use milk instead of stock, wholly or partly. It is also nice to add a few mixed herbs and a bayleaf when sautéeing the mirepoix. Serve with croutons (105).

188 Artichoke soup (Jerusalem artichokes)   **Serves 4**

Artichokes have a very strong flavour which is too rich for some people. The potatoes make the flavour less rich but if you do like artichokes leave them out and thicken the soup with a little roux (see Chapter 1).

Stage	Ingredients	Quantity	Method
1	Artichokes (C)	400 g	*Cook the artichokes and the potatoes in the vegetable stock.*
	Potatoes (C)	150 g	*When soft blend and season.*
	Vegetable stock	150 ml	
	Salt and pepper	To taste	
	Nutmeg, optional	½ tsp	
2	Cream	100 ml	*Stir in the cream just before serving.*

Variations

(a) Substitute vegetable stock wholly or partly with milk.

(b) Substitute artichokes with asparagus stalks to make Cream of asparagus soup. Cook the tips separately in boiling salted water and add to the soup just before serving.

Well, I think that is enough root vegetable or tuber-based soups. As you can see, they are extremely easy to make and should be very tasty too.

Cream of vegetable soups (using roux or potatoes as thickeners)

As the Thick Soup chart shows, many vegetables other than root vegetables do have some thickening properties. However, most will look and taste better if they are additionally thickened with either a roux or a neutral, natural thickener like potatoes. Potatoes, although excellent for robust soups, are a little clumsy when it comes to making more delicately flavoured soups. They tend to disguise flavour and have a predictable consistency. Roux are more flexible, they can make a soup as thick or thin as you want it and, more importantly, they can enhance flavour rather than concealing it. There is little point in using a roux for root vegetable soups as they don't need the thickening or subtle-tasting properties that a roux provides. For those of you who don't like to use flour or margarine, or are perhaps allergic to them, then potatoes can be substituted for roux in all of the next batch of recipes, although seasoning will, of course, have to be adjusted. Again, where vegetable stock is used, milk may be used wholly or partially instead.

189 Cream of cauliflower soup   **Serves 4**

An excellent way to use cauliflower that is a little older than it should be. However, this recipe is just as good with fresh young cauliflowers.

Stage	Ingredients	Quantity	Method
1	Butter/vegetable margarine	60 g	*Prepare the roux (Chapter 1) and allow to cool.*
	Wholewheat flour	60 g	
2	Vegetable stock	1¼ l	*Mix the boiling vegetable stock into the roux gradually, stirring continuously until sauce has thickened evenly.*
3	Cauliflower (I)	375 g	*Blanch the cauliflower, drain and add to the soup.*
4			*Bring the soup back to the boil gently and blend.*
5	Cream	100 ml	*Stir in the cream just before serving and adjust seasoning.*
	Salt and pepper	To taste	

Variations

(a) Beat cream with an egg yolk and fold into soup when it has been removed from the heat.

(b) Retain a few florets of cauliflower whole and add to the soup at stage 4.

(c) A dash of tamari will make this soup a little more savoury.

190 Cream of mushroom soup

As for cream of cauliflower soup (189), but stir-fry the mushrooms rather than blanching, then add them to the soup.

Variations

(a) Reduce 50 ml of white wine or vermouth with the mushrooms when you stir-fry them.
(b) Dash of shoyu.
(c) Handful of chopped parsley before serving.

191 Cream of onion soup

As for cream of cauliflower soup (189) and cream of mushroom (190).

Variations

(a) Sauté the onions with a dry sherry.
(b) Serve with parmesan cheese.

192 Cream of spinach soup

As for cream of cauliflower (189), but substitute spinach for cauliflower.

Variations

(a) Season with nutmeg.
(b) Stir-fry the spinach in butter with garlic.

193 Cream of lettuce soup

As for cream of cauliflower soup (189), but with the addition of 1 dsp of sugar, and substitute lettuce for cauliflower.

Variations

(a) Throw in a handful of mange-tout or fresh peas just before serving.
(b) Stir-fry the lettuce with a medium-sliced onion.

194 Cream of corn soup

As for cream of cauliflower soup (189), but use fresh or frozen corn. Retain some corn to add to the soup at stage 4.

195 Cream of celery soup

As for cream of cauliflower soup (189), but substitute celery for cauliflower. Again, the celery can be celery past its prime. Cut the celery into medium-sized chunks (A, B).

196 Cream of tomato soup   Serves 4

It is nice to use fresh tomatoes for this soup. But no need for them to be salad quality. The tomato skins should be removed at some stage in the cooking. This can be done in advance by making a small prick in the tomatoes and then plunging them into boiling water for about 40 seconds. The skins will then come off easily. The other method is to push the whole soup through a sieve when it has been cooked. If fresh tomatoes are not easily available, use tinned tomatoes or tomato purée. Remove the 'tinned flavour' by adding cider vinegar or lemon juice, and sugar/honey, after the rest of the ingredients have been stir-fried. The following recipe allows for 1 kg of tomatoes that have been skinned in advance.

Stage	Ingredients	Quantity	Method
1	Butter/vegetable margarine/oil	50 g	Heat the butter in a deep pan, add the onions, carrots and herbs and stir-fry until softening.
	Onion (G)	1 medium	
	Carrot (G)	1 large	
	Bay leaf	1	
	Thyme/oregano/basil	1 dsp	
2	Flour	60 g	Stir in the flour and cook for 1 minute, allow to cool.
3	Fresh tomatoes	1 kg	Add the tomatoes and mix in. Bring the stock to the boil and stir into tomato mixture. Add shoyu, bring to boil and blend.
	Vegetable stock	1 l	
	Shoyu, optional	1 dsp	
4	Salt and pepper	To taste	Reheat soup and adjust seasoning.
5	Cream, optional	100 ml	Decorate with a swirl of cream just before serving. Or mix the cream in.

Special point

Serve with cheesy garlic croutons (105) and sprinkle with chopped fresh chives, spring onion ends or parsley.

Variations

(a)   Add 4 cloves of minced garlic with the cream.
(b)   Substitute cream with sour cream or yoghurt.
(c)   Sprinkle with parmesan cheese.
(d)   Add a dash of Worcester sauce or Tabasco.

197 Mushroom bisque

Serves 4

Bisques are perhaps the richest of these soups. They don't rely on the flavour of the vegetable in the liquid of the soup, rather that the vegetables retain their shape and flavour. Mushrooms are the perfect example

Stage	Ingredients	Quantity	Method
1	Butter	50 g	Heat the butter in a pan and sautée the vegetables and herbs until softening.
	Carrot (G)	1 large	
	Onion (G)	1 medium	
	Bay leaf	½	
	Thyme	1 dsp	
	Parsley	5 g	
2	Flour	50 g	Stir in the flour and cook for one minute, allow to cool.
3	Brandy	25 ml	Add the brandy and mix in well.
4	Tomato purée	30 g	Stir in tomato purée, wine and boiling stock. Bring back to the boil.
	White wine	100 ml	
	Vegetable stock (1)	1 l	
5	Mushrooms, button, whole	300 g	Add the mushrooms, including the stalks in the stock and re-boil.
6	Butter	25 g	Remove from heat and stir in butter, cream and brandy. Adjust seasoning.
	Cream	50 ml	
	Brandy	Dash	

I think this recipe is enough to make even the most reluctant vegetarian start changing his ways.

Variations

(a)   Substitute mushrooms with florets of cauliflower (blanched).
(b)   Substitute mushrooms with whole green beans (blanched).
(c)   Substitute mushrooms with mange-tout.
(d)   Substitute mushrooms with asparagus (blanched).

Pulse, bean and grain-based thick soups

Pulses, beans and grains have formed the base of soups for centuries. They thicken naturally and have a delicious flavour in their own right. However, like root vegetables, they are not the most subtle of ingredients and need other strong flavours to keep the palate entertained. With most pulse and bean-based soups it is not necessary to prepare a special stock, the water in which they are cooked will do. It is always best to pre-cook the pulses, beans or grains as this gives you more ultimate control of the overall consistency and flavour of the soup. Milk is not a necessary addition to these soups, although a dollop of cream or sour cream at the end can round them off nicely.

198 Green split-pea and leek soup

Serves 4

As for potato and leek soup (184), but substitute 200 g of cooked split-peas for the potatoes.

Variations

(a) Add minced garlic to the soup just before serving.
(b) Add the juice of half a lemon to the leeks.
(c) Add 1 dsp tamari to the leeks.
(d) Finish off with cream, sour cream or butter.
(e) Substitute green split-peas with yellow split-peas, yellow lentils, red lentils or haricot beans.
(f) Substitute leeks with watercress, add watercress just before blending.
(g) Substitute leeks with spinach.
Serve with chopped parsley and croutons (105).

199 Little cheese soup

Serves 4

Probably the nicest soup ever invented and the simplest too.

Stage	Ingredients	Quantity	Method
1	Butter	30 g	Melt the butter and sautée the onions and carrots with the cayenne until soft.
	Onions (G)	1 medium	
	Carrot, grated	1 large	
	Cayenne	1 tsp	
2	Tomato purée	1 dsp	Stir in these ingredients and mix well with the carrots and onion.
	Yeast extract	2 tsp	
	Cooked red lentils	400 g	
3	Lentil water/ vegetable stock	1 l	Add the vegetable stock (boiling) to the lentils to achieve correct consistency. Remember the lentils will probably go on thickening. Bring to the boil and allow to simmer, season. Throw cheese into soup just before serving and allow to melt, do not reboil or the cheese will toughen.
	Salt and pepper	To taste	
4	Cheddar cheese, grated	120 g	

Serve with a handful of chopped parsley sprinkled on the top.

Variations

(a) Substitute yellow or orange lentils for red.
(b) Substitute cheddar cheese with mozzarella for a really dangerous soup.

200 Mulligatawny soup

Serves 4

I have often made this with the leftovers of yesterday's curry, especially when it is a lentil dahl (215). This is strictly a mulligatawny but a delightful soup neverthe-less. You will need to have a good quality mild curry powder.

Stage	Ingredients	Quantity	Method
1	Vegetable oil	50 ml	Heat the oil and stir-fry the mirepoix into the curry powder and garam masala. When it is hot add the shoyu.
	Mirepoix	200 g	
	Curry powder, mild	1 dsp	
	Garam masala	1 tsp	
	Shoyu	1 dsp	
2	Cooked green/brown lentils	200 g	Add the lentils and tomato paste and mix thoroughly.
	Tomato paste	1 tbsp	
3	Lentil water/vegetable stock (1)	1 l	Bring the stock to the boil and add to the mixture. Blend and adjust seasoning.
	Salt and pepper	To taste	

Serve with a little rice in each bowl, and/or dried fruit.

Variations

(a) Add 100 ml of cream, sour cream or yoghurt before serving.

(b) Add a few mushrooms and/or aubergine to the mirepoix, or anything you need to use up.

201 Cream of aduki soup

Serves 4

I think aduki beans are the nicest beans to use in soups, having a deep rich flavour that is free from the more beany taste and texture of larger and harder beans. Aduki beans may be left whole in a soup or blended for thickening purposes.

Substitute 300 g of cooked aduki beans for cauliflower in cream of cauliflower soup (189).

Variations

Aduki soups are probably nicer in their varied form. A soup made entirely of beans can be heavy going.

(a) Add 100 g of spinach to 200 g of aduki beans.
(b) Add 100 g of mushrooms to 200 g of aduki beans.
(c) Add 100 g of onions/watercress/spring onions/leeks to 200 g of aduki beans.
(d) Add 1 tbsp miso to the soup just before serving.
(e) Substitute aduki beans with haricot beans, lima beans or black beans.

202 Scotch broth

Serves 4

We are now heading rapidly toward thin soups, but somehow this soup and the next few soups seemed too substantial to be included in that section of the chapter. Scotch broth is really a barley soup – it is very substantial and ideal for a cold winter's day. It is very important to get a good tasty stock on the go for this one, you might want to boost it with a little Yeastex (vegetable stock 4). Pre-cook the barley and use the water as the base for the stock. The shape and size of the vegetables is very important for the overall look of the soup; keep them a regular shape and of similar size.

Stage	Ingredient	Quantity	Method
1	Vegetable margarine	50 g	Heat the margarine in a deep pan and add the root vegetables. Stir-fry until onions start to soften.
	Onion (G)	1 small	
	Carrot (diced)	1 small	
	Swede (diced)	1 small	
	Parsnip (diced)	1 small	
	Turnip (diced)	1 small	
	Potato (diced)	1 small	
	Leek (diced)	1 small	
2	Flour	50 g	Sprinkle flour over mixture and stir in thoroughly, allow to cool.

3	Vegetable stock (4)	1½ l	*Bring stock to the boil and pour gradually into vegetables, stirring continuously.*
4	Pot barley, cooked Salt and pepper Cauliflower (I, small)	200 g To taste	*Stir in the barley and adjust the seasoning. Reboil and add the cauliflower (blanched) just before serving.*

To serve: sprinkle with chopped parsley.

Variations

(a) Substitute barley with wholewheat.

(b) Add 50 ml of sherry with stock to make a really warming soup.

203 Corn chowder

Serves 4

Chowders are the real transition point between thick and thin soups, suitable for both winter and summer consumption. Chowders generally have more summery ingredients.

Stage	Ingredients	Quantity	Method
1	Vegetable stock/water Onion (G) Celery (diced) Potato (diced) Parsley	500 ml 1 medium 1 stick 1 medium 10 g	*Bring the stock to the boil and place the onions, celery, potato and parsley in it. Cook until vegetables are semi-cooked, about 5 minutes.*
2	Sweetcorn	100 g	*Add the corn and continue cooking for another couple of minutes.*
3	Bechamel (34) Salt and pepper	500 ml To taste	*Add the soup mixture to the bechamel sauce gradually, stirring all the time. Adjust seasoning.*
4	Shoyu Garlic, minced	Dash 3 cloves	*Add shoyu and garlic just before serving.*

To serve – add a knob of butter.

Variations

(a) Replace béchamel at stage 3 with tomato sauce.
(b) Add a little chilli.

Thin soups

Thin soups are ideal for summer, or as part of a larger meal at any time of the year. The two most important aspects of thin soups are the liquid, which will be a vamped-up stock, and the contents. Vegetable content of thin soups should be attractive to look at, yet quick to cook. Once you have created a tasty stock it should literally only take a few minutes to finish off the soup. Finely slicing or dicing the vegetables makes them not only a nice overall size and shape, but easy to cook too. These soups should be fresh, almost refreshing, so it is important not to overcook the vegetables – let them retain some texture and shape. If using pasta in your thin soups the same rule applies. It is not really necessary to thicken thin soups – a little potato in the stock may be all that is necessary or an egg yolk liaison. Seasoning, of course, is vital in soups which depend so much on flavour for their enjoyment. The following chart is similar to that used to illustrate the wide variety of thick soups that could be made.

Stocks	Flavourings	Ingredients	Chopping Techniques (all small)
Vegetable stock 1	Yeastex	*Vegetable:*	
Vegetable stock 2	Shoyu	Any, especially	A, A1,
Vegetable stock 3	Miso	fresh spring	B, B1,
Vegetable stock 4	Seaweed	vegetable.	C, (small)
Pulse water	Oils	*Others:*	D
Grain water	Tomato paste	Pulses	F, (small)
Bean water	Tahini	Grains	G,
Vegetable water	Herbs	Beans	H,
	Spices	Pastas	I (small).
	Sherry	Gnocchi	
	Marsala	Chopped	
	Brandy	omelette	
	Garlic	Chopped	
		pancake	

204(a) Maxistrone stock and variations   Serves 4

I have always called our minestrone 'maxistrone' to set it apart from those awful powdered minestrone mixes that have become so common. It is extremely easy to make. You will need a really tasty vegetable stock:

Stage	Ingredients	Quantity	Method
1	Oil	50 ml	*Sautée the mirepoix in the oil with the herbs and garlic.*
	Mirepoix (rough-cut)	300 g	
	Herbs/bay leaf	1 tbsp	
	Garlic	3 cloves	
2	Sherry		*Add the sherry and reduce by half.*
3	Tomato paste	2 tbsp	*Stir the tomato paste and shoyu in thoroughly.*
4	Vegetable stock (l)	150 ml	*Heat the vegetable stock separately and add gradually to the mirepoix. Allow to simmer for 30 mins, then strain.*

Special points

It is a good idea to make more than you need of this stock and keep it in a jar in the fridge. It can then give you instant soup with the addition of any vegetables or pasta you fancy.

Variations

(a) Substitute sherry with marsala.
(b) Omit the tomato paste.
(c) Omit the vegetables

204(b) Maxistrone soup

Serves 4

Stage	Ingredients	Quantity	Method
1	Butter/vegetable margarine	25 g	*Melt the butter or margarine in a deep pan. Add the vegetables and herbs and stir-fry for 5 minutes.*
	Onions (G)	25 g	
	Carrots (A, thin)	25 g	
	Turnips (A, thin)	25 g	
	Leeks (A, thin)	25 g	
	Celery (A, thin)	25 g	
	White cabbage (A, thin)	25 g	
	Oregano	1 dsp	
	Basil	2 tsp	
	Thyme	1 tsp	
2	Maxistrone stock	1½ l	*Bring the stock to the boil and add to the vegetables. Bring back to the boil and simmer.*
3	Short-cut macaroni/spaghetti	30 g	*Add the macaroni/spaghetti and cook until almost tender about 10 minutes.*
4	Cauliflower (I)	25 g	*Stir in the cauliflower, peas, garlic and parsley and cook for a further 3 minutes. Stir well before serving.*
	Fresh peas	25 g	
	Garlic, minced	3 cloves	
	Parsley	Sprig	

Serve with parmesan cheese and croutons (105).

Never adhere strictly to any maxistrone recipe; it's best to use up all those vegetables that may be left over in your store cupboard or fridge. Try to cut them into regular shapes, not too large.

Thin soups can be made more substantial with the addition of accompaniments like croutons, or thickened with an egg yolk liaison. The egg yolk method of thickening soups is probably the lightest available but, of course, totally unsuitable to vegans. We'll start the recipes with perhaps the most substantial of thin soups.

205 French onion soup

Serves 4

The emphasis in French onion soup is on savoury. French onion stock must set your savoury taste buds alight. It will be tempered by the sweetness of real French onions if you can get them (the red ones). Although essentially a thin soup, French onion soup is slightly thickened by the roux method as this enhances the flavour of the onions.

(a) The stock

Stage	Ingredients	Quantity	Method
1	Vegetable stock (l)	1½ l	Bring the stock to the boil and, if it isn't terribly savoury, add a little yeastex or shoyu.
2	Sherry Salt and pepper	100 ml	Add the sherry and simmer, adjust seasoning. If you are using real French onions use dry sherry, if English onions use sweet sherry.

(b) The soup

Stage	Ingredients	Quantity	Method
1	Butter/olive oil French onions (A, thin)	50 g/50 ml 1 kg	Heat the butter in a deep pan and add the onions, cook gently until the onions are beginning to colour.
2	Flour	30 g	Sprinkle the onions with the flour and mix well, allow to cool. Return to heat.
3	French onion soup stock Salt and pepper	1½ l To taste	Bring the stock to the boil and add gradually to the onions stirring gradually. Adjust seasoning and serve.

To serve: serve with cheesy garlic croutons or a thin slice of French bread toasted with gruyère cheese.

Variations

(a) Add 25 g of butter before serving.

(b) Add 100 ml of cream or sour cream before serving.
(c) Add a dash of brandy.
(d) Sprinkle with parmesan cheese.
(e) Substitute onions with celery/watercress/spinach/green beans.

206 Chinese vegetable soup

Serves 4

These, again, are extremely quick soups based upon stir-fried vegetables. In fact, you can use half quantities of the stir-fried vegetable recipe (177) but cut the vegetables smaller. Before the vegetables are completely cooked add 1½ litres of miso stock (3). Reheat but do not boil. Just before serving throw in:

(a) 2 sheets of nori seaweed (toasted or chopped).
(b) A handful of beansprouts.
(c) Fresh herbs and ground spices.
Just think of stir-fries as the base for soups, use any stock you like and start creating delicious quick soups.

207 Garlic soup

Serves 4

An example of a thin soup thickened with eggs.

Stage	Ingredients	Quantity	Method
1	Olive oil Garlic, whole	3 tbsp 4 heads	Sautée the cloves of garlic in the olive oil for a few minutes.
2	Vegetable stock (l) Salt and pepper	1 l To taste	Bring the vegetable stock to the boil and pour over the cloves of garlic – season. Simmer for 1 hour. Blend.
3	Egg yolks	2	Beat the egg yolks together in a bowl and add a little of the soup to them, mix thoroughly. Pour the egg mixture back into the rest of the soup, re-heat but do not re-boil as this will destroy the flavour and goodness of the soup. Serve with croutons.

Chilled soups

Most soups may be served cold to suit extremely hot weather conditions, or as appetisers for meals. Thick soups should be diluted with dairy produce such as cream, sour cream, milk or yoghurt after they have cooled down. Chilling can reduce the apparent flavour of a dish so you may wish to re-season with fresh herbs, garlic and spices, or flavour them with lemon juice, shoyu and tahini. You can even give extra texture by adding finely chopped salad vegetables, chopped hard-boiled eggs, olives or roasted nuts and seeds.

208 Vichysoisse   Serves 4

Vichysoisse is a good example of a hot soup turned cold by the addition of dairy produce.

Stage	Ingredients	Quantity	Method
1	Leek and potato soup (184)	1 l	*Prepare the soup and allow to chill. Make soup slightly thicker than normal.*
2	Cream	100 ml	*Stir in cream, sprinkle with chives and adjust seasoning. Chill again.*
	Chives, chopped		
	Salt and pepper	To taste	

Some chilled soups may simply be a salad vegetable in a thick dairy product e.g.

209 Cucumber and yoghurt soup   Serves 4

This is almost an extension of tsatziki dressing (68).

Stage	Ingredients	Quantity	Method
1	Cucumbers	2	*Grate or finely dice the cucumbers, add salt. Drain off liquid after a minute.*
	Salt		
2	Onion		*Chop the rest of the ingredients finely and mix with the cucumber.*
	Celery	Choose any	
	Green pepper	selection to	
	Parsley	make 150 g	
	Watercress		
3	Garlic	3 cloves	*Stir into rest of ingredients.*
	Mint, optional	Sprig	
	Lemon juice	½ lemon	
4	Natural yoghurt	750 ml	*Add the yoghurt and season with salt and pepper and cayenne.*
	Salt and pepper	To	
	Cayenne	taste	

Some chilled soups form the perfect excuse to use up left-over salad. In fact they can be based upon a salad that is blended with more salad dressing, for example Gazpacho.

210 Gazpacho

Serves 4

Stage	Ingredients	Quantity	Method
1	Garlic	10 cloves	*Blend together.*
	Stale bread	100 g	
	Olive oil	100 ml	
2	Tomatoes	250 g	*Chop these ingredients finely, toss in lemon juice and fold into*
	Cucumber	125 g	*oil mixture. Season and chill for 30 minutes. If too thick,*
	Green pepper	100 g	*adjust with French dressing (54) or Greek dressing (57).*
	Lemon juice	50 ml	
	Salt and pepper	To taste	

To serve: serve accompanied by croutons (105) and a selection of chopped salad vegetables.

The portions given in this chapter on soups are fairly large so do reduce them if you are going to follow with a large meal.

Chapter 11

Casseroles

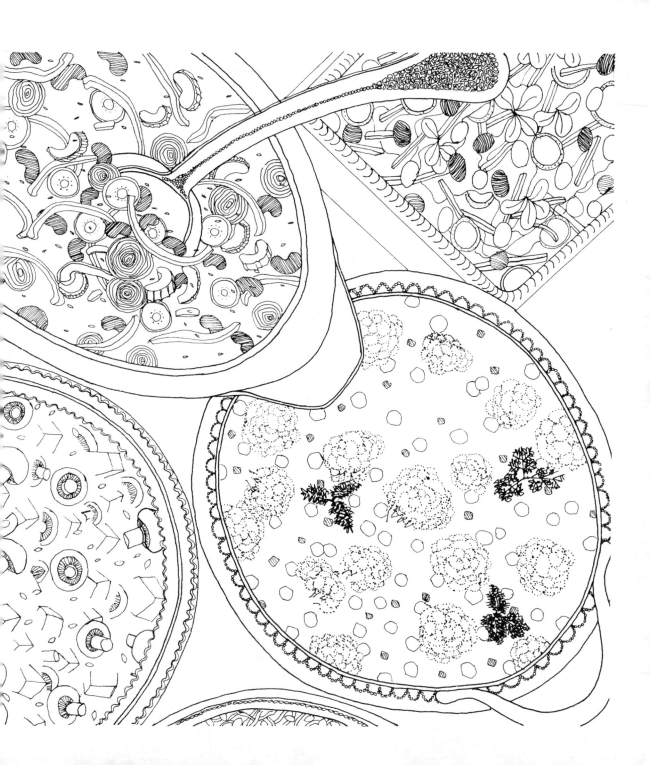

The main difference between vegetarian casseroles and meat casseroles is that, with vegetarian casseroles, other ingredients are added to a sauce whereas with meat casseroles, ideally, the ingredients should help to create the sauce themselves. In practice, however, they are both based on the same principle, except that meat casseroles take about four times as long to cook. The absence of meat with any flavour these days means that a separately created sauce will tend to dominate the finished dish anyway. Vegetarian casseroles are best cooked on the top of the stove in the same manner as soups (Chapter 10) or stir-fries (Chapter 9).

Many people find it really difficult to imagine cooking a casserole that is partially, if not entirely, made of vegetables. But, if you've read the rest of the book, you will have all the knowledge that is necessary already at your finger-tips. Your mind should drift back to these fundamental decisions:

1 Selection of ingredients

Select ingredients according to season, condition, taste, colour, texture, and relevance to the dish you are attempting to create. Balance one ingredient against another.

2 Selection of sauce

The sauce will determine the theme of the dish – so choose it carefully to enhance the end result. As Chapter 3 explains the thickening agent is often an under-rated factor in the dish as a whole. The thickness of any casserole sauce must take into account any additional liquid that may be secreted from the vegetables themselves.

3 Stir-frying or not stir-frying

Most vegetables will be partially stir-fried, and some may be blanched, before being added to a casserole sauce. This gives you total control over the end texture of the vegetables. Therefore, it is vital to choose a vegetable chopping technique as well as a regular size that is in line with the way you want each vegetable to cook. You must then set an order of cooking. Generally roots will always come first, followed by leaves, vegetable fruits and fungi. It is also very important to think of the texture of the overall dish and how the vegetable chopping technique and size of the different vegetables can complement each other and other ingredients like beans, grains and pulses.

4 Beans, grains, pastas and pulses

These ingredients must always be pre-cooked when used in a casserole. Their cooking times are too indefinite and variable to risk overcooking delicate vegetables. Care should be taken to cook them to perfection, overcooked they will act as a natural thickener to what may already be a perfectly thickened sauce, thus creating a stodgy mess. If you do happen to overcook them don't worry, you have two options either wash them or, better still, make your sauce thinner than you would normally and allow the beans, grains and pulses to do their work. Overcooked beans, grains and pulses washed or unwashed should always be added to the casseroles as short a time as possible before serving so that they don't overcook even more.

5 Overall

A casserole should always look attractive, nourishing and alive so remember, the sauce recipes in the sauce chapter are only guides; vary them as you wish. There is an enormous range of vegetables, beans, grains, pulses, pastas, flavours, fruits, herbs, spices, dairy produce etc. to choose from when deciding to make a casserole; use what you like best and what is easily to hand. I have chosen a few examples to illustrate different combinations of ingredients that have proved successful in the past. Try the same ingredients with a different sauce, or a different chopping technique, or both. Use different ingredients and proceed along similar lines, experiment with sauces. If you have read the rest of the book I think you will know what I mean by now.

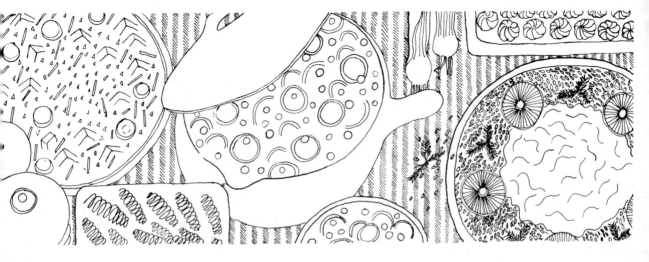

Equipment required

Ideally, you will need a casserole dish but don't panic if you do not have one, a saucepan will do. Nothing else is necessary except a lively imagination.

209 Ratatouille

Serves 4

Perhaps a classic among traditional vegetarian dishes. A very colourful dish that should be almost refreshing – a hot salad that can of course be served cold too.

Stage	Ingredients	Quantity	Method
1	Olive oil	2 tbsp	*Heat the oil in a deep pan and add the onions, cook for 5 minutes. Add the peppers and herbs and season to taste. Add the aubergines and garlic and stir-fry for another 5 minutes. Add the courgettes, stir-fry for a further 1 minute.*
	Onions, sliced	450 g	
	Red and green peppers (D)	450 g	
	Oregano/basil	3 tbsp	
	Parsley	1 tbsp	
	Aubergine (C)	450 g	
	Garlic, crushed	4 cloves	
	Courgettes (A, B)	450 g	
2	Ratatouille sauce (14)	½ l	*Heat the sauce separately. When it is hot add it to the vegetables.*
3	Mushrooms, button	100 g	*Add mushrooms and serve when re-heated.*

To serve: serve with rice and the alternative of grated cheese or parmesan.

Variations

(a) Substitute ratatouille sauce with red wine ratatouille sauce (16).

(b) At stage 2 put all ingredients into a bake tray and cover with a topping of your choice.

(c) Halve vegetable quantity and substitute red beans.

210 Hungarian red bean goulash

Serves 4

This is such a good goulash you would never miss the traditional bad cut of beef.

Stage	Ingredients	Quantity	Method
1	Oil	50 ml	*Heat the oil in a deep pan and add the onion, paprika and bay leaf. Cook gently for a minute and add the carrots, green and red peppers. Continue stir-frying for about 5 minutes.*
	Onions, sliced	2 medium	
	Carrot (B1)	1 medium	
	Green pepper (D)	1 medium	
	Red pepper (C)	1 medium	
	Paprika	1 tbsp	
	Bay leaf	1	
2	Cauliflower (I)	1 medium	*Quickly blanch the cauliflower in boiling water. Drain and add to stir-fries.*
3	Goulash sauce (11)	¾ l	*Heat the sauce separately and pour over the stir-fry mixture.*
4	Red beans (cooked)	200 g	*Stir in the beans and bring to the boil gently.*
5	Mushrooms, button	100 g	*Add the mushrooms and reboil. Adjust seasoning and consistency. Serve.*
	Salt and pepper	To taste	

To serve: serve with a blob of sour cream or yoghurt on a bed of rice perhaps.

Variations

(a) Substitute goulash sauce with Hungarian red wine sauce (47).

(b) Substitute any other sauce.

(c) Add any topping and serve as a bake – Boulangère topping is particularly good.

211 Black bean and green bean neapolitan

Serves 4

Stage	Ingredients	Quantity	Method
1	Olive oil	50 ml	*Heat the oil and add the onions and red peppers, cook until the onions are softening.*
	Red onions, sliced	2 medium	
	Red peppers (C)	2 medium	
2	Whole or halved green beans, blanched	450 g	*Add the green beans and mix in. Heat the sauce separately and pour it on to the green bean mixture.*
3	Neapolitan sauce (10)	¾ l	*Reboil.*
4	Mushrooms, sliced	120 g	*Stir in the mushrooms and black beans. Reheat the casserole and adjust seasoning and consistency. Serve.*
	Black beans, cooked	300 g	
	Salt and pepper	To taste	

To serve: serve with rice or pasta and a sprinkling of parmesan.

Variations

(a) Replace black beans with flageolet, red beans or macaroni.

(b) Use as a bake with a topping.

(c) Use other sauces at stage 3.

212 Pinto and cauliflower ghuvetch

Serves 4

This is another Hungarian dish and the emphasis is on dill and tomatoes. If you can, use fresh dill, but stir it in at the end.

Stage	Ingredients	Quantity	Method
1	Oil	50 ml	*Heat the oil and stir-fry the onions, green pepper and parsnips until onions are softening, but the peppers are still crisp.*
	Onions, sliced	1 medium	
	Green pepper (C)	1 large	
	Parsnip (B small)	1 medium	
2	Courgettes (B)	2 large	*Add the courgettes and stir-fry for another 3 minutes.*
3	Ghuvetch sauce (12)	¾ l	*Heat the sauce separately and pour on to the rest of the ingredients. Re-heat.*
4	Cauliflower(I)	1 medium head	*Blanch the cauliflower separately for 3 minutes in boiling salted water. Drain and add to the casserole with the beans. Bring whole casserole to boil again. adjust seasoning and consistency and serve.*
	Pinto beans	200 g	
	Salt and pepper	To taste	

To serve: sprinkle with parsley or fresh chopped dill weed.

Variations

Serve as a bake with a topping.

The pattern of work

If you have tried these first four recipes you will be beginning to understand the system used in creating fresh casseroles at home. Nevertheless, it helps if you always follow a pattern of work. Here is a typical work pattern.

1 Think of your beans, pulses and grains a day in advance. Soak them if necessary.
2 Put your beans, pulses, grains and pastas on to cook, allowing the appropriate time to cook.
3 Prepare and cook your casserole sauce.
4 While it is cooking take the chance to prepare the fresh vegetables for the casserole.
5 Stir-fry the chosen vegetables and hard fruits as suggested in Chapter 9, but allow 5 minutes further cooking in the sauce.
6 If the sauce has cooled, re-heat it and, when it is boiling, add it to your stir-fried vegetables.
7 Add the cooked beans with the sauce and bring back to the boil.
8 A minute or two before serving add mushrooms, par-cooked vegetables and soft fruits, as well as any delicate last-minute flavourings like miso or dairy produce (do not re-boil with these last two ingredients) and of course, fresh herbs and garlic.
9 Serve and eat as quickly as possible, most casseroles do not improve with prolonged cooking or simmering.

Given this as a typical work pattern which applies, in general, to all casseroles, I think we will devote the rest of the chapter to ideas rather than specific recipes. Quantities are up to you – generally, ¾ litre of sauce to 1½ kg of ingredients, but this will vary with the ingredients. The ingredients will be listed in order of usage with an indication of chopping technique followed by some good variations and accompaniments. Refer to p. 149 for inspiration. Always adjust the casserole for seasoning and consistency before serving. Remember all casseroles can be bakes and vice-versa.

213 Mexican chilli beans

Olive oil, Onions (sliced), Carrots (B, medium), Green peppers (D), Red peppers (D), Courgettes (B,B1, Medium and F), Mexican chilli sauce (21(b)), Black beans, Sweetcorn, Mushrooms, (whole button or sliced cup).

To serve

Serve with rice, or tortilla chips (137) and a small bowl of guacamole (85).

Variations

(a) Use chilli sauce (21a).
(b) Add a dash of sour cream or yoghurt before serving – but do mix in.
(c) Make the chilli as hot as you like it.

214 West Indian fruit curry

Coconut oil (if you are feeling rich), Onions (G), Green peppers (C), Apples (C, medium), Pineapples (C, medium), Courgettes (B1, medium), West Indian fruit curry sauce (22c), Kidney beans, Oranges (C, medium) Bananas (A, chunky), Mushrooms (whole button or sliced cup).

To serve

Serve with rice, or if omitting kidney beans from the recipe serve with a bowl of buttered blackeye beans.

Variations

See pp. 48–9. Blackeyes are a nice substitute for kidney beans in this recipe.

215 Lentil aubergine dahl

This is a delicious, spicy curry, but not hot with chilli. If you have any left over, use it for Mulligatawny soup (200) the next day. The overall appearance of this dahl should be regular.

Onions (G), Green peppers (G), Aubergines (C, small), Courgettes (C, small), Dahl sauce (226(b), Lentils (brown or green), Mushrooms (sliced).

To serve

Serve with yoghurt or sour cream and poppadoms or chapatti (138).

216 Chick-pea and cauliflower curry

A mild curry but it is easy to make it spicy with added chilli if you wish. It is important that the consistency of the sauce is just right. Too thin a sauce and somehow the chick-peas become too harsh. Too thick a sauce and the casserole will soon dry out, again leaving the chick-peas high and dry. Chick-peas need to be cooked evenly and smoothly with the sauce otherwise they can be very tough.

Sunflower oil, Onions (G), Green peppers (D), Courgettes (A1, medium), Mild curry sauce (22a), Caulif-lowers (I, par-cooked), Mushrooms (whole button or cup sliced).

To serve

Rice is not necessary if you use chick-peas. Try serving it with tahini and lemon dressing (73) or tsatziki (68), or cucumber raita (69). Otherwise try simply sour cream or natural yoghurt.

Variations

Apart from all the many obvious variations this dish is great as a bake.

217 Courgette and green bean rojak

This fruity, nutty casserole is irresistible. It originated in Indonesia and so is also quite spicy, but then that is, of course, in your hands. If you want to use dried beans use red, black or pinto.

Peanut oil (if possible), Onions (sliced thin), Apples (C, small), Pineapple (C, small), Courgettes (B, B1, F), Rojak sauce (22d), Cauliflowers (I, par-cooked), Green beans (whole, par-cooked), cucumber (H), Mushrooms (button whole, cup halved).

To serve

Another dish that's good with rice and, if it is very spicy, serve with yoghurt, sour cream or an appropriate dairy-based dip.

Variations

Other good vegetables to use in this dish might be auber-gines, broad beans, broccoli, carrots, celery, mangetout, potatoes, sweet potatoes, peppers (red or green), pars-nips, brussel sprouts, bananas.

218 Sweet potato and aubergine africaine

Similar to the Rojak but the Africaine dish is more commonly curried than chillied and owes its sweetness to the sweet potatoes; don't be frightened of using them.

Peanut oil, Onions (sliced, red if possible), Carrots (F), Green peppers (D), Sweet potatoes (C, medium), Aubergine (A1), Africaine sauce (22d), Kidney beans (few), Green beans (whole, par-cooked), Sultanas, Mushrooms (button whole, cup halved).

To serve

This dish does not need rice; serve with any traditional accompaniments to a curry.

Variations

As for Rojak (217). Also try reducing the vegetable content and adding wholewheat spaghetti in its place.

219 Sweet and sour haricot hot pot

This is really a hefty extension of a stir-fry. The addition of beans differentiates it from sweet and sour stir-fried vegetables (179). Follow this recipe (179), but increase the volume and thickness of the sweet and sour sauce used – to compensate for the weight and volume of haricot beans. Here, is a slightly different alternative.

Safflower oil, Onions (thin sliced), Carrots (H, small), Green peppers (H), Courgettes (H, B1), Sweet and sour sauce (20), Haricot beans (or flageolets), Pineapple (C, medium), Cucumber (H), Chinese Leaf (B, medium) Green beans (whole, par-cooked), Mushrooms (open cup sliced), Bean sprouts.

To serve

Rice is not necessary but quite nice in spite of the haricot beans.

Variations

(a) Substitute haricot beans with egg noodles (pre-cooked).

(b) Add soaked chopped apricots with the courgettes and whole roasted almonds just before serving for Imperial Sweet and Sour dishes.

220 Aduki and spinach blanquette

A really simple but delicious recipe, but be careful – it is dangerous to eat; you will see what I mean.

Vegetable oil, Onions (G), Garlic (minced), Carrots (B1), Bechamel sauce (34), Aduki beans, Spinach (cooked and drained), Mushrooms (button halved or sliced), Nutmeg, Roasted cashew nuts (chopped).

Special point

Make your bechamel sauce extra thick to allow for the water that will come out of the spinach.

To serve

Serve as it is – sprinkle with chopped parsley and roast sunflower seeds.

Variations

(a) Use other white sauces; tamari and cheese are especially nice; tomato sauces are generally not of the right consistency for spinach but do experiment.

(b) Add a little extra ground cloves at the end but only a touch.

(c) Make it richer with a dollop of cream or sour cream just before serving.

221 Brussel sprout and chestnut forestière

This is a rich satisfying dish excellent for a cold winter's evening. Use cooked dried chestnuts if you can; the quality is more consistent. Vegetable oil/margarine/ butter, Onion (G), Carrots (B1, fine), Swedes (B1, fine), Pumpkin, optional (B1, fine), Parship (B1, fine), Mushroom sauce (39), and Parsley sauce (40) (two last ingredients in equal quantities mixed together with seasoning adjusted appropriately), Brussel sprouts (whole, par-cooked), Chestnuts (whole, par-cooked), Mushrooms (whole/halved button), Fresh chopped parsley.

Special points

Chestnuts are extremely filling so don't over-estimate how much your diners can eat.

To serve

As it comes.

Variations

(a) It makes a fabulous bake with a suitable topping.
(b) Add cheese to the sauce and a little nutmeg.
(c) Add more tamari/shoyu to the sauce.
(d) Add sour cream just before serving.

222 Leek and butter bean citron

A savoury lemon sauce is excellent to get those taste buds working, and fennel seems to fit into this recipe as nowhere else.
   Vegetable oil/margarine/butter, Carrots (A1, fine), Celery (B1, fine), Fennel (B1, fine), Leeks (B, medium), Lemon sauce (42), Butter beans, Green beans (whole, par-cooked), fresh, chopped watercress.

Special points

Add a little lemon juice or lemon zest to the leeks when stir-frying, this gives an even more lemony flavour.

To serve

As it comes.

Variations

As for Brussel sprouts and chestnut forestière (221).

223 Cheesy wheatberry and broccoli casserole

Another really hearty casserole that can totally finish any plans of eating for the rest of the day. Wheatberries are like chick-peas in that they need a large amount of sauce of the right consistency to help them go down.
   Vegetable margarine/butter, onions (sliced), Carrots (H), Courgettes (H), Cheese sauce (38), Wheatberries, Broccoli (I) (pre-stir-fried), mushrooms (sliced).

To serve

As it comes; sprinkle with a little cheese or parmesan.

Variations

(a) Vary sauce
(b) Vary vegetables, sweetcorn, peas, celery, peppers, leeks and adukis are particularly good.

224 Cauliflower and mange-tout fondue

This is a delicious variation of the fondue principle, lots of fresh undercooked vegetables coated in a cheesy, white wine sauce.
   Butter, Carrots, (for colour) (F), Courgettes (B, medium), Mushrooms (whole button), Cauliflower (I, par-cooked), Garlic. Fondue white wine sauce (46b), Mange-tout.

To serve

Serve immediately – do not allow to cook any further. If you really want to be exotic, rub garlic butter over the inside of your serving dish.

Variations

Choose other vegetables like green beans, broad beans, broccoli, snow-peas, brussel sprouts, and aubergines. Butter beans are nice too.

225 Flageolet and courgette aurore

Just as Forestière was the blending together of mushroom and parsley sauce, Aurore is the blending together of a herby tomato sauce (9) and a white sauce (35). Aurore is even better if you use a red wine tomato sauce (32), but this is not absolutely necessary. Sauce combinations can often result in very exciting sauces, so do experiment.

Vegetable oil, Spring onions (A, fine), Carrots (B1, fine), Celery (B, fine), Red Wine Sauce (47), Courgettes (F, medium) (par-cooked), Flageolet beans, Mushrooms (sliced).

To serve

Serve as it is, sprinkled with chives or spring onion greens.

Variations

(a) Use broad beans, aubergines, broccoli, leeks, parsnips, swedes, brussel sprouts, shallots and beans such as red beans, black beans and blackeye beans.
(b) Finish off with a blob of sour cream.
(c) Add chilli or curry powder to the sauce when you make it.
(d) Add a handful of roasted almonds at the end.

226 Blackeye and mushroom strogonoff

In no way is this a cheap imitation of other strogonoffs. Even though strogonoff refers to a particular way of cutting meat the name has become synonymous with the flavour of mushrooms, cream and white wine. Butter, Onions (sliced), Green peppers (H), Strogonoff sauce (46c), Blackeye beans, Mushrooms (sliced), lots of them.

To serve

Serve with a dash of paprika on a bed of rice.

Variations

(a) Add a dash of brandy before serving.
(b) Substitute blackeye beans with another vegetable like broccoli, cauliflower or green beans.

227 Broccoli and broad bean bonne femme

A curious-sounding title but the subtle flavour of a bonne femme sauce complements the delicate nature of broccoli and broad beans. Butter, Onions (G), Carrots (B1, fine), Red peppers (C), White wine sauce (46), Broccoli (I, stir-fried), Broad beans (par-boiled), Mushrooms (sliced), White grapes (halved).

Special point

Don't add the grapes until literally 1 minute before serving.

To serve

Serve on its own or with rice.

Variations

Choose different vegetables according to availability, but do keep them light. Strongly flavoured vegetables destroy the subtlety of the sauce.

228 Kidney bean and courgette bourguignonne

Perhaps the richest of the casseroles – dark savoury flavours, a thick red wine sauce intermingled with mushrooms and shallots. Vegetable oil, Shallots, ideally, but onions will do (G), Carrots (B1), Green peppers (C), Leeks (G), Bourguignonne sauce (18), Kidney beans, Courgettes (B, partially stir-fried) Mushrooms (flat, sliced).

To serve

As it is, sprinkled with parsley.

Variations

(a) Use pinto beans or black beans.
(b) Use broccoli, cauliflower, spinach, chard, celery, green beans, parsnips, swede, potatoes, chestnuts.

229 West country casserole

An unusual dish but quite delicious, the sauce should be piquant, slightly clinging but not thick.
 Vegetable oil, Onions (sliced), Carrots (B1), Parsnips (B1), Swedes (C, small), Green peppers (H), Cider sauce (33), Butter beans, Cauliflowers (I, blanched), Mushrooms (button, halves).

To serve

Serve as it is sprinkled with parsley.

Variations

(a) Add a little orange juice and orange zest to the cider sauce for an Elizabethan flavour.

(b) Substitute cider with apple juice and a dash of lemon juice.
(c) Use broccoli, leeks, broad beans, courgettes, celeriac, marrow, mange-tout, potatoes, brussel sprouts, spinach, pumpkin, chunks of apple and slices of orange.

230 Irish stew

I can hear the clamour of outrage, cheek, how can you! Basically, I would suggest that the original Irish stew was only flavoured with the worst bits of lamb; basically, it is a potato casserole.

Vegetable margarine, Onions (sliced), Carrots (B1), Parsnips (B1), Swedes (C), Potatoes (C), Celery (B), Irish sauce (25), Green, brown or speckled lentils, Broccoli (I, partially stir-fried), Brussel sprouts (partially cooked), Mushrooms (flat, sliced).

To serve

Sprinkle with fresh parsley.

Variations

(a) Substitute lentils with aduki beans.
(b) Vary vegetable content as for West country casserole (229).
(c) Add a dessert spoon of mint to the Irish sauce.

231 Macro stew

For the macro-biotics amongst you, here is a stew that is really tasty. Safflower oil, Onions (sliced), Carrots (B1, thin), Green peppers (D, thin), Leeks (A), Hot Pot sauce (27), Aduki beans, Cauliflowers (I, par-cooked), Brussel sprouts (par-cooked), Chinese cabbage (B), Nori seaweed, Miso.

Variations

According to your interpretation of macro-biotics.

Conclusion

It has been difficult to decide what recipes to include in this chapter the variations are so limitless. I hope that the ones I have chosen have been varied enough in concept to show even the reluctant vegetarian that making a casserole is easy. Of course, in every case the sauce is the key to success. There are many many more sauces in Chapter 3 that haven't been mentioned yet. Some of these will appear in the next chapter and some I will leave for you to experiment with. Remember, everything you have done or learned in this chapter will help you in the next.

Possible variations for casseroles and bakes

Feature vegetable	Flavour vegetable	Fruit and bulk	Beans, nuts and flavouring
Aubergines	Onions – Spanish	Apples	Pinto beans
French beans	Onions – Red	Bananas	Red beans
Bobby beans	Onions – English	Grapes	Cashews
Broad beans	Okra	Oranges	Chestnuts
Brussel sprouts	Parsley	Pineapple	Almonds
Broccoli	Potatoes – red	Rice	Peanuts
Chinese Leaf	– white	Barley	Hazelnuts
Chard	– new	Wheat	Sunflower seeds
Carrots	– sweet	Buckwheat	Sesame seeds
Cabbage – green	Peppers – red	Macaroni	Tahini

Cabbage – white	– green	Tagliatelle	Miso
Celery	Chillies	Lasagna	Shoyu
Courgette	Pumpkin	Noodles	Yeastex
Corn	Parsnip	Spaghetti	Peanut butter
Celeriac	Peas	Aduki beans	Tomato paste
Fennel	Snow-peas	Black beans	Seaweed
Ginger	Spinach	Blackeye beans	Coconut
Garlic	Spring onions	Butter beans	
Leeks	Swedes	Chick-peas	
Marrow	Shallots	Flageolet beans	
Mange-tout	Sprouts	Green lentils	
Mushrooms – flat	Tomatoes – cooking	Brown lentils	
Mushrooms – open	Turnips	Speckled lentils	
Mushrooms – cup	Watercress	Haricot beans	

Other variables for casseroles and bakes (try different types of these)

Dried fruits
Other nuts
Sauces
Toppings (for bakes)
Herbs and spices
Thickening agents
Vegan (without dairy produce or honey)
Chopping technique
Alcohol
Oils
Vinegars
Sweetners

Chapter 12

Bakes

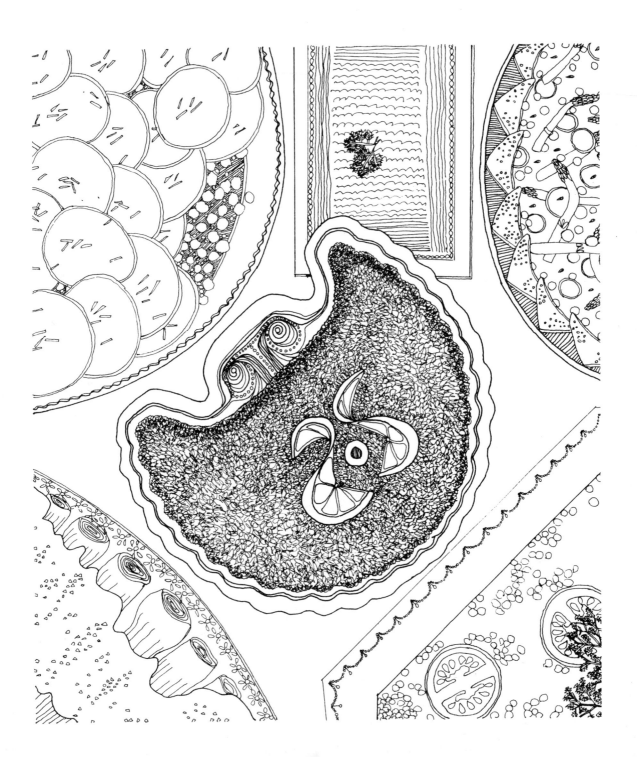

Probably more than any other in the book, this chapter will illustrate vegetarian dishes that are dishes in their own right. Past experience has shown that bakes are by far the most enjoyable and most variable of all savoury vegetarian cookery. Basically, bakes differ from casseroles in that they are always finished off in the oven and usually have a topping. Some bakes are no more than casseroles with a topping as you will see, while others could be nothing other than a bake. Generally, I have included a selection of some of the more popular dishes that spend at least some of their life sitting in an oven. Bakes, to many people, are a more recognizable food form, especially when they have a rich and tasty topping; it is probably because they look so good that even the most reluctant vegetarian would find them immediately appealing (apart, perhaps, from the anomalous quiche). In winter, they are especially satisfying, wholesome, nutritious and tasty too. I think the secret with most bakes is in the topping – choose the right topping, cook it to perfection and it will do miracles for what is underneath.

Equipment required

You will need only something to cook the bake in – attractive ovenware pottery is nice. A grater or blender helps too.

Toppings

Many of the toppings used for bakes are identical to those used for quiches. I refer you to grated cheese (164), cheese and breadcrumbs (au gratin) (165), cheese and blue cheese (166), breadcrumbs (167), cheese, carrot and breadcrumbs (168), cheese with seeds or chopped nuts (169), cheese and herbs (170), cheese and oats (171), pastry (173). If you wish to decorate your topping then, again, use the decorations suggested in (174). Of course there are many more combinations and permutations of even these toppings, so try to develop these ideas further.

In addition to the toppings suitable for quiches, there are many that are only suitable for bakes (unless you want to experiment that is). When choosing a topping it is most important to decide whether it is the best one for the bake, as it is possible to enhance the flavour and texture of the bake with the topping. For instance a spicy bake may benefit from having a light cool yoghurt-based topping. The consistency of the bake is important too – if it is runny it may be in need of a thicker more absorbent topping or a binding topping to hold it together. If it is very thick, then the topping should help lubricate its passage to your stomach. Try to choose a topping that will stay on top, toppings that sink can have a disastrous effect on the final consistency of the bake.

When you have chosen a topping for your bake you must next decide how long it will take to cook and add this time to the overall cooking time of the rest of the bake. Dairy-based toppings should end up a light golden brown, potatoes and pastry should also colour. Crumble toppings are more difficult to judge and will take longer to cook at a medium temperature than perhaps you might suppose. Here are some previously successful toppings. The name of the topping can also lend its name to the bake.

232 Boulangère

Use old potatoes if possible (reds are good all rounders).

Method

Par-boil enough potatoes, drain and allow to cool for 5 minutes. Slice the potatoes into ¼ in thick rounds. Place these on the top of the bake and sprinkle with grated cheese (164). The whole should be baked until the potatoes are tender and the cheese is golden brown (you will need a moderate oven).

Variations

(a) Garlic and herbs – After you have par-cooked the potatoes and sliced them, sautée them in butter or vegetable margarine with crushed garlic and sweet herbs (oregano, basil, marjoram). Season with salt and pepper. The potatoes will now be almost cooked and will therefore take less time in the oven on top of the bake. If gratinating with cheese use a higher temperature oven.

(b) Breadcrumbs – after placing the sliced potatoes on the bake, brush with oil or garlic oil and sprinkle with breadcrumbs (167). This in turn may be sprinkled with herbs and/or gratinated with cheese.

(c) Lyonnaise – proceed as for garlic and herbs (a) but replace the garlic and herbs with finely sliced onion and cook until onions are starting to soften.

(d) À l'anglaise – After carefully placing potatoes on top of the bake, filling any obvious gaps, pour on top any of the dairy-based toppings (236).

Other variations

Use parmesan cheese in addition to cheese or mixed with breadcrumbs. Use mozzarella cheese instead of cheddar or in addition. Use sweet potatoes instead of ordinary potatoes.

233 Mashed potatoes

Use old potatoes (whites are best). Mashed potatoes offer unlimited variations for topping a dish. If you are very clever you can even pipe them on to the top of the bake to make a dish really attractive. Because potatoes have fantastic thickening properties and yet are fairly bland but with some taste, they form the ideal topping for more runny bakes, making the perfect buffer for a really tasty sauce.

Method

Cook the potatoes until soft then mash or blend them with milk and butter until you have achieved a smooth consistency. The variations are all instead of, or in addition to, milk and butter, depending on what overall consistency you want to use. Season with salt and pepper plus nutmeg, chilli, garlic, herbs, shoyu, miso, or tahini.

Variations

(a) Add sour cream, cottage cheese, cream cheese, parmesan, blue cheese, ricotta, yoghurt or cream, grated cheddar cheese or eggs.

(b) Dilute with basic quiche mix (147) or variations thereof.

(c) Separate the eggs and fold in egg yolks with cheese and milk. Whisk the whites until peaking and fold in to potato mixture just before spreading on top of the bake – cook in a moderately hot oven.

(d) Substitute mashed potatoes wholly or partially with mashed swedes and proceed as before (swedes 'need' nutmeg).

234 Pastry toppings

Bakes topped with pastry obviously make pies. Pie bases may be dry or moist served with a sauce separately or already have the sauce in them. Pies which contain a sauce make the pastry cook a lot slower than pies that are only moistened. Most casserole recipes may be turned into pies with the addition of a pastry topping.

Method

Use recipe for vegan pastry (143) as it rolls out well, but other pastry recipes may be tried. Pour the base of the pie into a dish (it may or may not be lined with pastry also). Roll out the pastry until reasonably thin then roll it up around the rolling pin. Carefully unravel this over the pie tin and trim around the edges. You may wish to pinch the edges for decoration. Use an egg and milk glaze (133) and decorate with pastry shapes made out of the trimmings. If your pie tin is rather wide place a pastry pigeon in the middle before covering with pastry.

Variations

(a) Use different pastries or simple breads to suit the filling. For instance a Mexican bean filling is best covered with a corn bread pastry (137) to make Tamale Pie (250).
(b) Cut the pastry into strips and weave an attractive topping.

Special point

Pastry toppings are cooked when they sound hollow on tapping, but still give a little. If glazed they should be a light golden brown colour. Dry-based pies will take 20 minutes to cook in a moderate oven, whereas wet-based pies take at least 40 minutes in a slightly cooler oven.

235 Noggin toppings

For want of a better description, these toppings are made with a basic quiche mix (147) or variations thereof. Because they are wet and their base will also often be wet, they do take at least 45 minutes to set in a moderate to high oven. When using a noggin topping try to create a flat and non-porous surface on which to pour the topping mixture, otherwise, it may become absorbed into the base, creating more of an omelette than a bake – if this does happen don't worry too much it will still be delicious. Use potatoes or large slices of aubergines/courgettes or a thick layer of spinach or cabbage, perhaps even a bean pâté to create this surface. Soufflé variations of noggin toppings are particularly spectacular. Add to and decorate noggin toppings in the same way as you would a quiche.

236 À la creme

These toppings are really a novel way of serving a bake that needs a sauce, with the sauce, rather than serving the sauce separately. Hot pâtés or roasts are particularly well suited to these types of topping.

Method

Choose a suitable sauce for the base of the bake. Particularly good are the thick bechamel (34)-based sauces, especially tamari sauce (35) and cheese sauce (38). These toppings may also be gratinated with cheese for added colour. Cooking time should be sufficient to heat everything thoroughly without drying out the sauce or base. Any gratin top should be brown – use a medium oven.

237 Cobblers

An unusual topping that is good for fairly moist but not runny bakes.

Method

Make a scone mixture (141), cut into rounds and place on top of the base so that the entire surface is covered. Bake in a moderate oven until the scones are cooked.

Variation

Use different scone mixes – gratinate if you wish.

238 Crumble toppings

Very simple and very 'ethnic' toppings, but can be stodgy so don't overdo them. Best used with warming wintery bakes – these toppings have the advantage of being vegan. Cream sauces in the bakes can make them too filling with a crumble topping so use tomato, wine or simple sauces.

Method

Mix mainly regular oats, some jumbos, sesame seeds, sunflower seeds, poppy seeds, chopped nuts, breadcrumbs, flour with vegetable oil or vegetable margarine, season and flavour with herbs and spices. Spread evenly but not too thickly over the surface of the bake. Cook in a moderate oven until all ingredients are crumbly and starting to colour.

Variations

Add cheese.

You can probably think of a lot more toppings yourself now. The rest of the chapter will be devoted to recipes themselves. Bakes are usually served as a main meal; if you wish you can reduce the quantities in some of them and serve them as starters.

Baked casseroles

These bakes are simply casseroles with a topping. We will approach them in the same way as we did casseroles.

239 Boston bean crumble

A warming wintery dish.
Vegetable margarine, Onion (sliced), Carrots (B1, thin), Green peppers (H), Boston sauce (24), Black beans, Courgettes (B, medium), partially stir-fried), Cauliflower (I, blanched), Mushrooms (whole or halved buttons). Topping – Crumble (238).

240 Courgette and green pepper noggin

A hint of the Caribbean.
Coconut oil, Red onions (sliced), Sweet potatoes (C), Pineapple (C), Aubergine (A1, small), Creole sauce (7), Garlic (minced), Green pepper (C), Courgettes (B1, medium, partially stir-fried), Sweetcorn (optional). Topping – Noggin (235), especially good with sour cream or yoghurt noggin.

241 Aubergine and mushroom scallopini

Very Italian.
Olive oil, Onions (sliced), Red peppers (H), Aubergines (B, medium), Scallopini Sauce (19), Courgettes (B1, medium, partially stir-fried), Mushrooms (whole or halved button).
Topping – Cheese (164) or other cheese variations – parmesan is a good addition. Could decorate with slices of tomato too.

Simple bakes

Although very simple these are also extremely delicious. They are similar to baked casseroles, except that they rely more heavily on a mouth-watering topping.

242 Cauliflower and lentil au gratin

Serves 4

Stage	Ingredients	Quantity	Method
1	Vegetable oil	50 ml	Heat the oil in a deep pan and add the leeks, stir-fry until
	Leeks (G)	2 medium	softening.
2	Shoyu	1 tbsp	Add the shoyu, coat leeks.
3	Béchamel sauce	¾ l	Heat the sauce separately and add the leeks.
4	Green lentils	400 g	stir in the lentils. Add the cauliflower and mushrooms.
	(cooked)		Remove from the heat and pour into bake tray.
5	Cauliflower (I, blanched)	1 large	
	Mushrooms (button, whole raw)	120 g	
6	Cheese and breadcrumbs (165)	120 g	Sprinkle evenly over the top. Bake in an oven at 200°C for 30 minutes or until topping is browned.

Variations

(a) Good with any béchamel-based sauce.
(b) Vary topping – cheesy flavour is always nice.

(c) Use aduki beans instead of lentils, vary vegetable content.

243 Scallopped vegetables

Serves 4

Stage	Ingredients	Quantity	Method
1	Vegetable oil	50 ml	Heat the oil in a deep pan. Add the vegetables and stir-fry for 5
	Onions (sliced)	2 medium	minutes with the ginger.
	Celery (B)	4 sticks	
	White cabbage (H)	1 small	
	Fresh ginger	20 g	
2	Tamari sauce (35)	¾ l	Bring the sauce to the boil gently and add to the vegetables.
3	Sweetcorn (frozen)	250 g	Stir in the sweetcorn and mushrooms, but do not cook any
	Mushrooms (open cup, sliced)	250 g	longer. Turn into bake tray.
4	Cheese and breadcrumbs (165)	120 g	Sprinkle evenly over top. Bake in an oven at 200°C for 30 minutes.

Variations

Use carrots, broad beans, peppers, Chinese leaf, cauliflower, broccoli and green beans.

244 Leeks and roots au fromage

Serves 4

An unbelievably economical yet delicious dish, only takes 5 minutes to prepare too! It is important to slice the root vegetables really thinly, about the only thing a food processor can do better than you apart from blending.

Stage	Ingredients	Quantity	Method
1	Vegetable oil	50 ml	Heat the oil, stir-fry the vegetables with the mixed herbs until
	Carrots (A thin)		starting to soften. Add the shoyu and allow the vegetables
	Parsnips (A thin)		to absorb it.
	Swedes (A thin)		
2	Shoyu		

3	Leeks (B medium)	450 g	Add the leeks and continue stir-frying for about 7 minutes.
4	Tamari sauce (35) (optional)	¼ l	Add the sauce and mix in well; remove from heat.
5	Mushrooms (flat, sliced)	90 g	Stir in the mushrooms and pour mixture into bake tray. Try to keep the root vegetables flat.
6	Cheese and sunflower seeds (169)	120 g	Sprinkle evenly over the top and bake at 190°C for 40 minutes or until root vegetables are tender and the topping is golden brown.

Variations

(a) Use cauliflower instead of leeks.
(b) Emphasize mushrooms.
(c) Use more sauce.
(d) Use different cheese-based topping or make it à la creme.

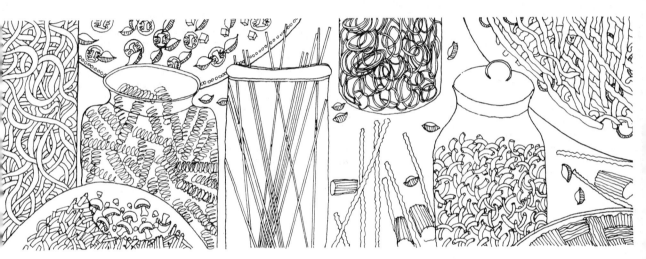

Pasta bakes

Pasta bakes are always extremely popular. There are several kinds of pasta you can buy; we use wholewheat or spinach. To cook it, simply immerse it in plenty of boiling salted water for about 15 minutes. Test it after 10 minutes, it should be edible yet retain some texture (i.e. *al dente*). Overcooked pasta is soft and pappy. There are many, many variations – just think Italian. Again, for vegetables, use courgettes, green peppers, tomatoes, red onions, garlic, aubergines, olives, spinach, chillies, green beans, mushrooms, corn, broccoli. For herbs, use oregano, bay leaf, basil, marjoram, parsley, and thyme. For spices, use chilli, cayenne and coriander. For dairy produce, use mozzarella, cream cheese, ricotta cheese, parmesan cheese and gruyere. Use olive oil and lemon juice – imagine you are on holiday in Italy.

245 Lasagna al Vittoria   **Serves 4**

Named after the best vegetarian chef I ever knew; this was one of her specialities. Basically, a series of layers of pasta, sauce, vegetables, pasta, sauce, vegetables, etc.

Stage	Ingredients	Quantity	Method
1	Olive oil	50 ml	*Heat the oil in a pan. Partially stir-fry the vegetables and add the tomato sauce; then stir in garlic and oregano. Set to one side to cool.*
	Onion (sliced)	1 medium	
	Green pepper (C)	1 large	
	Aubergines (B1)	1 large	
	Courgettes	2 large	
	Tomato sauce A	½ litre	
	Garlic	4 cloves	
	Oregano	1 tbsp	
2	Béchamel sauce (34)	½ l	*take the béchamel sauce from the heat then beat in the eggs, parmesan and chilli.*
	Eggs	2	
	Parmesan cheese	1 tbsp	
	Chilli (optional)	1 tbsp	
3	Lasagna, cooked	10 slices	*Grease a baking tin, then line it with 3 strips of lasagna, pour a third of the vegetable mixture on to the lasagna and sprinkle with a third of the cheese, cover with another layer of lasagna slices and repeat the process twice. Finally pour the béchamel sauce on and another sprinkling of cheese. Bake in a medium hot oven until golden brown and the egg béchamel has just set. Be careful not to overcook.*
	Grated cheese	250 g	

Variations

(a) Alter the tomato mixture and substitute with other sauces perhaps. Spinach is nice, as is buckwheat.
(b) Replace the lasagna with thinly sliced vegetables, (as in recipe 244) for a lighter dish.

(c) Use other types of lasagna – spinach lasagna is excellent. Note – Served in individual cocottes this makes a good starter.

246 Macaroni con spinacci   **Serves 4**

Another simple yet delicious dish; it takes about 10 minutes to prepare.

Stage	Ingredients	Quantity	Method
1	Butter	30 g	*Heat the butter in a deep pan and add the onions; allow them to soften before adding the spinach.*
	Onions (sliced)	1 medium	
	Spinach (chopped)	450 g	
2	Cheese sauce, thick	¾ l	*When the cheese sauce is hot add it to the spinach and stir in the garlic.*
	Garlic, minced	5 cloves	
3	Macaroni, cooked	300 g	*Remove the mixture from the heat and stir in the cooked macaroni, pour mixture into baking tray.*
7	Cheese and breadcrumbs and parmesan	120 g	*Sprinkle evenly over the top of bake. Bake in a moderate oven for approximately 15 minutes (enough time to let the cheese gratinate).*

247 Aubergine and sour cream tagliatelle

Serves 4

Sour cream and aubergines were just made for each other.

Stage	Ingredients	Quantity	Method
1	Vegetable oil	50 ml	*Heat the oil in a deep pan. Add the onions and allow to soften.*
	Onions (sliced)	1 large	*Add the aubergine and garlic and cook for another 5 minutes.*
	Aubergines (Bl)	1 large	
	Garlic	5 cloves (or more)	
2	Béchamel sauce (34)	½ l	*Make a light béchamel, remove from heat and fold in sour*
	Sour cream	¼ l	*cream and eggs. Adjust seasoning.*
	Eggs	2	
	Salt and pepper	To taste	
3	Tagliatelle (cooked)	500 g	*Add the tagliatelle to the aubergines and pour the sauce over them. Stir in well and pour into baking dish.*
4	Mozzarella cheese, breadcrumbs and parmesan	180 g	*Sprinkle evenly with topping and bake in a moderate oven for 30 minutes.*

Variations
(a) Vary vegetable content.
(b) Vary type of pasta used.

(c) Use tomato-based sauce or one with alcohol.

248 Pastitsio

This is a Greek dish in origin and uses an unlikely combination of lentils and pasta – they really go well together. Don't ever use beans with pasta – they are far too heavy; lentils have the right size and texture. Basically, follow the same recipe as for lasagna al Vittoria (245), but replace the lasagna with equal quantities of macaroni and green, brown or speckled lentils. Also add 1 teaspoon of coriander to the tomato sauce.

Pies

These are pastry pies and they are wonderfully versatile. Pies may have pastry underneath, pastry on top, may be shaped into individual pastries or tarts, or rolled up like welly rolls (100). They can be rather filling so do provide a sauce somewhere along the line.

For some dishes you may wish to use potato pastry, buckwheat pastry or cheese pastry – depending on what overall effect you want to achieve. Try adding sesame seeds or sunflower seeds, chopped nuts and herbs to your existing pastry recipe for flavour and decoration. Otherwise, decorate the pastry like bread (after glazing) with poppy seeds, sesame/sunflower seeds, wheatmeal, mustard seed and fenugreek. Here are two recipes for pies; one is a conventional 'dry' pie served with separate sauce and the other is a 'conceptual' pie where the pastry crust is designed to complement the casserole base.

249 Di's veggie pie

Serves 4

Di is another of the great vegetarian cooks who trained under the creator of Lasagna al Vittoria.

Stage	Ingredients	Quantity	Method
1	Vegetable oil	50 ml	*Heat the oil and add the onions and carrots. Cook for 5 minutes then add the cabbage and herbs. Try to keep the vegetables of uniform size. Add the mushrooms and shoyu and cook for 1 more minute; remove from heat.*
	Onion (G)	1 large	
	Carrots (G)	2 medium	
	Green cabbage (G)	1 medium	
	Mushrooms (button, halved)	120 g	
	Mixed herbs	1 dsp	
	Shoyu	1 tbsp	
2	Lentils, brown	300 g	*Add the lentils to the mixture, adjust the seasoning and turn into a greased pie dish.*
3	Vegan pastry (143)	225 g	*Roll the pastry out as thin as possible, but so that it is still manageable. Roll it up on the rolling pin and out over the pie tin.*
4	Soft glaze (133)	25 ml	*Brush surface with glaze and sprinkle with sesame seeds. Bake in a hot oven for 15 minutes until pastry is golden brown and hollow but yielding.*
	Sesame seeds		

To serve

Serve with a really tasty cream sauce, i.e. parsley (40), mushroom (39), onion (41) and variations, white wine (46) and variations, cheese (38), tahini (36), tamari (35), or with any piquant sauce.

Variations

(a) Vary vegetable ingredient, e.g. broccoli, leeks, courgettes, spinach and cauliflower.

(b) Use green/speckled lentils or aduki beans.

(c) Vary the pastry topping; for instance, use cheese pastry to top a ratatouille base (209).

250 Tamale pie

Serves 4

This is a Mexican dish in which the pie crust is integral with the pie filling; it is almost like having a chilli with a tortilla.

Stage	Ingredients	Quantity	Method
1	Mexican chilli beans (213)	1½ l	*Prepare as for a casserole but do not cook thoroughly as this dish spends half an hour in the oven. Also make it slightly thicker than it would be in a casserole.*
2	Cold water	400 ml	*Blend these ingredients together to form a thick but smooth paste and spread over surface of casserole.*
	Cornmeal	350 g	
	Salt	1 tsp	
	Chilli	½ tsp	
3	Grated cheese	120 g	*Sprinkle over the surface and bake in a moderate to low oven for 30 minutes or until corn pastry is cooked.*

Potato topped bakes

These bakes are made really substantial with the addition of a potato topping, and they are incredibly popular too. Remember to adjust the consistency of the potato topping to suit the base of the bake underneath.

251 Shepherdess pie

Serves 4

Stage	Ingredients	Quantity	Method
1	Vegetable oil	50 ml	Heat the oil and stir-fry the root vegetables with parsley until quite hot. Add the shoyu, season and add the leeks. Cook for another five minutes on a medium heat. Remove from heat.
	Onion (sliced)	1 medium	
	Carrot (Bl small)	1 medium	
	Parsnip (Bl small)	1 small	
	Swede (C small)	1 small	
	Parsley (chopped)	1 bunch	
	Shoyu	1 tbsp	
	Leeks (B)	450 g	
2	Béchamel sauce	1 l	Add the béchamel sauce to the vegetables, then stir in the aduki beans. Adjust the seasoning and turn the whole lot into your baking dish leaving room for the potatoes.
3	Aduki beans, cooked	250 g	
	Salt and pepper	To taste	
4	Mashed potatoes (234)	500 g	Spread the potatoes evenly over the surface being careful not to press too hard. Piping the potatoes is a particularly good way of avoiding this.
5	Grated cheese (164)	120 g	Sprinkle over the potatoes and place in oven at 350°F (180°C, Gas mark 4), for about 10 minutes or until the potatoes have browned.

Variations

(a) As for Cauliflower and Lentil au gratin (242).
(b) Use a tomato-based sauce for the vegetables, or a tomato and alcohol-based sauce.

252 Moussaka

Serves 4

A lovely Greek dish open to several interpretations. Again we have found the traditional lamb is not really worth thinking about – the dish is great without it.

Stage	Ingredients	Quantity	Method
1	Olive oil	50 ml	Heat the oil in a deep pan, add the onions and garlic and cook gently until onions are softening. Add the green peppers and courgettes and cook for 5 minutes.
	Onions (sliced)	1 medium	
	Garlic (crushed)	5 cloves	
	Green peppers (H)	1 large	
	Courgettes (B thin)	250 g	
2	Oregano	1 heaped tbsp	Finally stir in the oregano and tomato paste.
	Tomato paste	1 tbsp	
3	Aubergine (A thick)		Oil a bake tray and bake the aubergines in a hot oven until starting to soften, but not soft.
4			Line another bake tray with some of the cooked aubergines then add a layer of the other vegetables. Repeat this process until all the mixture is used up.

5	Mashed potatoes (233)	500 g	*Add the quiche mix to the potato mixture and perhaps a little*
	Quiche mix	200 ml	*yoghurt or sour cream, but don't make it too runny. Spread*
			evenly over and bake.
6	Grated cheese (164)	120 g	*Sprinkle with grated cheese and quickly bake in the oven for 10*
			minutes at 190°C.

Variations

(a) Use boulangère topping (232) instead of mashed potatoes.

(b) Use boulangère topping in alternate layers with the aubergine.

(c) Substitute green or brown lentils for part of the vegetable bulk.

(d) Experiment with different additions to mashed potato and boulangère toppings.

253 Cauliflower and courgette boulangère   Serves 4

Good boulangères need plenty of rich sauce.

Stage	Ingredients	Quantity	Method
1	Vegetable margarine	50 ml	*Stir-fry the vegetables until partially cooked.*
	Onion (red, sliced)	1 medium	
	Carrot (A, medium)	1 medium	
	Green peppers	2 medium	
2	Chausseur sauce	1 l	*Add the sauce and remove from the heat.*
3	Cauliflower (I)	1 large	*Blanch the cauliflower and partially stir-fry the courgettes*
4	Courgettes (B)	450 g	*before adding to the rest of the vegetables. Pour vegetable*
			mixture into bake tray leaving room for topping.
5	Boulangère topping	500 g	*Place the potatoes evenly over the top of the bake base. Brush*
			with oil.
6	Cheese and breadcrumbs	120 g	*Sprinkle over potatoes and bake in a medium oven for about*
			40 minutes.

Variations

(a) Boulangères are best with alcohol-based sauces, or thin but creamy white sauces.

(b) Vary the vegetable content and topping.

Hot pâtés

I have already mentioned in Chapter 6 that many of the pâtés may be served hot as pâtés or loaves. Like cold pâtés, hot pâtés use a fairly bland base on which to build flavours. Most of the remainder of the recipes in this chapter involve what is really a hot pâté in one form or another. Many people find a dish composed entirely of a pâté too filling. The next recipe is really the transitionary phase between a hot pâté and a more conventional bake, alleviating the bulk of the pâté with stir-fried vegetables and an intrinsic sauce.

254 Blackeye bean and mushroom pâté à la creme

Serves 4

Stage	Ingredients	Quantity	Method
1	Vegetable oil	50 ml	Heat the oil in a deep pan and stir-fry the vegetables until almost cooked. Add the shoyu and tip the ingredients into a bake tray; spread evenly.
	Carrots (A thin)	2 medium	
	Swede (A1 thin)	1 medium	
	Broccoli (I, optional)	240 g	
	Shoyu	1 tbsp	
2	Vegetable oil	50 ml	Heat the oil in a pan and add the onions, mushrooms and herbs; then stir-fry until onions are soft.
	Onion (sliced)	1 medium	
	Mushrooms (sliced)	240 g	
	Mixed herbs	1 dsp	
3	Blackeye beans, well cooked	700 g	Add the vegetables to the blackeye beans and mash together. If you have an electric beater this is best, a blender will do but loses some of the texture. If the mixture is too thick add stock to moisten. Season.
	Salt and pepper	To taste	
4			Spread the pâté over the broccoli and root vegetables evenly.
5	Béchamel sauce	½ l	Pour béchamel on top of pâté and sprinkle with breadcrumbs. Bake for 40 minutes at 180°C or until coloured. Be careful not to overcook.
	Breadcrumbs	120 g	

Variations

(a) Use different pâtés.
(b) Use different vegetable bases.
(c) Use different sauces (white ones are best).
This pâté à la creme is basically a layer bake and once you have accepted the idea of introducing layers into hot pâtés the variations are enormous. Next is a layer bake in its own right; you will see how its construction is similar to a lasagna.

255 Buckwheat and cabbage layer bake

Serves 4

This is basically a buckwheat pâté (which is incidentally excellent as a cold pâté), layered with white cabbage (stir-fried or steamed slightly), and finished off with a sauce and cheese on top. If you wish you can serve the sauce separately.

Stage	Ingredients	Quantity	Method
1	Vegetable oil	50 ml	Heat the oil in a pan. Stir-fry the vegetables and garlic until onion going soft. Add the shoyu, chilli and sugar/honey and continue to cook gently.
	Onions (G)	1 large	
	Green peppers (G)	1 medium	
	Garlic (crushed)	3 cloves	
	Mushrooms (flat, rough chopped)	180 g	
	Shoyu	2 tbsp	
	Chilli	1 tsp	
	Sugar/honey	1 tsp/2 tsp	
2	Peanut butter (smooth)	2 tbsp	Stir in the peanut butter and tomato paste to coat the mixture well.
	Tomato paste	1 tbsp	
3	Buckwheat (cooked)	450 g	Remove from heat and add the buckwheat. Mix in well and add the grated cheese.
4	Grated cheese, optional	120 g	
5	White cabbage	1 small	Remove the core of the cabbage and steam until leaves can be removed easily.
6			Grease a bake tin and line it with white cabbage leaves (they may need to be cut a little). Next, add a layer of buckwheat mixture, repeat process twice leaving a layer of cabbage on top.
7	Aurore sauce (225)	½ l	Pour the sauce over the cabbage and sprinkle with cheese. Bake in a moderate oven until cheese has gratinated.
	Grated cheese	120 g	

Variations

As I have said the variations are enormous; here are a few.

(a) Different fillings – barley, rice, millet, cracked wheat, nuts, pulses, beans etc.

(b) Different layers – lasagna, sliced root vegetables.

(c) Different sauces – choose any in Chapter 3.

(d) Different toppings – see pp. 117–18.

Roasts

Roasts are much abused archetypal food of the average vegetarian – or so some reluctant vegetarians like to believe. It is not surprising they have a bad name, because so often they are dull and lifeless, served without a sauce and barely warm – they can be very hard going. A good roast must not only be full of flavour itself, it must be reasonably moist, properly cooked and served piping hot with a suitably tasty sauce for lubrication. Roasts can also form the fillings of layer bakes, stuffings for numerous vegetables and shaped they make excellent burgers, rissoles and balls. For roasts are basically hot pâtés again; they require a bulky base but it is important to make them as light as you can. There is a temptation to always use up leftovers in roasts and while this is definitely a valid option, care should be taken to adjust the texture and flavour of any leftovers to suit the roast – not the other way around. The ideal roast will have a light, but truly tasty background, interspersed with definitely textured ingredients.

Soufflés

Any roast may become a soufflé by the same technique as that outlined for loaves in Recipe 95. While these soufflés in no way compare for lightness with traditional soufflés, they are definitely a lot lighter than the average roast.

The addition of eggs to roasts is not necessary, except again they do make them lighter; vegans may substitute tofu for eggs. Cheese is an option which your ethics will, of course, decide. Many other forms of dairy produce can be added to roasts but most become lost in the overall flavour.

256 Nut roast with xavier sauce

Serves 4

This recipe uses peanuts (they are the cheapest nuts), but any selection of nuts will do.

Stage	Ingredients	Quantity	Method
1	Vegetable oil	50 ml	*Heat the oil in a pan and stir-fry the vegetables and herbs, add the spinach last and then the shoyu. Remove from the heat.*
	Onion (G)	1 large	
	Carrots (G)	2 medium	
	Parsnip (G)	1 large	
	Mixed herbs	1 tbsp	
	Spinach (chopped)	225 g	
	Shoyu	2 tbsp	
2	Breadcrumbs	350 g	*Fold in the breadcrumbs and peanuts and eggs. If you don't use eggs, the mixture may be a little dry. Moisten with stock or additional shoyu. Adjust seasoning. Turn into oiled bake tray and smooth into corners. Bake for 45 minutes in a moderate oven.*
	Peanuts, roasted (grated)	150 g	
	Eggs	3	
	Salt and pepper	To taste	
3	Xavier sauce (49)	½ l	*Heat the sauce and serve it with the roast.*

Special points

1 When the roast is ready it will have coloured and will be firm to touch – but not hard.
2 Try to keep the size of the vegetables fairly uniform – this helps cooking and appearance.

Variations

Use millet or Bulgar in place of breadcrumbs; vary the herbs and vegetables; vary the sauce with which it is served. Tomato and celery sauce (15) is particularly nice with roasts, especially when it has been thickened naturally.

257 Barley roast with tahini sauce

Serves 4

Make sure you cook the barley well for barley roast, otherwise your jaw will get more than its usual exercise.

Stage	Ingredients	Quantity	Method
1	Vegetable oil	50 ml	*Heat the oil in a pan. Stir-fry the onions and carrots. When onions soften add the rest of the vegetables. When all the vegetables are hot add the shoyu and parsley, remove from heat.*
	Onion (G)	1 medium	
	Carrot (G)	1 medium	
	Green pepper (G)	1 large	
	Flat mushrooms (G)	225 g	
	Parsley (chopped)	3 sprigs	
	Shoyu		
2	Barley (cooked)	450 g	*Stir in the barley and adjust seasoning.*
	Salt and pepper	To taste	
3	Cheese (grated)	225 g	*Add the cheese and eggs. If mixture is too dry add a little stock.*
	Eggs	2	

4			*Pour mixture into oiled bake tray.*
5	Grated cheese	120 g	*Sprinkle with grated cheese and decorate with tomatoes. Bake*
	Tomatoes (A thin)	2 medium	*in a moderate oven for 35 minutes until gratinated.*
6	Tahini sauce	½ l	*Serve roast with tahini sauce.*

Variations

Vary vegetable content and serve with the sauce of your choice.

258 Wheatberry roast with cheese sauce (38)

As for barley roast (257) but substituting wheatberry for barley.

Variation

Add tomatoes and courgettes (diced) to the vegetable base.

259 Rice roast with mushroom sauce (39)

As for barley roast (257) but, if serving with mushroom sauce, substitute spinach for mushrooms in the recipe.

260 Chestnut roast with red wine sage sauce

As for nut roast (256) but substitute peanuts with chest-nuts. For sauce add sage to the red wine sauce (32) at the stir-fry stage. This dish is an excellent Christmas dish.

261 Lentil roast with leek sauce (41b)

As for barley roast (257) but substitute barley with lentils (use green or brown lentils)

262 Channa roast with dahl sauce (22b)

As for barley roast (257) but substitute chick-peas that have been mashed or blended for the barley and do not use a cheese topping.

263 Mushroom roast with tamari gravy

The best of all pure vegetable roasts.

Stage	Ingredients	Quantity	Method
1	Vegetable margarine	30 g	*Melt the margarine in a pan and add the vegetables, herbs and*
	Onion (G)	1 large	*chilli. Cook gently for 10 minutes then add the shoyu.*
	Red or green pepper (C medium)	1 large	
	Mixed herbs	1 tbsp	
	Chilli	Pinch	
	Shoyu	1 tbsp	

2	Mushrooms (thin sliced)	250 g	*Stir in the mushrooms but retain a third for later. Cook until mushrooms are soft. Remove from heat.*
3	Breadcrumbs	150 g	*Mix in the breadcrumbs and two-thirds of the cheese and the rest of the mushrooms.*
	Cheese (grated)	125 g	
4	Egg (optional)	1	*If the mixture is dry add the egg.*
5	Tomato (thin sliced)		*Pour mixture into greased bake tin and sprinkle with the rest of the grated cheese and decorate with slices of tomato and mushrooms. Bake for 20 minutes in a moderate oven or until cheese is cooked.*
6	Tamari gravy (35)	½ l	*Serve with tamari gravy.*

Variations
Vary the sauce and the topping.

Balls, burgers and rissoles

These are really created in the same way as roasts but, if anything, should be slightly less moist. They must, however, bind together well. A ball can be a burger and can be a rissole, it depends upon what shape you make them and how you cook them. Shape them by hand or with a spoon to make individual portions of 180 g–220 g. They may then be left as they are, brushed with oil or an egg wash, or even egg wash followed by a coating of breadcrumbs or regular oats. You can then bake them, grill them, shallow or deep fry them. They are best served with a tasty sauce or relish, on their own as a starter or with a salad or hot vegetables as a main course. Use any of the roast recipes to make balls, burgers or rissoles. Here are a couple of specially nice variations.

264 Soya burgers

Possibly the best way to eat soya beans; they are also vegan.

Stage	Ingredients	Quantity	Method
1	Vegetable oil	1 ml	*Heat the oil and add the onion, celery and garlic, cook until almost soft. Then add the shoyu.*
	Onion (G)	1 medium	
	Celery (G fine)	1 stick	
	Garlic (minced)	5 cloves	
	Shoyu	1 ml	
2	Tahini	2 tbsp	*Add the tahini and stir in well.*
3	Breadcrumbs	100 g	*Remove from heat and add the breadcrumbs and soya beans. Allow to cool. Shape into four rounds, burger-shaped. (It is easier if you coat your hands in flour.) Brush with oil and bake for 15 minutes, fry for 10 minutes or deep fry for 5 minutes*
	Soya beans (cooked and mashed)	400 g	

Variations

(a) Substitute soya beans with lentils (brown or green).
(b) Substitute soya beans with adukis.
(c) Substitute soya beans with tofu for tofu burgers.
(d) Add chopped spinach to onions and celery.
(e) Substitute breadcrumbs with wheatgerm.
(f) Use sage, thyme, parsley for flavour.

(g) Add an egg instead of tahini.
(h) Add cheese to the mixture.
(i) Use recipe for buckwheat pâté in buckwheat layer bake (255) to make buckwheat balls – coat in breadcrumbs.
(j) Use recipe for nut roast to make nut rissoles.

Stuffed Vegetables

Choose any of the recipes for roasts and burgers to form the stuffing for a suitable vegetable. When you have prepared the space for the stuffing, simply fill it with the chosen recipe. You can then if you wish gratinate it with cheese or cheese and breadcrumbs.

265 Stuffed peppers

Red or green peppers may be used for this recipe.
To prepare: thinly slice off the stalk end of the pepper and scoop out the pips. Don't lose the end you have sliced off as this will make an attractive topping to the pepper. Fill

the pepper well with the stuffing. Sprinkle cheese on the top and a slice of tomato. Return the stalk end to its rightful place. Now repeat the process for the rest of your peppers. Choose a pan that will hold all the peppers packed tightly together. When they are firmly in position pour boiling water or stock into the pan carefully avoiding the tops of the peppers. Cook on top of the stove for 10 minutes before placing the peppers into a medium hot oven for another 20–30 minutes (depending on their size). Peppers should be tender. Serve with the sauce of your choice – spicy ones are nice.

266 Stuffed marrows

If extremely large, cut marrows into rings and remove seeds. Blanch for a few minutes in boiling water. Smaller marrows may be cut in half lengthwise before scooping out the pips. Younger marrows do not need to be blanched. Fill the hole where the pips were with the stuffing of your choice and proceed as for peppers. Make sure white flesh is tender before serving. Good with most sauces.

267 Stuffed tomatoes

Big (beef) tomatoes are best. As for peppers, remember to retain stalk end. Tomatoes only take 20 minutes to cook. Garnish with parsley.

268 Stuffed cabbage

As for Buckwheat and Cabbage Layer Bake (255) but keep the cabbage leaves whole and use them as a receptacle for the stuffing. Large leaves are best, but it is possible to overlap 2 or 3 smaller leaves with the same effect. Sprinkle the stuffing with grated cheese and decorate with a slice of tomato or mushroom. Fold the leaves over the top to make a complete parcel. Coat the bottom of a bake tray with a little tomato sauce (A) (5) and arrange the cabbage parcels in it. Bake in a moderate oven for 30 minutes. Serve with a really tangy sauce like tomato and celery (15).

269 Stuffed pancakes

Make a pancake using recipe 139 and fill it with a selection of stir-fried vegetables (177). Beansprouts, peppers, mushrooms, water chestnuts are especially nice. Sprinkle with cheese and fold the pancake over. Make sure there is no excess liquid. Bake in a hot oven for 5 minutes before serving with the sauce of your choice – cheesy white wine (46b) is really good.

Chapter 13

Sweets

Introduction

Sweets are probably the one part of the menu that everyone, even those of you who are still reluctant, may be interested in. All sweets are or can be vegetarian; they can also be extremely sickly and stodgy. We try to make sweets that are more wholesome by using natural ingredients as far as we can, though not to the detriment of the quality of the end product. It is possible to adjust conventional recipes and ingredients with that aim in mind without losing any of the overall direction of the dish. Successful sweet cookery relies heavily on obeying basic formulae, but always remember it is possible to alter a formula to suit your own ends and adapt a dish with your own tastes in mind, so long as whatever you adjust is compensated for in one way or another.

If you are interested in using less refined ingredients for preparing sweets then you will be amply rewarded in terms of taste and the benefit felt through your diet. White flours, white sugars, flavourings, chemicals and other more conventionally used ingredients sit heavily in your stomach and contain no real goodness. However, in order to use unrefined ingredients successfully you will have to make a few changes in the way you organize your kitchen and the sort of ingredients you use. So the first part of this chapter will be devoted to the ingredients and how best to use them.

Equipment required

Whisk (manual or electric), sieve (the round, flat ones that look like a drum are best), baking tins and flan tins, baking sheets, metal spoons, and wooden spoons, spice mills, a blender, grater, mixing bowls, rolling pin, pastry knife, measuring jugs/spoons/cups, grease-proof paper, muslin, tinfoil, pastry brush.

Alternative ingredients

1 Flours

We have already discussed flour to some extent in the section on pastry and recipes for pastry will be referred to Chapter 8. For sponges it is best to sift 100% wholewheat flour before use as this will help create a lighter sponge. Extremely light sponges can be made by sifting and then making up the quantity of flour required with soya or cornflour. Sponges made with wholewheat flour have a light brown colour, rather like conventional coffee cake. If you wish, use un-bleached white flour, although personally I prefer the flavour of the wholewheat flour.

2 *Sweetners*

This is always the most controversial subject in wholefood cookery. Basically, all sweetners are refined in some way and all sweet things are bad for you. The only true natural sweetners are fruits. However, it is impossible to make a successful light sponge for instance, without using a refined sweetner, so you have to make a series of decisions.

(a) *'If I want to use sugar I will use the best, least refined, which is demerera.'* Demerera is granulated and will need the presence of heat to cream with butter or margarine properly, e.g. for the base of a sponge. Sugar is also by far the cheapest sweetner so you may decide to use it for economic reasons. However, when using sugar in conjunction with natural sweetners like fresh sweet fruit, the amount you use can be reduced substantially, so that the overall flavour is of the fruit and not the sweetner.

(b) *'If I don't like the idea of using sugar in any form, can I use honey?'* Honey is more expensive than sugar, but there are many varieties to choose from, each with a different flavour. Some honeys have so strong a flavour that, if you are not careful, it may dominate the dish. It is best to use clear honey as this is semi-fluid already. By warming it before use you will find it easier to measure, and to cream. Sponges made with honey are usually heavier and moister but will keep longer. Store honey in a tightly sealed jar in a dark cool place. Honey is a liquid so, in order to use it most successfully, reduce the amount of liquid stated in the recipe to compensate for the volume of honey.

Remember, although honey is better for you than sugar, it is still not good for you. But don't worry too much about things that aren't good for you, just make them as wholesome as possible. The same principle applies to honey as it does to sugar, where you can supplement the sweetners of a dish with natural fruit do so. (Genuine maple syrup is a good alternative to honey).

(c) *'Alternatively, may I use molasses or malt?'* These are less expensive than honey and may be used in the same way; they have the added advantage of being less refined. However, they have extremely strong flavours and cannot be used in a sweet that demands subtlety. They are best used in heavy spicy sweets. Malt, although a form of sugar, has no sweetness at all and so should always be used with a sweet fruit like dates.

(d) *'Natural sweetners are what I would prefer to use if I can.'* Fruit juices like orange, apple and pineapple add not only sweetness to desserts, but also contribute flavour. Unlike other sweetners the sweetness of fruit need not dominate. However, they also add liquid and this must be compensated for. Fruit purées can be used not only for sweetening but binding also. In the cooking process they release pectin which will act in a similar way to eggs; the result however is a lot heavier and moister and so using fruits either as juices or purées has its limitations, especially when cooking sponges.

3 Setting agents

Don't use gelatine – agar agar is just as good if prepared properly and it may be used for exactly the same purposes. Agar agar, unlike gelatine, must be boiled for at least 5 minutes to release all its setting properties and after use, chilled thoroughly to set.

For thickening, use arrowroot rather than cornflour; it is not so glutinous, has no colour or flavour and it can therefore alter a dish without changing the appearance or taste.

Eggs, of course, have many uses in the sweet department apart from acting as a setting agent. Always store eggs out of the fridge and do try to use free-range eggs. Free-range eggs may seem more expensive but, in actual fact, give better value for money in the long run.

Pectin is perhaps the most natural of all setting agents, but the high temperature at which it is released limits its use in a lot of dishes.

Most of the setting agents may be used on their own or in conjunction with other ingredients for glazes.

4 Raising agents

We have already discussed the use of yeast, bicarbonate and baking powder in the bread section. For making more wholesome sweets you may not wish to use baking powder as it contains a chemical called sodium pyrophosphate which is harmful. Baking powder is made from bicarbonate of soda and cream of tartar; an alkali and an acid, which in the presence of liquid and heat, creates a controlled amount of carbon dioxide. The carbon dioxide then aerates the substance within which it is held. By substituting cream of tartar with a natural acid as is found in sour cream or yoghurt you will achieve the same reaction. Because sour cream and yoghurt are liquid you have to compensate for that liquid in another part of the recipe. If you are vegan, use molasses instead of sour cream/yoghurt.

Eggs are also used as raising agents. When whipped they will retain pockets of air. In cooking, the air expands and so makes the dish rise. If you separate the yolks from the whites the effect is even more spectacular; whipped egg whites retain much more air and so rise even further. When adding eggs to a butter and sugar cream they should be added slowly, beating all the time to ensure that the aerating process is thorough. Eggs will not aerate if they have been stored in a fridge prior to use.

5 Fats and oils

These are basically the same in chemical terms, except that oils can usually be heated to higher temperatures than fats before they break down. We use butter, vegetable margarine (hard and soft), vegetable

oil, corn oil, or sunflower oil. Butter contributes richness to the end product, but vegetable oils and margarine are chosen because they do not have any distinctive flavour, some oils have very strong flavours and these should not be used. The shortening properties of butter, vegetable margarine and oils have already been discussed (see Chapter 8). They also act as preservatives, especially when used in a sponge mixture. The addition of a fat or oil to a sponge will slightly decrease its capability to rise and is not always necessary. However, without these ingredients, a sponge will quickly dry out if not eaten straightaway. Recent research shows that high-cholesterol fats are harmless when eaten with unrefined foods. For very light sponges, it is best to use a small amount of melted butter or margarine; oil does not have the same effect as it gets too hot too quickly.

6 Dairy produce

Always use fresh dairy produce and always keep it in your fridge. Use whipping cream for lighter dishes and double cream for heavy ones where more support is needed. Use your nose to determine how fresh your produce is. Care must be taken not to curdle dairy produce through the addition of acid or the application of heat. It is always best to try and prepare your sweets in the coolest part of the kitchen, especially in summer.

7 Flavourings

Try to keep unnatural flavourings down to a minimum. I would suggest vanilla essence, almond essence and concentrated coffee (e.g. Camp coffee) as the only necessities but, if possible, use ground almonds and vanilla pods, depending on the recipe. Many of the hard-line whole-fooders don't like to use chocolate, but I think that makes life a little too hard – use cocoa powder for chocolate flavour and block chocolate for toppings. Carob is no substitute for chocolate, but is often used in its place. It should be remembered that, unlike cocoa, carob is a flour and part of its bulk should be compensated for in the recipe when it is used. Carob is best if cooked with water and honey before use.

Fruit juices, flower waters and alcohol may be used for flavouring, but their liquid volume must be compensated for in the recipe. You can buy natural fruit juice concentrates and thereby avert the problem of added volume. Flower waters may be bought at any large chemist – we usually use orange or rose water – and they have a very subtle flavour which is easily meshed with spices or strong sweetners. Alcohol may be used in many ways in sweets. Always use real alcohol; concentrates have a chemical taste. Spirits or fortified wines are best used to flavour sponges as they have a lot of flavour in a small volume; try dark rum, Kirsch, brandy, port, sherry and vermouth, madeira and marsala or, alternatively, marinate some of the ingredients in alcohol before using them in the dish. If marinating, you may use larger volume alcohols like wine and some dark beers. Alcohol also acts as a preservative, but is more commonly used for this purpose in heavier dishes. It is possible to flavour a dish after it has been prepared simply by carefully introducing a strong flavour to it. Many cakes are successfully flavoured by this method and we usually use a spirit, a fresh fruit juice, or a flower water – by gently piercing the surface of the cake all over it is then possible to sprinkle the flavour of your choice over the surface and allow it to be absorbed; this not only flavours the cake but moistens it too.

Zests introduce a fresh flavour to sweets and no added volume (they are particularly useful where this is a critical factor). To get the best flavour from a zest wash the fruit well and avoid cutting or grating into the pith of the fruit for this is bitter. Zests too may be marinated for additional flavour. Zests can also introduce the flavour of citrus to dishes which would curdle if the actual juice was used – a good example is an egg custard; to add lemon juice to an egg custard would risk curdling the mixture. Lemon zest adds the flavour quite safely with no risk of curdling.

Spices are, of course, the most common flavouring in sweets, but use only sweet spices and always add them at a stage when they will be mixed in evenly with the rest of the mixture, usually at the beginning. Choose from ginger, cinnamon, coriander, mace, nutmeg, cardamom, caraway, cloves and try to grind the spices freshly for use.

Dry fruits and nuts also add their own particular flavour and texture to dishes. It is best to soak or marinate dry fruits before use; nuts will not impart much flavour unless they are ground – but do give the dish texture.

Similarly, fresh fruit may be used whole, or sliced or puréed in the same way as fruit juices. However, because they will be fairly bulky they must become an integral part of the dish and be compensated for in the rest of the recipe. If using whole fruit, it is important to buy high quality produce, bearing in mind whether it will be eaten raw, partially cooked, or totally cooked, and whether it will be used for decoration purposes or just for flavour or both (see Chapter 2). A lot of vegan sweets rely heavily on the flavour and binding properties of fresh fruit. Fresh fruit is also delicious if marinated before use, a process which takes much less time with soft fruits than with hard fruits. If you are really desperate use frozen fruits for flavour or unsweetened tinned fruits but, as with vegetables, it is always best to ride with the seasons.

People have written whole books, many inches thick, on the subject of sweets and cakes. This book is necessarily less voluminous but here follows a selection of some of my favourites. First we will explore how to make them look nice with glazes, toppings, fillings and decorations.

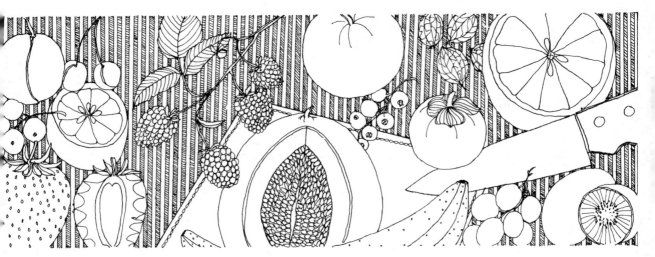

Sweet glazes

We have already covered egg and milk glazes, in Chapter 8. They are designed to add only colour and shine to pastry, while sweet glazes may be clear, coloured, flavoured or just sweet and they perform a dual purpose. Not only can they make the surface of a sweet look nice, but they can also protect what is underneath. This is especially important when using fresh fruit that may oxidize if exposed to the air for any length of time; a glaze seals the surface of a dish completely. Sweet glazes are composed basically of water, sugar and a thickening agent. Any or all of these ingredients may be varied or added to to create special glazes, for instance, here are some alternatives to these ingredients.

(a) Water – fruit juice, diluted fruit purées, wine, sherry, milk, cream, sour cream.

(b) Sugar – honey, molasses, malt, maple syrup.
(c) Thickening agents – arrowroot, cornflour, fruit purées, eggs, agar agar, butter, honey and sugar.

Here are some recipes for glazes that use honey rather than sugar, try different types of honey to flavour the glaze. Remember glazes are really simple jams.

270 Simple glaze

Stage	Ingredients	Quantity	Method
1	Honey	100 ml	*Dissolve the honey with the water until desired consistency is*
	Water, hot	25 ml	*reached. Heat to about 175°F (80°C).*

Variations

(a) Substitute honey with demerera sugar.
(b) Substitute water wholly or partially with fruit juice or sweet wine.

271 Black or red currant glaze

Stage	Ingredients	Quantity	Method
1	Redcurrants	225 g	*Cook the redcurrants with the water. Pass them through a fine*
	Water	1 tbsp	*strainer.*
2	Honey	50 ml	*Reheat and add the honey, simmer for 10 minutes.*

Variations

(a) Substitute for honey with sugar.
(b) Substitute for water with fruit juice or wine.
(c) Use dry apricots, figs, dates, fresh pineapple (finely chopped), raspberries, strawberries, gooseberries, plums, cherries and any other soft fruits.
(d) Cheat and use jams or jellies in place of fruit and sweetner.

272 Arrowroot glaze

Stage	Ingredients	Quantity	Method
1	Arrowroot	1 tsp	*Mix a little of the orange juice with the arrowroot to form a*
	Orange juice	100 ml	*paste. Bring the rest to the boil and add it gradually to the*
	Sugar/honey	To taste	*arrowroot again stirring continuously. Sweeten to taste and*
	Orange zest	Half orange	*add a little orange zest. Use while hot.*

Variations

(a) Use any other fruit juice.
(b) Use a diluted fruit purée, fresh or dry.
(c) Use wine or add alcohol to the juice.
(d) Use jam or jelly in place of sugar or honey.

273 Agar agar glaze

Stage	Ingredients	Quantity	Method
1	Agar agar	25 g	*Bring the agar agar to the boil in the hot water and boil for 5*
	Hot water	70 ml	*minutes.*
2	Honey/sweetener	180 g	*Add the sweetener and the lemon juice. Use while hot or allow*
	Lemon juice	half lemon	*to chill before use.*

Variations

(a) Use fruit juices or diluted fruit purées instead of water.

(b) Use jams or jellies in place of conventional sweeteners.

274 Chocolate or carob glaze

Stage	Ingredients	Quantity	Method
1	Sugar	125 g	*Melt the sugar in the water until it reaches 220°F (110°C).*
	Water	200 ml	
2	Cocoa/Carob	30 g	*Add the cocoa or carob and colour with a little caramel.*

Sweet sauces, compôtes and purées

These may be regarded as the next logical step on from glazes as they use many of the principles that glazes themselves are based upon. Sweet sauces, compôtes and purées may be used hot or cold and, unlike most glazes, they present the opportunity of using spices and other flavourings. The amount you cook these fillings will depend largely on the nature of the fruit (see Chapter 2). Their applications are as diverse as they are numerous, and they provide powerful sources of taste, flavour and colour in anything from sorbets to crumbles.

Purées

Purées are perhaps the easist of all fillings, and may also be used as toppings or as sauces in their own right. Purées are most easily made in a blender, but a finer result can be achieved by using a sieve. Some fruits need to be cooked before puréeing; others need to be sweetened prior to puréeing and so may require cooking; yet other fruits have delicate flavours and may not benefit from cooking or sweetening. Try to use as little sugar, honey or maple syrup as you can, let the flavour of the fruit be enhanced rather than swamped. There is no point in using your best fruit for puréeing – it is sheer waste. Purées concentrate flavour and colour only. Use as little water, juice or alcohol as possible when making purées as this dilutes the flavour of the purée itself. They may be stored in the fridge for only a day or so unless sugar, honey or alcohol have been added to them, which will preserve them for over a week.

275 Peach purée

Soak 200 g of dry peaches over night. Place in a deep pan and just cover with water or the remaining soaking juice. Add 65 ml of honey or the equivalent in sugar. Bring to the boil and simmer for 30 minutes. Allow to cool, then blend until smooth. If the mixture is too thick for your purposes, dilute with water or juice until it is the desired consistency.

Variations

(a) Substitute peaches with dried apricots, pears, prunes, dates, figs, bananas, sultanas and raisins.
(b) Substitute for water with fruit juices (apple, orange, pineapple, etc.) or sweet wine.
(c) Add a little alcohol to the mixture before puréeing.
(d) Add a few spices before cooking.

276 Apple purée

Makes ½ litre

Slice 1 kg of cooking apples and place in a deep pan. Add 100 ml of water, the juice of half of a lemon, and 40 g of sugar or the equivalent in honey. Place the lid on the pan and bring to the boil; cook rapidly until apples are tender. Purée in a blender. Add 25 g of butter to the mixture while it is still hot (optional).

Variations

(a) Use any hard fruit, especially pears and gooseberries, plums, damsons, cranberries, pineapple, quince (needs more sugar).
(b) Vary the cooking liquor, use different juices, cider, wine or a little additional strong alcohol before puréeing.
(c) Add spices prior to cooking especially cloves, cinnamon and ginger.
(d) Add other fruits to the apples especially blackberries, blackcurrants, gooseberries, rhubarb, redcurrants and cooking cherries.

277 Raspberry purée

This recipe applies to fruits that are naturally sweet and soft. Usually, they need no added sweetening and no cooking. It is a good way of using up soft fruit that is still good but has perhaps discoloured (some soft fruits may need a little honey). Take 375 g fresh or frozen raspberries and add 2 tbsp honey. Purée in a blender. If you do wish to cook these use very little water and sweeten to taste. Adjust the consistency with a little water, fruit juice, alcohol (like kirsch) or wine.

Variations

(a) Replace raspberries with strawberries, loganberries, cherries (with stones removed), bananas, kiwi fruit, peaches, nectarines, apricots. Note – if any of the fruit used is slightly under-ripe it will need to be poached in a little cooking fluid prior to being puréed.
(b) Remove any bruises or marks before puréeing as they can taint the entire dish.
(c) Soft fruits like these have very subtle natural flavours and should not be used with spices or other dominant flavourings (unless you like them like this).

Compôtes

Compôtes are always cooked, or par-cooked if they are going to go through another cooking (see hot sweets). Really, they are exactly the same as purées except that they are not blended or passed through a sieve. The fruits involved may remain whole or be sliced depending on how long they take to cook and what role they will play in the ensuing dish. When fully cooked, compôtes are usually eaten as they are, while partially cooked compôtes form the filling for many hot sweets. They may be composed only of dry fruits, of fresh fruits or a combination of both. They are often flavoured by their cooking liquor and other flavourings, unless you wish the flavour of the fruit to predominate. Here is a master recipe.

278 Blackberry and apple compôte

Serves 4

Stage	Ingredients	Quantity	Method
1	Honey	120 ml	*Mix together and bring to the boil.*
	Apple juice	½ l	
2	Blackberries (whole)	300 g	*Place blackberries and apple into a deep pan and cover with the boiling syrup. Re-boil and simmer for 25 minutes. Allow*
	Apples (F Fine)	400 g	*to cool and then chill.*

Special point

When using compôtes as fillings for hot or cold sweets that are going to be cooked again, reduce cooking time to 10–15 minutes, depending on fruit. To retain the texture of soft fruits, like blackberries, do not add them to the compôte until you are about to finish cooking the dish as a whole.

Variations

(a) Vary fruit, using dry fruit, hard fruit, soft fruit.
(b) Add spices and other sweetners.
(c) Add different juices.
(d) Add alcohol, either strong wine or cider.
(e) Add other ingredients like roasted nuts.

Here are some good ideas for compôtes. Apple (cooking), Apricots, Cherries (cooking), Figs, Raspberries, Blackcurrants, Redcurrants, Gooseberries, Plums, Blackberries, Pears, Prunes, Greengages, Rhubarb, Pineapple, and any dried fruits, Strawberries, Blueberries, Damsons, Oranges and Lemons.

When attempting combination compôtes it is nice to balance a hard fruit like apples with a soft fruit like blackcurrants. Dried fruits will go equally well with fresh hard fruits or in combinations of themselves. Here are a few for you to try. Use the same method and quantities as in blackberry and pear compôte (278). Dry fruit must always be soaked before use.

	Main fruit	Secondary fruit	Cooking liquor (+ honey/sugar)	Spices/other ingredients
279	Banana		Rum + orange juice	Mace
280	Apple	Blackcurrant	Apple juice	Cinnamon
281	Pear		Orange juice	Ginger
282	Rhubarb	Apple	Apple juice	Cloves
283	Apple	Apricot	Apricot juice	Cinnamon
284	Pineapple	Orange	Orange juice	Mace
285	Gooseberry	Fig	Apple juice	Ginger
286	Plum	Apple	Apple juice	Cinnamon
287	Morello cherry	Date	Cherry water	
288	Greengage	Pear	Orange juice	Ginger
289	Rhubarb	Strawberry	Water	
290	Figs, Dates, Peaches, Lexias	Prunes, Apricots	Apple juice	

As you can see the combinations are numerous; you will find your own favourites and of course, be governed by what is in season.

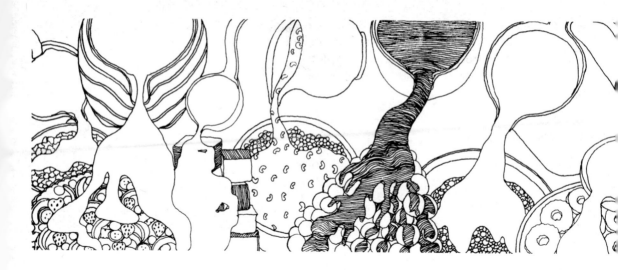

Sweet sauces

These are often a cross between a glaze and a purée. There are r
many varieties, some of them old classics. With a few of them u
your belt you will be able to rattle off delicious hot and cold swe
no time at all. Sweet sauces are sometimes used to accompany a
sometimes they make up most of the dish, and sometimes they fc
delicious background for the main ingredients in the dessert, pr
ing a tasty, yet not overwhelming, common denominator in the di
a whole. Sweet sauces use the whole range of thickening ag
flavours, and ingredients. Here are a few sweet sauces – the most
is a simple arrowroot-thickened sauce (cornflour may be used inst

291 Blackberry sauce

Stage	Ingredients	Quantity	Method
1	Honey (syrup)	3 dsp	*Melt the honey over a low flame and add the blackber*
	Blackberries (whole)	300 g	*lemon juice, and lemon zest. Heat gently.*
	Lemon zest	1 tsp	
2	Water	50 ml	*Heat the water separately and add to the blackberries.* *and bring to the boil.*
3	Arrowroot	2 tsp	*Make the arrowroot into a smooth paste with cold wat*
	Salt	Pinch	*add to the blackberries with the salt. When thickened r* *from heat. This mixture will set as it cools.*

Note: Harder fruits will take longer to cook; you may wish
to pre-cook them and purée them before adding any
water.

Variations

As with fruit purées and compôtes.

292 Lemon curd sauce

Stage	Ingredients	Quantity	Method
1	Water	400 ml	*Bring all ingredients to the boil.*
	Lemon juice	50 ml	
	Honey/sugar	70 ml/85 g	
	Salt	Pinch	
	Lemon peel	3 tsp	
2	Cornflour	25 g	*Prepare a paste with the cornflour and add to the liquid when it is boiling. Allow it to thicken.*
3	Egg yolks	2	*Beat the egg yolks well and add a little of the lemon sauce to it whisking vigorously. Then whisk the egg/lemon mixture back into the lemon sauce. Stir continuously for another 2 minutes and use immediately.*

Variations

(a) Substitute lemon with orange, pineapple or limes.
(b) Substitute water with a fruit juice.
(c) Add other soft fruits to the sauce after it has been made.
(d) If making lemon meringue pie separate the yolk from the white and use the white for the meringue.

293 Egg custard

Serves 4

This sauce is baked, usually with other ingredients in it, rather like a sweet quiche. Cooking time will vary according to the other ingredients as will the oven temperature.

Stage	Ingredients	Quantity	Method
1	Milk	¾ l	*Warm the milk in a deep pan. Cream the eggs and sugar together in a bowl. Add the milk stirring continuously. Sprinkle with the nutmeg. Pour into your baking dish and bake in an oven for 40 minutes at 325°F (165°C, Gas mark 3).*
	Eggs	5	
	Sugar/honey	90 g/50 ml	
	Nutmeg	Pinch	

Variations

(a) Add vanilla, almond or coffee essence or chocolate powder.
(b) Add the zest of orange or lemon.
(c) Add cream to the milk or perhaps yoghurt or sour cream.

Note: this recipe may be used for créme caramel.

294 Cornflour custard

Commonly known as custard. it is extremely versatile and may be served separately or as part of a dish. It sets when it is chilled. Don't use packet custards as they are disappointing in comparison.

Stage	Ingredients	Quantity	Method
1	Milk	700 ml	*Make a smooth paste with a little milk and the cornflour. Bring the milk to the boil and add the paste stirring continuously. When it has thickened, add the honey (if using sugar add it to the milk at the beginning).*
	Cornflour	1 tbsp	
	Honey/sugar	1 dsp/tbsp	
2	Egg yolks	4	*Whisk the egg yolks; add a little of the sauce whisking continuously; add this back to the milk sauce.*
3	Vanilla essence	Dash	*Add a dash of vanilla essence, serve immediately.*

Variations

(a) Flavour with citrus fruit zests.
(b) Flavour with chocolate powder.
(c) Flavour with almond and coffee essences.

(d) Flavour with strong alcohol like brandy.
(e) Add dried fruits like sultanas.
(f) Flavour with carob.

295 Butterscotch sauce

Stage	Ingredients	Quantity	Method
1	Water	50 ml	*Boil the water and honey together (112°C) until a little for*
	Honey/sugar	150 ml/150 g	*a soft ball when dropped into cold water.*
2	Butter	60 g	*Remove from heat and stir in the butter.*

This will keep in the fridge for up to a week.

Variations

Add chopped nuts with the butter.

296 Cider sauce and other sweet sauces

Other sweet sauces are just a question of sweetening, spicing and thickening, as with blackberry sauce (291). Try different variations to suit the dish you are making. In place of blackberries try cider (sweet variety needs no extra sugar), this also takes the place of water. In addition to water use brandy; fresh ginger for a ginger sau⟨ maple syrup (with water and thickening); carob powd⟨ chocolate powder or grated chocolate and so on. Sor may need no extra sweetening, others should sweetened according to taste.

297 Caramel sauce

Simply use water and sugar (or honey) boiled until it is golden brown. Quantities – 100 g sugar to 75 ml water.

Whips and fools

Whips and fools are fruit purées usually with the addition of a dai product. They are quick to make and really refreshing on a h summer's day. Do not make them too sweet.

298 Gooseberry fool

Serves

Stage	Ingredients	Quantity	Method
1	Gooseberry purée	500 g	*Substitute the apples in apple purée with gooseberries (27 Allow to cool.*
2	Whipping cream	¼ l	*Whip the cream and fold into the gooseberries. Serve in gl⟨ bowls decorated with cream, biscuits and poached whole gooseberries.*

Variations

(a) Use any purée.
(b) Supplement cream wholly or partially with yoghurt or sour cream.
(c) Instead of using a purée, use a sauce like coffee, chocolate, butterscotch or simply a little caramel – these are called whips rather than fools

Fools are really good for using up leftover fruits and desserts. Always serve well chilled.

Hot sweets

Hot sweets are particularly well appreciated on cold winter's days. They should be nourishing and sustaining and always served hot and fresh; re-heated hot sweets are somehow never the same. There are many varieties of hot sweets; most have a topping or a bottom, some have both. They are usually filled or flavoured with a fruit compôte, purée or sauce. Some have a sauce served separately and some are simply 'hot sweets'.

As we go through recipes for hot sweets we will be trying, in particular, to demonstrate different kinds of toppings and bases. We have already discussed pastry (see Chapter 8) and this is widely used as both topping and base in hot sweets. As with all our other foods, the important thing is to grasp the basic concepts and then start to experiment on your own. All recipes are to serve 4 – use a 9 in flan tin where appropriate.

299 Rhubarb and strawberry crumble

Crumble-topped hot sweets are by far the most simple and quickest of all hot sweets to make; yet they never cease to be popular. There are a wide variety of crumble toppings and these are sprinkled liberally on a partially cooked fruit compôte – the whole is then baked until the fruit is totally cooked and the crumble has gently coloured.

Stage	Ingredients	Quantity	Method
1	Butter/vegetable margarine	2 tbsp	*Rub the butter into the flour until it resembles breadcrumbs. Add the sugar and spices and mix in well.*
	Wholewheat flour	120 g	
	Sugar	60 g	
	Cinnamon	1 tsp	
	Nutmeg		
2	Rhubarb and strawberry compôte (289)	½ l	*Partially cook the rhubarb as directed but leave the strawberries out.*
3			*Add the strawberries to the rhubarb and cover liberally with crumble topping, bake for about 45 minutes at 375°F (190°C, Gas mark 5).*

To serve

Serve on its own or with custard, a sauce, cream or yoghurt.

Variations

(a) Wholly or partially substitute crumb mixture with breadcrumbs – this makes a quick Charlotte.
(b) Wholly or partially substitute crumb mixture with cakecrumbs. Old cakes are especially good.
(c) Wholly or partially substitute crumb mixture with regular oats, jumbo oats, wheatmeal, oatmeal, coconut, dried fruits, chopped nuts, leftover flapjacks (346), sesame seeds and sunflower seeds. Dry ingredients should be rubbed with vegetable oil before use. Crumbles with a larger nut content may be called crunchies.
(d) Use any compôte.

300　Banana and blackcurrant crumble cake

This may be served hot or cold and is an extension of the crumble idea. Bananas need no prior cooking. The mixture used is much drier than for crumble.

Stage	Ingredients	Quantity	Method
1	Shortcrust flan case (146)	250 g	*Blind bake the flan case and line with bananas sprinkled with lemon juice to prevent discolouration. Substitute blackcurrants for blackberries in sauce recipe (291), pour over bananas.*
2	Bananas (B thin)	3 medium	
	Lemon juice	squeeze	
3	Blackcurrant sauce (291)	100 ml	
4	Basic crumble mix (299)	200 g	*Sprinkle crumble mix evenly on bananas and sauce and pat down. Bake for 40 minutes at 350°F (180°C, Gas mark 4), or until crumble is golden.*

To serve

Cut into wedges and serve with creamy yoghurt or custard.

Variations

(a) Use different pastry base.
(b) Use different filling – always make sure that they are drier than standard compôtes by halving the liquid.
(c) Use different crumble toppings.

301　Treacle apple tart

This is identical to the crumble cake concept except for the topping made by mixing 60 g of breadcrumbs with 240 g of golden syrup. Make a dry compôte of partially cooked, thinly sliced apples (add cinnamon and lemon juice to the apples when cooking) and arrange as evenly as you can on a pre-cooked flan case. Spread on the breadcrumb mixture and bake for 30 minutes at 400°F (200°C, Gas Mark 6) or until apples have cooked and topping is golden brown. Serve hot or cold and vary as with crumble cake (300).

302 Pear and ginger pie

This must have a pastry topping and can have a pastry base too.

Stage	Ingredients	Quantity	Method
1	Shortcrust pastry (146)	500 g	*Grease an 8 in. pie tin and line it with just over half of the pastry. Blind bake partially.*
2	Pear and ginger compôte (281)	¾ l	*Partially cook the compôte and pour onto pie base.*
3			*Use an upturned egg-cup to support the centre, and roll the rest of the pastry over it. Pinch the edges together.*
4	Egg wash	A little	*Brush with egg wash and bake in the oven for 40 minutes at 400°F (200°C, Gas mark 6).*

To serve

Allow to cool slightly before cutting. Serve in wedges.

Variations

(a) Use different pastries.

(b) Use different fillings.

(c) Sprinkle with sesame or sunflower seeds, after glazing.

303 Orange meringue pie

This is the close cousin of lemon meringue pie. You already know how to make the base and the filling, but the meringue is another important string to your bow. Meringue pies may be served hot or cold.

Stage	Ingredients	Quantity	Method
1	Flan case (146)	As stated	*Prepare the flan case.*
2	Meringue topping		
	Egg whites	3	*Whisk the egg whites with the salt until peaking. Add the warm honey.*
	Salt	Pinch	
	Warm honey	3 tsp	
3	Orange custard sauce (292)	½ l	*Use orange instead of lemon in recipe 292. Substitute orange juice for the water but retain the lemon juice.*
4			*While still hot pour the orange sauce into the flan case.*
5			*Spread the meringue mixture evenly over the surface – it helps if it is still warm. Flick the surface of the meringue up in peaks as this helps it to cook more evenly and quickly. Bake for 15 minutes at 325°F (160°C, Gas mark 3).*

Special points

The meringue should be at least 25 cm thick and spread right to the edges of the dish to seal the orange sauce completely.

Whenever preparing meringues be scrupulously clean as the slightest amount of grease or dirt can make them fail.

Variations

(a) Use lemon or pineapple, peaches, nectarines, strawberries, gooseberries, rhubarb, raspberries or any combination in place of orange.

(b) Add a little butter with the honey when making the orange sauce.

304 Pineapple chiffon pie

As for orange meringue pie, substituting 450 g of crushed pineapple for the orange juice and folding the egg whites into the pineapple custard sauce.

305 Gooseberry and fig charlotte

A really good way of using up left-over bread. You will need a deep tin or ovenware bowl.

Stage	Ingredients	Quantity	Method
1	Wholewheat bread Butter	7 thin slices 50 g	*Melt the butter and dip the slices of bread into it. Grease a 5 in. cake tin and line it with the bread – if the bread overlaps it will take longer to cook.*
2	Gooseberry and fig compôte	¾ l	*Fill the centre of the charlotte with a moist but not wet compôte and bake in a hot oven for 45 minutes or until the bread is golden brown. Turn the charlotte out of its mould to serve.*

To serve

Serve with a sauce like rum and raisin sauce or cider sauce.

Variations

Use different compôtes, but make sure that they are not too wet.

306 Pear and chocolate egg custard

These sweets are so simple but extremely fattening; the vanilla essence removes the egg flavour.

Stage	Ingredients	Quantity	Method
1	Ripe pears (halved)	4	*Grease a 7 in. pyrex dish and line it with the pears.*
2	Egg custard (293)	1 l	*Pour the egg custard over the pears and sprinkle with nutmeg. Cook for 45 minutes at 325°F (165°C, Gas mark 3) in a dish filled with warm water, in the oven. When it is golden brown and has set, take out of the tin and pour hot chocolate sauce over it. Eat immediately.*
3	Chocolate sauce (274)	100 ml	

Variations

(a) Use different fruits – bananas are good.
(b) Line the dish with a little caramel (297) before adding the pears.
(c) Use different-flavoured egg custards.

307 Apfel strudel

One dish in which wholewheat pastry flour is a real asset but it does require considerable patience.
    Try to prepare the filling at least half an hour in advance; the longer it marinates the tastier it will be, especially if you use alcohol – rum is nice.

Stage	Ingredients	Quantity	Method
1	Raisins	50 g	*Marinate all the ingredients in just enough apple juice or cider to cover.*
	Sultanas	50 g	
	Roasted walnuts (chopped)	50 g	
	Lemon juice and zest	2 tsp	
	Cinnamon	2 tsp	
	Honey	1 tbsp	
	Apple juice and/or cider		
2	Apples, cooking (grated)	600 g	*Drain off any excess liquid from the dry fruits and retain for the pastry. Stir the apples into the mixture.*
3	Butter	100 g	*Melt half of the butter and toss the breadcrumbs in it. Cook until they are crisp and golden. Fold into fruit mixture.*
	Breadcrumbs	50 g	
4	Wholewheat flour	200 g	*Sieve the flour and salt together. Make a well in centre and add the egg and oil. Gradually stir in the water using a fork, work the dough until it no longer sticks to the sides of the bowl. Turn out onto a floured board and knead well until it is elastic. Leave under a warm cloth for about an hour.*
	Salt	½ tsp	
	Egg (beaten)	1	
	Vegetable oil	30 ml	
	Warm water	45 ml	
5			*Warm the rolling pin and flour a large clean towel. Put the dough on the towel and roll it out into a rectangle, as thinly as you can. Strudel pastry should be translucent when it is of the correct thickness. Melt the remaining butter and brush over the pastry, then spread the filling evenly over the dough leaving 2.5 cm all the way around the edges.*

Take the two corners of the teatowel nearest to you and roll the dough up into a tight log. Grease a baking sheet and place the log on it bending it into a crescent shape. Bake in a hot oven for 15 minutes then turn the heat down and continue baking for a further 35 minutes. Dust with icing sugar or ground coconut. Serve hot or cold in slices.

Variations

Use different fillings for the strudel – choose any compôte, but do make it spicy and add alcohol too.

308 Chocolate sponge with chocolate mint sauce

Hot sponges are rather like crumbles in terms of the unlimited variations they present. They may cover a fruit compôte or purée or they may simply be well flavoured themselves. The presence of a fruit compôte under a sponge mixture will increase the overall cooking time considerably. Alternatively, you may wish simply to poach or marinate a fruit and then set it, only just moist, into the sponge mixture. Hot sponges are very filling and are best served with plenty of cream, yoghurt or a hot sweet sauce. Hot sponges are usually made with the traditional pound cake recipe, but you may wish to experiment with Genoese and lighter types of sponges also. Remember, everywhere baking powder is used you can substitute bicarbonate of soda and sour cream or yoghurt to make up the overall volume. Hot sponges with tightly packed fruit bases can be turned out when cold and served as upside down cakes in squares or oblongs. Cook these sponges in the tins that you used for crumbles. Sift the flour used for the sponges before use. The bran that is left behind may be saved for porridge or flapjacks. Egg quantities are given in grams to allow for different sizes; weigh them as you crack them.

Stage	Ingredients	Quantity	Method
1	Butter	250 g	*Cream the butter and the sugar together until there are no lumps and the mixture is a brilliant white in colour. You may require to heat the bowl slightly by placing it over hot water. Beat the eggs together and add gradually to the butter and sugar mixture. Be careful not to let the mixture curdle.*
	Sugar/honey	250 g	
2	Eggs	250 g	

3	Wholemeal flour	190 g	*Sieve the flour, cocoa powder and baking powder together.*
	Cocoa powder	60 g	*Fold gently into the batter. Grease the baking tin well and*
	Baking powder	1 tsp	*pour the mixture in. Cook in a moderate oven for 45 minutes*
			or until firm to touch. Serve immediately.

Chocolate mint sauce

Put 2 tbsp of sugar or honey into a small pan over a low heat with 150 g of grated plain chocolate and a little finely chopped spearmint (or mint liquor). Stir until mixture is smooth and add 60 g of butter. Serve with the sponge while still hot.

Variations

(a) Substitute cocoa powder with coffee powder, carob powder or ground almonds. Or add spices and essences.

(b) Line the baking tin with a partially cooked fruit compôte or poached fruit (drained). Try to avoid a lot of liquid. Cook for up to 15 minutes longer (you may have to cover the sponge with tinfoil to stop the top of the sponge burning).

(c) Decorate the top of the sponge with fruit and/or nuts before placing it in the oven.

(d) Serve with any other sweet sauce. You may wish to add a few roast chopped nuts like cashews, almonds or walnuts to the sauce for added texture.

(e) Line the tin with a little sauce or purée before adding the sponge mixture. This will also increase cooking time – may necessitate covering sponge with tinfoil.

(f) Use different sponge mixtures – see cake section.

There are many many more hot sweets that are easy to make, soufflés, pancakes, rice puddings (hot and cold), bread and butter puddings, baked stuffed apples, baked bananas. But I think those I have demonstrated should have helped you to develop a feeling for creating dishes using the knowledge you have gained.

Cold sweets

These are great at any time of the year. Always try to emphasize the fruits that are in season, through your cold sweet. Fruits of first class quality should be used for display and presentation purposes as well as flavour, while additional flavour may be introduced through fruit purées, compôtes and sauces. The presentation of cold sweets is all important; not only should they taste good, they should look good too. There is a wide variety of decorations you can use for cold sweets, some of which are listed below.

Decorations for hot sweets, cold sweets, cakes and munchies

Choose from: flaked almonds, ground almonds, whole almonds (toasted), glacé cherries, dried fruits, glazes, ground coconut, fresh fruits (must be glazed), walnuts, chopped walnuts (should be blanched), pecans, chopped pecans, whipped cream, little meringues, hazelnuts (whole), whole grains, and cracked grains, pastry shapes, chocolate (chips, flakes, chunks), melted chocolate, roasted coffee beans, flaked grains and toasted grains. And anything else you might think is appropriate.

Now, without further ado, let's move on to some recipes. Most of the recipes for hot sweets can only really be served hot, while several of the recipes for cold sweets may be served hot too if you wish (this will be stated for individual recipes). Each recipe will represent a particular type of sweet; obviously, it is possible to take ideas from one recipe and put them into another, particularly toppings, sauces, combinations and presentations.

Don't worry if you are not a whizz-kid with a piping bag; dollops of cream can be made to look just as attractive sprinkled with grated chocolate or nuts, etc.

Make sure if a sweet is to be served cold that it is cold. Cold sweets that do involve cooking should be allowed to cool naturally before being chilled in the fridge. Here are a few cold sweets that I have found to be very successful in the past.

309 Strawberry cheesecake

This is a cooked cheesecake – uncooked cheesecakes are extremely difficult to make without the addition of the dreaded gelatine. Agar agar will not set cream sufficiently well to recommend it. Recipe for a 9 in flan tin.

Stage	Ingredients	Quantity	Method
1	Cottage cheese	450 g	*Blend all the ingredients together.*
	Sour cream	150 g	
	Sugar/honey	170 g	
	Vanilla essence	1½ tsp	
	Lemon zest	½ lemon	
	Egg yolks	6	
2	Egg whites	6	*Whisk the egg whites until peaking and fold into mixture.*
3	Sweet pastry (145)	250 g	*Grease the flan tin and line it with the pastry – blind bake.*
4			*Pour the cheese mixture into the flan case and bake in a moderate oven until it has set (about 40 minutes). Allow to cool then chill in the fridge.*
5	Redcurrant glaze (271)	50 ml	*Glaze the surface of the cheesecake with half of the glaze.*
6	Strawberries	450 g	*Halve the strawberries and arrange on the top of the glaze. Glaze the tops of the strawberries with the rest of the glaze.*

Variations

(a) Biscuit base – Instead of shortcrust pastry use a biscuit base made from 250 g margarine, 150 g sugar or honey and 550 g of wholewheat digestive biscuit crumbs. Simply melt the margarine (butter) and sugar together and stir in the biscuit crumbs until all the liquid is absorbed. Grease the flan tin and spread the biscuit base over it. Push lightly into the corners. Otherwise use a shortcake base (see 318).

(b)   Make a compôte with the strawberries (especially if they are past their best).

(c)   Substitute strawberries with compôtes of fresh fruits such as cranberries, blackberries, blueberries, black-currants, redcurrants, gooseberries, apricots, peaches, nectarines, pineapple etc.

(d)   Use any glaze or fruit sauce.

(e)   Divide the cheese mixture in half. Add 100 ml chocolate sauce, or just 50 g of plain melted chocolate, to one half (cocoa, water, margarine, sugar, grated chocolate and milk). Pour the chocolate mixture into the flan case first, then pour in the plain mix. Swirl gently with a knife for Chocolate Swirl Cheesecake.

(f)   Add more lemon zest for lemon cheesecake, likewise use orange zest for orange cheesecake. Glaze with lemon or orange glaze or sauce.

310 Tofu cheesecake

This is a real treat for vegans. Use vegan pastry to line the flan tin. Do not use any artificial sweetner either.

Stage	Ingredients	Quantity	Method
1	Tofu	450 g	*Blend all the ingredients together and use as for cheesecake mixture (309).*
	Soya milk	100 ml	
	Lemon juice and zest	½ lemon	
	Dates	150 g	
	Apple juice (concentrate)	100 ml	
	Vanilla essence	1 tsp	
	Salt	Pinch	
	Vegetable oil	Dash	

311 Banana sour cream pie

As for strawberry cheesecake (309) but substitute the cottage cheese with equal quantities of sour cream and bananas. Proceed as for strawberry cheesecake. Glaze decorate with slices of banana dipped in lemon juice and glaze again.

Variations

(a)   You may wish to keep bananas as part of the base but decorate the top with another fruit, say raspberries for raspberry and banana sour cream pie.

(b)   You may omit the bananas completely but the bulk must be made up with sour cream, or you can use cottage cheese or cream cheese but it then becomes more like a cheesecake.

312 Banana toffee pie

Irresistibly bad for you.

Stage	Ingredients	Quantity	Method
1	Flan case (14)	250 g	*Coat the bananas in lemon juice and line the flan case with them.*
	Bananas (sliced)	3 large	
	Lemon juice	Squeeze	
2	Butter/margarine	80 g	*Melt the butter and sugar together to make a syrup. Allow to cool slightly.*
	Sugar/honey	70 g	

3	Eggs	2	Beat the eggs with the vanilla essence and add to the cooled syrup.
	Vanilla essence	Dash	
4	Flour	100 g	Add the flour, baking powder and salt.
	Baking powder	1½ tsp	
	Salt	Pinch	
5			Pour this mixture over the bananas and bake until set in a moderate oven (about 30 minutes). Serve hot or cold.

Variations

(a) Substitute some of the flour with an equal quantity of breadcrumbs.

(b) Bananas are best for this recipe but any fruit will do, especially hard fruits (par-cook them first).

313 Bakewell tart

A classic sweet using an almond sponge, a jam or glaze and pastry. Always try to use ground almonds, almond essence just isn't the same.

Stage	Ingredients	Quantity	Method
1	Sweet pastry flan case (14)	250 g	Blind bake the flan case. Cream the butter and the sugar until smooth and white. Beat the eggs separately with the essence and add slowly to the mixture whisking continuously.
2	Butter	250 g	
	Sugar/honey	250 g	
	Eggs	4	
	Almond essence	2 drops	
3	Wholewheat flour	75 g	Sieve the flour and baking powder and fold into the egg mixture gently. Finally fold in the ground almonds thoroughly.
	Baking powder	1 tsp	
	Ground almonds	115 g	
4	Raspberry jam	50 g	Spread the jam over the base of the flan case and pour the almond mixture over it. Decorate with whole almonds and bake for an hour in a moderate/hot oven or until mixture is firm to touch (see cake section).

Serve hot or cold.

Variations

(a) Use more ground almonds and equivalently less flour.

(b) Substitute raspberry jam with any fruit compôte, sauce, glaze, or purée, especially those that involve soft fruits.

(c) Substitute the raspberry jam layer with a thick fruit layer – use less almond mixture. Use hard fruits, partially cooked, in tightly packed thin slices.

(e) Flavour the almond sponge with chocolate, carob, coffee, spices or citrus juices.

314 Gainsborough tart

Stage	Ingredients	Quantity	Method
1	Sweet pastry flan case (145)	250 g	Blind bake the pastry case and line with the purée.
	Rhubarb purée (270)	75 g	
2	Butter/margarine	150 g	Cream together as for sponge mix. Beat the eggs and add slowly to the buttercream whisking all the time.
	Sugar/honey	250 g	
	Eggs	5	

3	Dessicated coconut	450 g	*Fold in the coconut and baking powder. Pour into flan case and*
	Baking powder	1¼ tsp	*bake in a moderate oven for 30 minutes until firm and golden*
			brown.

Variations

Use other purées, jams, sauces or glazes.

315 Cranberry maple pie

This is made in the same way as pear and ginger pie (302) except that you use a flan tin and the pastry topping is optional. Here is the filling.

Stage	Ingredients	Quantity	Method
1	Sugar/honey	115 g	*Bring all ingredients to the boil and simmer until cranberries*
	Wholewheat flour	1½ tbsp	*are just cooked.*
	Salt	Pinch	
	Cranberries	300 g	
	Maple syrup	1½ tbsp	
	Lemon juice and zest	1 lemon	
	Water	½ l	
2			*Pour into flan case and cover with pastry. Bake for 30–40 minutes.*

316 Shoo-fly pie

A traditional American breakfast cake.

Stage		Quantity	Method
1	Raisins	100 g	*Soak raisins overnight.*
2	Flan case, sweet pastry (14)	250 g	*Line the flan case with the drained raisins.*
3	Flour	450 g	*Rub the margarine into the flour and spices until it forms a*
	Cinnamon	2 tsp	*crumb consistency.*
	Nutmeg	1 tsp	
	Ginger	1 tsp	
	Margarine/butter	225 g	
4	Sugar/molasses	225 g	*Boil together and cool, then pour over the raisins. Sprinkle*
	Raisin water	300 ml	*crumb mixture over the water and raisins. Bake on the top*
	Bicarbonate of soda	1 tsp	*shelf of the oven at a moderate heat for 20 minutes. Then move*
			to middle shelf for another 25 minutes, or until firm to touch.

317 Honey pear custard pie

This is really an extension of an egg custard (293) but it is probably one of the most common ways of setting cold sweets and flans.

Stage	Ingredients	Quantity	Method
1	Flan case, sweet pastry (14)	250 g	*Unbaked.*
2	Firm pears cored and halved	6	*Line the flan case with the pears.*
3	Egg custard (293) using honey	300 ml	*Stir the rest of the ingredients into the egg custard. Pour over the pears. Bake at 400°F (200°C, Gas mark 6) for 45 minutes or until set.*
	Vanilla	½ tsp	
	Nutmeg	Pinch	
	Flour	2 dsp	
	Salt	Pinch	
	Honey	30 g	

Variations

(a) Use other fruits – hard fruits are best.
(b) Add a crumble topping (see 299) to the flan halfway through cooking.
(c) Use other flavourings – chocolate egg custard is nice.

318 Loganberry shortcake

An extremely versatile and quick way of preparing a cold sweet. Recipe is for a 9 in flan tin.

Shortcake recipe

Stage	Ingredients	Quantity	Method
1	Butter/margarine	150 g	*Cream together and add the rest of the ingredients.*
	Sugar/honey	100 g	
	Vanilla essence	½ tsp	
	Lemon zest	1 tsp	
2	Flour	250 g	*Sieve the flour and fold in gradually, stir in baking powder. Spread the mixture evenly over flan tin (greased) and bake in oven for 10–15 minutes at 340°F (170°C, Gas mark 3–4).*
	Baking powder	½ tsp	

Filling

3	Raspberry purée (277)	50 ml	*Coat the shortcake with the purée and arrange the loganberries on it.*
4	Loganberries	250 g	*Pour this glaze over the loganberries making sure each is well coated. Chill.*
5	Redcurrant agar (271)	100 ml	

Variations

(a) Vary fruit, purée and glaze.
(b) Add flavourings to the shortcake.
(c) Use egg custards and jam instead of fruit purées.
(d) Cook the whole shortcake with a fruit topping in the oven with a suitable sauce.

319 Peach and nectarine flan

Flans are perhaps the most versatile of sweets. A pastry case containing fresh fruit, which can be cooked or uncooked, depending on the fruit. Take care to arrange the fruit attractively, overlapping sliced fruit. If using fruit purées or compôtes only, then decorate with whipped cream or pastry.

The recipe is the same as for shortcake (318) replacing the shortcake with sweet pastry (14), but other pastries are just as good. For this flan, alternative slices of peach and nectarine for attractive colour contrast and glaze with a light red glaze (redcurrant 271).

Variations

As for shortcake (318). It is more common with deep flans to add a layer of egg custard to the flan case before blind baking them, for this helps the flan cut and gives it bulk. Always glaze flans.

320 Sherry trifle

Not just a good way of using up leftover sponge and fruit, it can be delicious in its own right. Use an attractive bowl for trifle or a glass dish so that you can see the layers. We do not use jelly for obvious reasons, but nobody misses it.

Stage	Ingredients	Quantity	Method
1	Genoese sponge (322)	250 g	*Cut into squares and line bottom of dish, sprinkle with sherry.*
	Sherry	100 ml	
2	Blackberry and pear compôte	½ l	*Cover with compôte.*
3	Cornflour custard	300 ml	*Pour hot custard over sponge/compôte and allow to cool. Chill and set.*
4	Whipping cream	100 ml	*Whip the cream and fold in the yoghurt. Spread evenly over the custard and smooth over.*
	Natural yoghurt	100 ml	
	Flaked almonds (toasted)	30 g	*Sprinkle with almonds.*

Variations

(a) Instead of the sponge use any leftover cakes, flapjacks or crumbles.

(b) Use different fruit compôtes or fresh fruits or leftover fruit salad.

(c) Use different flavour custards or omit completely for 'Tipsy Cake' (increase volume of sherry here).

(d) Use madeira, marsala, port or brandy instead of sherry.

(e) Use any whip or fool to cover or just plain whipped cream.

(f) Omit custard and substitute with 400 g of grated apple or apple purée (276) and with the addition of cloves and cinnamon you have Danish Apple Cake.

(g) Add cooked meringue (303) to sponge base.

(h) Instead of fruit compôte choose a poached fruit and add a sweet sauce, like pears with chocolate sauce.

Chapter 14
Cakes and Munchies

The important thing about cakes and munchies is that they should combine, in a fairly small space, flavour with colour and texture. Most important they should be no effort to eat. If you have read the book so far you will already be experienced in fruit preparation, some simple pastries, yeasted goods, sweet sauces, purées, compôtes, glazes, setting agents, raising agents and other aspects of sweet cookery. In fact, I have also previously given a sample recipe for a basic pound cake (308) and shortbread (318). You will use this knowledge in the creation of cakes and other sweet snacks. Many of the sweets discussed in the sweet chapter can in fact be adapted to form sweet snacks. First of all, however, I think it would be useful to discover a little more about sponges, as these form the base for most cakes and for munchies.

Equipment required

You will need all the equipment used for sweet preparation plus some cake tins, moulds, cutters, piping equipment. It is most important to make do with bare essentials until you feel confident enough to tackle more adventurous dishes. Always take great care of your equipment; it will save a lot of wasted time and ingredients in the long run. Avoid washing cake tins if you can and never scour them; it is worth buying good quality equipment to ensure even cooking and durability. Always use a fine whisk.

Sponges

Successful sponge cookery is the key to making good cakes and many other sweet snacks. To make a good sponge you must simply obey the formula that has, over the years, been developed for that particular sponge. There are essentially five different forms of sponge, each with specific cake forms in mind. All are combinations of egg, sugar, flour and occasionally butter. Butter not only preserves a sponge, it also makes it moister, but butter sponges are consequently heavier than sponges without butter. If you wish you may substitute butter with vegetable margarine (soft is best for sponges) and, in a few instances vegetable oil (these will be explained later). Vegetable oil is generally not desirable because of its high flashpoint. Light sponges may be flavoured with essences or concentrated juices; if a powder is used then it must form part of the total weight of the flour in the recipe. Some sponges may be flavoured after cooking. If you use the sour cream/bicarbonate method of raising the cake, substitute the same amount of bicarbonate as baking powder in the recipe, but decrease the volume of eggs by the same amount as the sour cream, likewise if you use honey rather than sugar to sweeten the cake. Always use 100% wholewheat flour for sponges; for light sponges it must be sifted, but this is not necessary with heavier sponges. Cornflour or soya flour may be added to the flour up to a ratio of 50/50 which will make the resulting sponge very light.

Eggs come in many different sizes so they must be weighed to obtain the right quantity. Always use eggs at room temperature, never chilled.

Making the sponge

For light and semi-light sponges, those which are most commonly used for sponge cakes and swiss-rolls, there are two different methods of aerating the mixture.

(A) Beat the eggs and sugar together in the presence of heat (a bowl of hot water will do) until all the sugar has dissolved, then fold in the flour.

(B) Separate the eggs and whisk the yolks with half the sugar and the whites with the other half – until peaking. Stir the two together carefully before folding in the flour.

In both cases any butter is added after the flour, melted but only warm not hot.

321 Sandwich sponge cake formula

Eggs	300 g	40%
Sugar	250 g	30%
Flour	250 g	30%

Best for sandwich cakes.

322 Genoese sponge cake formula

Eggs	300 g	50%
Sugar	150 g	25%
Flour	150 g	25%

Best for light sponges and swiss rolls.

323 Pound cake formula

Eggs	250 g
Sugar	250 g
Flour	250 g

Best for fruit cakes, heavy or light.

In all the above formulae, butter is added if necessary in proportion to the sugar. In sponge-making method A, up to 80% of the weight of the sugar; in method B up to 50% of the weight of the sugar. So, it depends on how sweet you like your cake.

Five types of cake

324 Recipe for a basic sandwich cake

Stage	Ingredients	Quantity	Method
1	Eggs	300 g	*Whisk the eggs and the sugar together in a bowl over some boiling water until the mixture is thick and white. The whiteness indicates that it is thoroughly aerated.*
	Sugar	250 g	
2	Flour (sifted)	250 g	*Fold in the flour carefully with a metal spoon.*
3	Butter (melted)	125 g	*Pour in the melted butter, and fold in carefully. Flavour as required. Grease cake tin and line with greaseproof paper. Grease paper. Pour in sponge mixture and allow to settle. Bake in oven for 15–20 minutes. When cooked it will have risen by at least twice its volume and will spring back when gently pressed. Turn on to cake rack and cool.*

Variations

(a) For chocolate sponge, add 30 g of cocoa powder as part of the flour quantity and sieve together. Add the same amount of warm water before adding the flour. This will absorb the cocoa flavour. Likewise for carob and coffee powder.

(b) For an almond sponge, add ground almonds. These may be added as part of the flour weight and because they are sweet as part of the sugar weight. Bias it mostly to the flour weight.

(c) For swiss rolls – use the same recipe but use method B for mixing and add a teaspoon of cinnamon with the flour. You may wish to add some ground nuts as part of the flour weight. Grease a baking tray, line with greaseproof paper and grease again. Spread the mixture over the baking tray to form a thin sheet. This will take less time to cook than other butter sponges, because it is thin.

(d) For lemon and orange flavour add the zest of 1 fruit with the sugar.

(e) For other flavours add vanilla, almond or coffee essence – a few drops with the sugar.

(f) For alcohol flavours, add after the cake is cooked.

325 Recipe for basic light Genoese sponge

Heat oven to 375°F (190°C, Gas Mark 5). This sponge is best used for light gateaux and layer cakes or swiss rolls.

Stage	Ingredients	Quantity	Method
1	Eggs	600 g	*Whisk the eggs and the sugar as in recipe 324.*
	Sugar	300 g	
2	Flour (sieved)	300 g	*Fold in the flour.*
3	Butter (melted)	200 g	*Add the butter and pour mixture into greaseproof lined tin or onto baking sheet for swiss roll. Bake for 10–15 minutes.*

Variations

(a) As for basic sandwich cake.

(b) Use method A or B for mixing. B is best for swiss rolls, but add a little warm water with the sugar to make the sponge less brittle and easier to roll.

326 Recipe for basic heavy Genoese

A much more substantial cake that may be used in the same way as a sandwich sponge. It is also good for hot puddings. Heat oven to 350°F (180°C, Gas Mark 4).

Stage	Ingredients	Quantity	Method
1	Butter	500 g	*Beat together butter and sugar until light.*
	Sugar	500 g	
2	Eggs beaten	625 g	*Add the eggs gradually to the mixture whisking continuously. Add any flavours required.*
3	Flour (sieved)	560 g	*Fold in the flours. Proceed as for other sponges.*
	Soya flour/cornflour	65 g	

Variations

(a) As for other sponges.
(b) Add baking powder (2 tsp) with the flour.
(c) Use methods A or B for mixing.

(d) Substitute sponge crumbs for flour.
(e) Add marachino with the egg yolks, or rose water.

327 Basic recipe for pound cake

Probably the easiest of all cakes, pound cakes are usually a pound in weight. They use equal quantities of ingredients, and rise with the addition of baking powder. They are usually used with fruit.
Heat oven to 350°F (180°C, Gas Mark 4)

Stage	Ingredients	Quantity	Method
1	Butter	125 g	*Cream the butter and sugar together until light and creamy.*
	Sugar/honey	125 g	
2	Eggs	125 g	*Add the eggs slowly to the mixture.*
3	Flour (sifted)	125 g	*Fold in the flour and baking powder. Bake according to content, if there is a lot of fruit bake in a slower oven for a longer period – up to 2½ hours – larger cakes will take longer. (Line cake tin with greaseproof paper.)*

Variations

(a) Add fruit in different proportions, traditionally, in the same quantity as the rest of the ingredients. In the above recipe this would be 100 g, making the rest of the ingredients 100 g each and the overall weight 500 g. Here are the most successful ways of proportioning fruit in a fruit pound cake based on the above recipe. Use any selection of fresh or dried fruits.
   (i) Light fruit cake – 20% fruit of whole weight of cake.
   (ii) Medium fruit cake – 33%.
   (iii) Medium heavy fruit cake – 45% (good for birthday cakes).
   (iv) Heavy fruit cakes – 50/55% (good for cakes that need to be preserved).
(b) Use fruit juices, alcohol, zests, spices, and different sweetners to flavour, and to bind these cakes without the use of eggs.
(c) For vegan cakes, substitute eggs with a cooked fruit purée (thick). Use honey instead of sugar, substitute part of the fruit weight with nuts and coconut. Substitute part of the flour weight with regular oats. Use oil instead of butter.

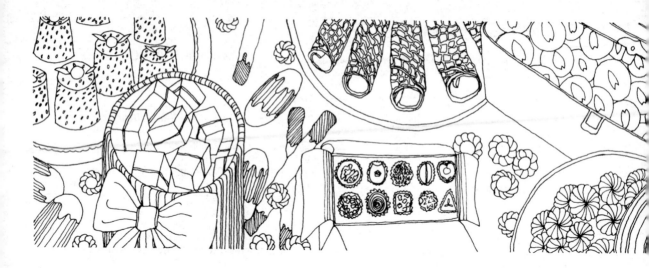

Toppings and fillings for cakes and munchies

After taking so much care preparing delicious cakes and munchies it seems a shame that most people top and fill them with a mixture of icing sugar, that is very sweet, and butter or margarine, with a chemical flavouring. If you do use icing sugar, use it in moderation; its only real attribute is as a sweet thickener. Here are some more earthy but tasty toppings.

328 Cream toppings and fillings

Use double cream if you are going to add it to something else; if not, whipping cream will do. Don't interfere with it if you can afford not to. Here are some various cream toppings.
(a) 1/3 double cream, 2/3 yoghurt, honey to sweeten/ otherwise use cream cheese with double cream.
(b) Add lemon or orange zest.
(c) Add sour cream in addition or instead of yoghurt.
(d) Add a spice like cinnamon.

329 Glazes

Use any glaze, jam or a thick sauce. It is good practice to glaze cakes and munchies before adding the main topping.

330 Purée

Use any purée; dry fruit purées are particularly good.

331 Fruit

Use whole, halved or sliced poached fruit (if it needs poaching); glaze before and after.

332 Fruit purées mixed with cream

Simply fold whipped cream into a suitable quantity of fruit purée.

333 Peanut butter with cream/sour cream and honey

Again simply fold whipped cream (or sour cream and honey) into a suitable quantity of peanut butter.

334 Tahini with honey

For decoration use any of the decorations already mentioned. Try to keep them simple and relevant.

Here are some recipes which demonstrate how the sponges already mentioned may be used, and giving a few different ones.

335 Chocolate gateau

Follow recipe 324. When the cake is cooled cut it in half and fill with chocolate cream (328). Replace the top half and glaze completely with Chocolate Glaze (275). Allow to set in a cold place. Decorate with chocolate cream and chocolate chips.

Variations

(a) Use carob or coffee powder and adjust topping accordingly.
(b) Substitute part of the flour weight with chopped nuts (almonds, walnuts, hazelnuts, or pecans) – Coffee Walnut Cake.

336 Very lemon cake

Follow recipe 324. While the cake is still hot puncture the surface evenly with a fork and introduce the juice of half a lemon into the sponge. Top with a lemon cream and decorate with thin slices of lemon dipped in honey.

Variations

(a) Use orange instead of lemon.

(b) Use lemon and orange in equal quantities.
(c) Add ground cinnamon (1 teaspoon) and cloves (½ teaspoon) to the flour. Proceed as for lemon cake, but fill with an apple purée (27) that has been flavoured with cloves. This is called Chinese apple cake. The surface of the cake is dusted with coconut powder.

337 Carob honey cake

Use method B for preparing the cake mix. Use recipe for heavy Genoese sponge, substituting sugar with honey. Add carob flour to make up 33% of the total flour weight. Also add 1 teaspoon of cinnamon and 1 teaspoon of vanilla essence with the eggs. Top with carob cream topping, made with margarine, honey, milk, carob flour and vanilla essence.

338 Honey cake

Stage	Ingredients	Quantity	Method
1	Butter	350 g	Melt together the ingredients and allow to cool.
	Water	50 ml	
	Sugar	290 g	
	Honey	220 g	
2	Eggs	5	Beat the eggs gradually into the mixture.
3	Flour	450 g	Fold in the flour thoroughly. Cook in a medium oven for 40 minutes.

Top with melted honey and sprinkle with toasted sesame seeds.

Variations

Add chopped walnuts as part of the flour quantity.

339 Cinnamon strudel cake

Stage	Ingredients	Quantity	Method
1	Flour	250 g	Grease a 500 g or 1 lb loaf tin. Rub the margarine into the flour and baking flour. Add the dates.
	Margarine	50 g	
	Baking powder	2 tsp	
	Dates	100 g	
2	Honey	100 g	Beat together and mix well with the flour. Pour into tin.
	Milk	125 ml	
	Eggs	2	
3	Sugar	100 g	ʾ ᴊix together and pour over mixture in tin. Bake at 350°F (180°C, Gas mark 4), for about 1 hour.
	Butter	25 g	
	Walnuts (chopped)	100 g	
	Cinnamon	1 tsp	

340 Date and walnut cake

Stage	Ingredients	Quantity	Method
1	Flour	300 g	Rub the margarine into the flour with the baking powder and mixed spice.
	Margarine	150 g	
	Baking powder	1 tsp	
	Mixed spice	2 tsp	
2	Dates	300 g	Add the dates and the walnuts.
	Walnuts (chopped)	120 g	
3	Eggs	2	Beat the eggs, milk and honey together and add to the date mixture gently. Bake for up to 1½ hours at 350°F (180°C, Gas mark 4).
	Milk	4 tbsp	
	Honey	120 g	

Variations

(a) Substitute eggs, milk and honey with a fruit purée for a vegan cake.

(b) Top with tahini and honey topping.

341 Coconut carrot cake

Heat oven to 180°C.
1. Use recipe for heavy Genoese sponge (326), and mixing method A.
2. Substitute mostly the flour and a little bit of the sugar (or honey) quantities with: 125 g chopped hazelnuts or walnuts; 125 g grated carrot, 125 g desiccated coconut, 2 tsp cinnamon, dash vanilla essence, 2 tsp baking powder.

Variations

Omit the coconut and add more nuts or more flour. Topping – cream and cream cheese (328). Decorate with grated carrots tossed in honey and lemon.

342 Fresh fruit cake (vegan)

Heat oven to 350°F (180°C, Gas Mark 4).

Stage	Ingredients	Quantity	Method
1	Vegetable oil	200 ml	*Mix all the ingredients together and push into a greased cake tin. Mixture should be moist. Bake for 40 minutes – 1 hour. Allow to cool in the tin for 15 minutes.*
	Peanuts	100 g	
	Cashew nuts	100 g	
	Lexias	225 g	
	Coconuts	225 g	
	Oats	225 g	
	Fruit purée	175 g	
	Salt	Pinch	
	Vanilla	1 tsp	
	Flour	450 g	

Topping – Honey glaze (127) or Tahini and honey.

343 Apple sauce cake

Stage	Ingredients	Quantity	Method
1	Sugar/honey	225 g	*Beat together. Note – add raisins, nutmeg, cloves and cinnamon when preparing the apple purée.*
	Vegetable oil	100 g	
	Apple purée (276)	675 g	
2	Flour	450 g	*Mix dry ingredients together and fold in wet ingredients. Bake as for vegan fruit cake (342).*
	Bicarbonate	2 tsp	
	Salt	½ tsp	
	Cinnamon	1½ tsp	
	Allspice	¼ tsp	
	Raisins	225 g	
	Nuts (any)	100 g	

344 Chocolate banana rum gateau

Use recipe for heavy Genoese sponge (326) and mixing method A. Reduce the weight of the eggs by the weight of 2 small bananas. Beat these in with the eggs plus a dash of dark rum. The cocoa powder is substituted for some of the flour weight. It may take slightly longer to cook. Topping – Banana cream and flaked chocolate.

345 Swiss rolls

Use recipe for light Genoese cake (325) with the addition of a little water with the egg yolks; use mixing method B (see technique in recipe 324 stage 3). Bake for 7–10 minutes in a hot oven 400°F (200°C, Gas Mark 6). Turn the sponge out onto some grease-proof paper covered with ground coconut. Quickly roll up the sponge in the greaseproof paper. Allow to cool. When cool spread with a cream or fruit purée filling and roll up again. Trim the edges. Leave the seam of the roll underneath for presentation. Dust with more ground coconut and serve in slices.

346 Basic flapjacks

These originated in Scotland as a sort of portable porridge. They are made from oats and, if cooked correctly, should almost melt in your mouth. They can take on any flavour and so are extremely versatile. I always mix regular oats with jumbo oats in a ratio of 3 to 2. Flapjacks are also called oat bars, oat slices or oat cookies and they are really simple. Eaten hot they fall to bits but are absolutely delicious. The test of a good flapjack is the muffled sound of someone eating it. Flapjacks may be made with honey, sugar, malt or molasses, or combinations of all these ingredients. Use a flan dish to cook them in (9 in) for this recipe. Grease the flan dish first.

Stage	Ingredients	Quantity	Method
1	Butter/margarine	300 g	*Melt the butter with the sugar and honey in a deep pan.*
	Sugar	225 g	
	Honey	50 ml	
2	Regular oats	560 g	*Stir in the oats and remove from the heat. Fold the Jumbo oats in gently, making sure all of them are well coated. Turn the mixture into your flan tin and gently press out, make sure there are no gaps around the edges. Cook for twenty minutes at 350°F (180°C, Gas mark 4) or until golden brown. Cut while hot. Allow to cool.*
	Jumbo oats	375 g	
	Salt	1 tsp	

Variations

Enormous scope for variations
(a) Add any flavouring, zest, spice, powder or essence to the oats.
(b) Substitute some of the weight of the oats with dried fruits, nuts, hard fruits, seeds.
(c) Add pastes like tahini and peanut butter.
(d) Make 'oat slices' by sandwiching a fruit purée mixture between layers of oat mixture before cooking.
(e) Make 'oat bars' by smoothing a fruit purée over the top of the flapjacks, before or after cooking.

Some good combinations

Coffee, lemon and honey, date and malt, orange and lemon, ginger, sunflower, sesame and tahini, rum and raisin, peanut and sultana, cashew and lexia, apricot oat slices, fig oat bars, almond and cinnamon flapjacks, etc.

347 Chocolate brownies

Chocolate brownies are simply a chocolate sponge mixture (324, Part 1), poured into a flan tin rather than a cake tin – as a result they take less time to cook – 30 minutes.

Variations

(a) Add nuts as part of flour bulk.
(b) Use carob instead of chocolate.
(c) Add dry fruit (raisins, sultanas) as part of the flour bulk.
(d) Use other flavourings, essences, etc.
Note – Cut into squares or oblongs.

348 Turkish coffee bars

Sound more like somewhere to go than something to eat.

Stage	Ingredients	Quantity	Method
1	Sugar	225 g	*Mix all the dry ingredients together. Stir in butter thoroughly.*
	Flour	450 g	*Divide in half. Press one half into greased 9 in. tin.*
	Melted butter (margarine)	115 g	
	Instant coffee	60 g	
	Cinnamon	2 tsp	
	Nutmeg	½ tsp	
2	Sour cream	200 ml	*Mix together and add to other half of above mixture. Pour on*
	Bicarbonate	1 tsp	*the top of base. Bake at 350°F (180°C, Gas mark 4) for*
	Egg (beaten)	1	*25 minutes.*
	Nuts (chopped)	120 g	

349 Butterscotch nut brownies

Grease 9 in flan tin.

Stage	Ingredients	Quantity	Method
1	Butter	150 g	*Heat together in a pan. Allow to cool slightly.*
	Honey	95 g	
2	Eggs	3	*Beat in the eggs and the vanilla essence.*
	Vanilla essence	½ tsp	
3	Flour	150 g	*Fold into the mixture.*
	Baking powder	2 tsp	
	Salt	1 tsp	
4	Walnuts (chopped)	300 g	*Add the walnuts. Turn into a flan tin and bake at 350°F (180°C, Gas mark 4) for 30 minutes.*

Variations

(a) Add different flavours.

(b) Use other nuts – hazelnuts are good.

350 Chocolate jumbles

Grease a 9 in flan tin – this is a really simple recipe.

Stage	Ingredients	Quantity	Method
1	Dessicated coconut	150 g	*Mix the dry ingredients together.*
	Flour	300 g	
	Cocoa	3 tsp	
	Sugar	150 g	
	Baking powder	1¼ tsp	
2	Melted butter	150 g	*Add the butter and mix in well. Press into flan tin and bake for 15–20 minutes at a medium heat.*
3	Chocolate icing (274)	100 g	*pour over surface while still hot. Continue to cook for another 5 minutes.*

351 Fig shorties

Simply shortbread (318) with a fig purée spread over it after cooking (see 276). Use any other fruit purée.

352 Banana nut bread

As for chocolate banana gateau (344) but omit the chocolate and rum.

Increase the banana/flour ratio by using 4 medium bananas. Add ½ tsp of baking powder.
Add the juice of half a lemon to the bananas.
Add 50 g chopped walnuts in place of flour (50 g).
Reduce volume of eggs to allow for the liquid volume of the banana mixture.

Variations

Use dates, figs, apples, peaches, apricots, etc. in place of bananas. Banana breads are cooked in a loaf tin at 375°F (190°C, Gas Mark 5) for 45 minutes or until cooked. Because of the high fruit content they do sometimes take longer. Sweet breads are usually denser moister cake mixtures.

353 Bath buns

Grease a baking sheet and heat oven to 375°F (190°C, Gas Mark 5).

Stage	Ingredients	Quantity	Method
1	Fresh yeast	25 g	*Make a yeast culture with the yeast, liquid and flour. Allow to work for about 20 minutes in a warm place.*
	Tepid milk	150 ml	
	Tepid water	60 ml	
	Flour	100 g	
2	Flour	350 g	*Sieve and mix together.*
	Salt	1 tsp	
	Sugar	50 g	
3	Cool melted butter	50 g	*Add to the flour mixture with the yeast culture to form a soft dough. Knead until smooth.*
	Egg (beaten)	2	
	Sultanas	175 g	
	Mixed peel	25 g	
4			*Cover and allow to rise until double in size. Knock back. Divide into 18 buns. Spoon buns on to greased baking sheet and allow to rise again until double in size. Brush with egg and sprinkle with sugar. Bake for about 15 minutes until golden brown. Turn onto wire rack.*

Variations

Chelsea Buns – Make same dough but do not include the dried fruit and sugar at stage 3. Allow to rise. Roll out the dough and sprinkle with the dried ingredients. Roll up (like swiss roll) and cover to rise again. When doubled in size brush with warm honey and bake for 30 minutes at 375°F (190°C, Gas Mark 5). Brush again with honey just before they have finished cooking.

354 Apricot linzertorte

This is very special.
Heat the oven to 375°F (190°C, Gas Mark 5).

Stage	Ingredients	Quantity	Method
1	Flour	150 g	*Sift together.*
	Cinnamon	½ tsp	
2	Butter	75 g	*Rub in the butter to form crumbs.*
3	Sugar	50 g	*Mix in the sugar, almonds and lemons.*
	Ground hazelnuts	50 g	
	Lemon zest	1 lemon	
4	Egg yolks (beaten)	2	*Beat into the mixture to form a stiff dough. Knead lightly.*
	Lemon juice	1 lemon	*Take ²/₃ of the dough and roll out into a 20 cm square. Press into your greased tin.*
5	Apricot purée	300 g	*Fill flan with purée. Roll out reserved pastry. Cut into a circle or into strips and place over apricot fillings. Bake for 30 minutes. Allow to cool.*

Variations
Use other fillings.

Index